✠ HAMLET ✠

BY WILLIAM SHAKESPEARE

Other works by Kenneth Branagh

Beginning

Much Ado About Nothing:
Screenplay, Introduction, and Notes
on the Making of the Movie

⊞ ·HAMLET· ⊞

BY WILLIAM SHAKESPEARE

SCREENPLAY AND INTRODUCTION

BY

KENNETH BRANAGH

Film Diary by Russell Jackson

Photographs by Rolf Konow and Peter Mountain

W. W. Norton & Company

New York London

First Edition

The text of this book is composed in Monotype Bembo
with the display set in Trajan
Composition by Shaun Webb Graphic Design
Manufacturing by The Haddon Craftsmen, Inc.
Book design by Shaun Webb Graphic Design

Library of Congress Cataloging-in-Publication Data

Branagh, Kenneth.
Hamlet / by William Shakespeare ; screenplay and introduction by Kenneth Branagh ;
production diary by Russell Jackson ; photographs by Rolf Konow and Peter Mountain.
p. cm.
Includes screenplay based on the play by William Shakespeare.
ISBN 0-393-31505-3 (pbk.) ISBN 0-393-04519-6 (limited ed.)
1. Hamlet (Motion picture) I. Shakespeare, William, 1564-1616.
Hamlet. II. Title.
PN1997.H254B7 1996
791.43'72--dc20   96-35077
CIP

W. W. Norton & Company, Inc., 500 Fifth Avenue, New York, N.Y. 10110
http://www.wwnorton.com

W. W. Norton & Company Ltd., 10 Coptic Street, London WC1A 1PU

1 2 3 4 5 6 7 8 9 0

For Martin Shafer – Thank you.

✠ C O N T E N T S ✠

✠ INTRODUCTION ✠

by Kenneth Branagh

As I write this, I am one month away from completing a project which has consumed me, to varying degrees, for the last twenty years.

I first encountered *Hamlet* when Richard Chamberlain, T.V.'s Doctor Kildare, played the title role on British television. I was eleven years old and from a background (Irish, Protestant, working-class) which had given me little preparation for watching Shakespeare. I was sufficiently distracted on that Sunday evening to leave my overdue homework uncompleted. I felt very uneasy when the Ghost of Hamlet's father appeared. There were no great special effects to heighten the audience's fear, but the atmosphere of the scene was unsettling. I was dragged away from the screen shortly afterwards to a tardy bedtime. It continued to affect me as I tried, unsuccessfully, to sleep. I wasn't sure that I had liked what I saw (the play I mean, not the performances) but it certainly stayed with me. Enough for me to resort to Shakespeare as an excuse when I was carpeted the following morning for my poor homework.

Over the following few years, *Hamlet* took on different shapes. One was a picture of Laurence Olivier on the cover of an old L.P. record, lying (unused) in a corner of the English Department Stock Room. Later still, the record itself was played in class, the master's sepulchral reading of 'To Be Or Not To Be' set against Walton's eerie score. I knew nothing of 'fardels' or 'bodkins', but I knew that here was 'something'. By the age of fifteen, though, Shakespeare had still taken no special hold of my imagination. I was interested in soccer and girls. Shakespeare was for swots.

Surprisingly, however, what did grab my attention at this time was a television serialization of Robert Graves's *I, Claudius*. I was particularly impressed by the actor playing the title role. His name was Derek Jacobi, and I noticed, with some excitement, a small ad in the entertainment section of our local newspaper announcing that Derek Jacobi 'of T.V.'s *I, Claudius* fame' was to appear in *Hamlet* at the New Theatre, Oxford.

I rang to book my ticket. A new adventure for me. My theatre-going had been limited to a couple of organized school trips prior to this. But I wanted to see this man in the flesh. I still hadn't read the play, so for all I knew, I might be treated to some of the stuttering which had impressed me so much in his television performance. I travelled to Oxford, some half an hour away by train, my first real independent outing as an adolescent. The pavement outside the theatre was thronged with ticket holders, and I discovered it was the very first performance of this production by the Prospect Theatre Company. Excitement was in the air, and from my first glimpse of the poster, with a haunted Jacobi staring into some bleak beyond, I was aglow with anticipation.

Much later I read a remark by the distinguished critic Kenneth Tynan, who said 'the difference between a good play and a great play is that after the experience of a great play we understand a little more about why we are alive'. My theatre-going experience at that point gave me little scope for comparison but I was convinced as I left the theatre that evening that I had experienced – not just watched, but truly experienced – something unique. The story was gripping, and I wanted at every moment to know 'what happened next'. Much of the language I did not understand and yet the actors' commitment to each line convinced me that I knew what they were feeling. As Ophelia lost her reason, I was moved to tears. I was passionate in my longing for Claudius to receive his come-uppance, and the sword fight at the end was as thrilling as any football match.

But as I travelled home that summer evening twenty years ago my overwhelming feeling was of having connected with an extraordinary energy. In the play itself and chiefly in the character of Hamlet I experienced the insistent hum of life itself. He was passionate, humorous, cruel, intelligent, courageous and cowardly, but unmistakably and gloriously brimming over with life. In the production and in Jacobi's performance I had been taken on an emotional rollercoaster. It made me reflect on my relationships with my parents, the prospects of my adolescent love affair. It set my heart and my head racing. I felt I had encountered a genuine force of nature, and on that journey home and for sometime afterwards, its memory made me glad to be alive. But then I was fifteen.

Nevertheless, the damage was done. I began to read the play, to read more of Shakespeare. I resolved to become an actor. Tempting though it is to re-write one's personal history with the benefit of hindsight, I believe that much of what has followed in my life was affected by that experience.

My training at the Royal Academy of Dramatic Art was the next point at which I could pursue this passionate interest. At twenty, having 'collected' as an audience member the performances of a dozen other Hamlets (including the films by Olivier and Kozintsev), I gave my first performance of the role. Regarding its success, I would borrow Richard Briers' self-assessment of his own RADA Prince - 'I may not have been the best Hamlet but I was the quickest'. But the experience taught me much about the practical demands of the role: massive physical exertion culminating in a complicated fight that an exhausted actor at the end of the play would happily do without. I felt the thrill of playing the role, but at the end of the run I knew little more about the Prince of Denmark than I had five years earlier.

There was a stronger sense of this four years later in 1984, when I played Laertes in a production for the Royal Shakespeare Company. It was invaluable to watch the central character (played by Roger Rees) from a different vantage point. I was able to observe much more clearly what is said about him by others, and worry less about the Prince's own words. Here too was a chance to view the whole play, but from within. I was made aware of the double family tragedy. All of the Polonius clan and all of the royal family - dead, at the finale. And in Fortinbras's accession to the throne there is the sense of a national tragedy - the end of an era. The weight of sadness is felt across the whole play, not confined to one man.

Derek Jacobi stepped back into my 'Hamlet' life once more, when in 1988 he directed me in the role for The Renaissance Theatre Company. As a director of the company I had originally asked him to produce *Richard II* with another actor, but he suggested *Hamlet* and asked me to play the title role. My actor's vanity got the better of me and I said yes.

Even so, I was unready. I produced a hectic Hamlet, high on energy but low on subtlety and crucially lacking depth. I was aware that something Jacobi himself had brought effortlessly and effectively to the role was life experience. He had the confidence as an actor to do less. A longer exposure to the 'whips and scorns of time' in his own life gave him an easy weight which underlined the depths of Hamlet's thinking and gave a necessary counterpoint to the frenzied and frantic elements of Hamlet's personality.

The chief lesson of the production was that I should do it again and that the time must be right. It had to be when I still fulfilled the age requirements for the Prince but when I had the courage to bring a slightly older and more complex self to the role. When I had the confidence to let the acting energy take care of itself and, as Hamlet, to live more completely in the moment. As the years went by, I was never less than fascinated by other actors' Hamlets. The play still held its attraction for me, but it remained artistically as unfinished business.

On radio in 1992 I had my first taste of the full text, and a splendid opportunity to explore the play's language with a focus and significance that was uniquely offered by the medium, in which the spoken word dominates. With the full text, the gravitational weight of the play seemed to increase. While arguments will always rage about exactly what constitutes a 'full text' I had no doubt that this version offered rich opportunities for the actors, particularly in the supporting roles. I felt I understood much more about Polonius with the inclusion of the often cut scene with his 'agent' Reynaldo. The complexity of Claudius's manipulations in the full version of the scene where he plots with Laertes, helped to flesh out a richer portrait than the conventional stage villain. And there were, to my taste, fascinating excursions on the state of the Elizabethan theatre, and jaundiced summations of the legal profession and of court life. On top of the domestic tragedy which engulfs a royal family the play seemed an all-embracing survey of life. It was harsh, vigorous and contemporary in feel.

I resolved that were I to attempt the role again, it should be using this full text.

The opportunity arose when Adrian Noble invited me to play the title role in a new Royal Shakespeare Company production which opened in 1992. He concurred with me that we should use what some critics have referred to as the 'eternity' version. Now, at thirty-three, the part seemed at last to be 'playing me'. There were no surprises in the obstacle course of great set pieces, and I felt as if I had been in training for this attempt. The performance matured as it had not before, and continued to surprise me, not least by the way in which the full text offered a much more comfortable playing experience for the actor. It was more imaginatively paced. One could take advantage of the 'breaths' that Shakespeare had given the actor. Paradoxically it was much less physically exhausting to play, and the cumulative weight of the longer evening made for an immensely powerful finale.

By this time I had had two experiences of filming Shakespeare and my film-maker's instincts made me long - even as I explored it within a fine production like Adrian's - to take the play into the cinema in its fullest form. I longed to allow audiences to join Fortinbras on the plain in Norway, to be transported, as Hamlet is in his mind's eye, back to Troy and see Priam and Hecuba. I felt that all my experience with the play and with Shakespeare was leading me in one direction.

My attempts to finance a film version had been in motion since the opening of *Henry V*, but the perpetual reluctance of film companies to finance Shakespeare had frustrated each attempt.

In 1995 Castle Rock Entertainment finally agreed to follow this dream, by financing a full-length version which would perhaps be followed by an abridged version at a more traditional length. The pages that follow, record the attempt.

The screenplay is what one might call the 'verbal storyboard'. An inflexion of a subjective view of the play which has developed over the years. Its intention was to be both personal, with enormous attention paid to the intimate relations between the characters, and at the same time epic, with a sense of the country at large and of a dynasty in decay.

The style is a development of my other Shakespeare film work. Among its principles are a commitment to international casting; a speaking style that is as realistic as a proper adherence to the structure of the language will allow; a period setting that attempts to set the story in a historical context that is resonant for a modern audience but allows a heightened language to sit comfortably. Above all, we have asked for a full emotional commitment to the characters, springing from belief that they can be understood in direct, accessible relation to modern life.

As I mentioned before, at the time of writing, the film is yet to be completed. The sound and music mix are in their final stages. So I for one am unsure of the results. I've brought as much intelligence as I can to its execution but in the end mine is not an intellectual approach, but an intuitive one. For better or worse, I am still connected to the feeling that had overwhelmed me all those years ago, when first I saw the play live. For audiences familiar or unfamiliar with the story, that's what I'd like to pass on.

That I should have pursued the play's mysteries so assiduously over twenty years continues to puzzle me. But, it's what I do, and this is what I've done. As the great soccer manager Bill Shankly once said, describing the importance of football, 'It's not a matter of life and death. It's much more important than that.' Certainly for me, an ongoing relationship to this kind of poetry and this kind of mind is a necessary part of an attempt to be civilized. I am profoundly grateful for the opportunity to explore it.

The hold it has over me will not lessen its grip. Michael Maloney, who plays Laertes in the film, told me recently of an impending production in which he will play the Prince. I found myself as excited as ever to discuss interpretation, casting, language - everything. For I believe I've come happily to realize that of course I cannot explain *Hamlet*, or even perhaps my own interpretation of *Hamlet*.

This film is simply the passionate expression of a dream. A dream that has preoccupied me for so many years. I cannot really explain that either. The reasons are in the film. The reasons are the film.

Goethe said, 'A genuine work of art, no less than a work of nature, will always remain infinite to our reason: it can be contemplated and felt, it affects us, but it cannot be fully comprehended, even less than it is possible to express its essence and its merits in words.'

After twenty years, I'm happy to say, I think I know what he means.

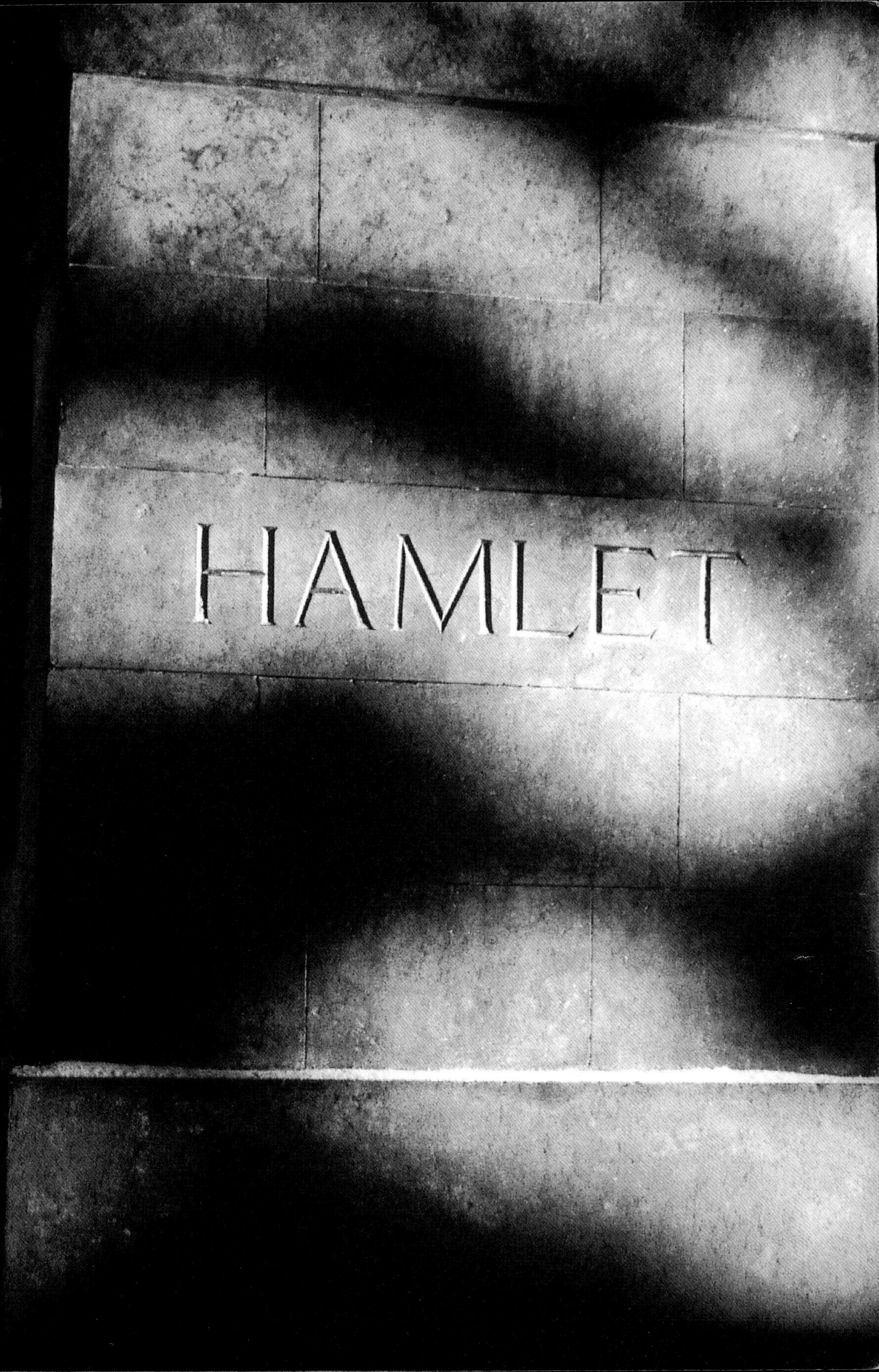
HAMLET

✠ CAST ✠

Attendant to Claudius	**Riz Abbasi**	Cornelius	**Ravil Isyanov**
English Ambassador	**Richard Attenborough**	Claudius	**Derek Jacobi**
		Attendant to Gertrude	**Rowena King**
Attendant to Claudius	**David Blair**	Fortinbras's Captain	**Jeffrey Kissoon**
Ghost	**Brian Blessed**	Attendant to Gertrude	**Sarah Lam**
Hamlet	**Kenneth Branagh**		
Polonius	**Richard Briers**	Marcellus	**Jack Lemmon**
Priest	**Michael Bryant**	Barnardo	**Ian McElhinney**
Attendant to Claudius	**Peter Bygott**	Laertes	**Michael Maloney**
		Fortinbras's General	**Duke of Marlborough**
Gertrude	**Julie Christie**		
First Gravedigger	**Billy Crystal**	Old Norway	**John Mills**
		Sailor Two	**Jimi Mistry**
Stage Manager	**Charles Daish**	Prologue	**Sian Radinger**
Hecuba	**Judi Dench**	Prostitute	**Melanie Ramsay**
Reynaldo	**Gérard Depardieu**	Second Gravedigger	**Simon Russell Beale**
Guildenstern	**Reece Dinsdale**		
Yorick	**Ken Dodd**	Young Lord	**Andrew Schofield**
Attendant to Gertrude	**Angela Douglas**	Fortinbras	**Rufus Sewell**
		Rosencrantz	**Timothy Spall**
Lucianus	**Rob Edwards**	Young Hamlet	**Tom Szekeres**
Horatio	**Nicholas Farrell**	First Player	**Ben Thom**
Francisco	**Ray Fearon**	Voltemand	**Don Warrington**
Doctor	**Yvonne Gidden**	Second Player	**Perdita Weeks**
Priam	**John Gielgud**	Osric	**Robin Williams**
Player Queen	**Rosemary Harris**	Ophelia	**Kate Winslet**
Player King	**Charlton Heston**	Sailor One	**David Yip**

✠ THE SCREENPLAY ✠

PART ONE

Exterior / MONUMENT Night

Darkness. Uneasy silence. The deep of a Winter's Night. A huge
plinth, with the screen-filling legend carved deep in the stone,
HAMLET. The Camera creeping, like an animal, pans left to reveal,
a hundred yards away, ELSINORE, a gorgeous Winter Palace.
Effortlessly elegant, yet powerful in its coat of snow. The bell
begins to toll the first deep ring of the midnight hour, as we

Cut to:

Exterior / SENTRY POST Night

We see the lonely FRANCISCO as he passes before the huge palace
gates. A brazier steaming. Quick unsettled cuts to FRANCISCO's POV
of unending darkness, reinforced by the intimidating sounds of
the night.

Cut to:

Exterior / MONUMENT Night

The immense statue of a military hero. We glimpse only part of the
sculpture as the Camera climbs higher, for we are chiefly aware, a
way off, of the confident twinkling-windowed eyes of this majestic
seat of government; a Versailles-like tribute to the power of the
Danish Royal Family, here in the midst of the Nineteenth Century.
Each toll of the bell seems deeper and louder as still the Camera
moves, tracking right now to lose the palace behind the stone
countenance of OLD HAMLET. The sculptor has caught the glamour
and ferocity of the late King's face, and noted also a hint of sadness.

Exterior / SENTRY POST Night

A noise. Tight on FRANCISCO, terrified, straining to hear where or what it might be. FRANCISCO slowly points his halberd out into the darkness. We inter-cut between the Sentry Post and the Monument until

Cut to:

Exterior / MONUMENT Night

The Camera now cranes down to take in the detail of the granite uniform in all its splendour. The last stroke of midnight hits as we settle on the huge hand, which holds a sword hilt and just as we would seem to cut, a great rasping noise like fingernails on a blackboard sears through the night and we see the statue's hand pull the sword from the scabbard with a savage rip!

Cut to:

Exterior / SENTRY POST Night

FRANCISO frozen in terror.

BARNARDO O/S
Who's there?

FRANCISCO whips around to his left, but not quickly enough.
CRASH! A body, from right of frame, bundles him forcibly to
the ground.
On the frozen ground they struggle, dangerous flashing blades in the
gloom. FRANCISCO gets the upper hand.

FRANCISCO
Nay, answer me. Stand and unfold yourself.

The other, equally terrified, pants out an answer.

BARNARDO
Long live the King?

Beat. Almost relief. Silence. Heavy breaths.

FRANCISCO
Barnardo?

BARNARDO
He.

Massive relief. FRANCISCO continues, with no little understatement.

FRANCISCO
You come most carefully upon your hour.

He helps his comrade up to his feet. Both now rather embarrassed by
this unorthodox changing of the guard.

BARNARDO
'Tis now struck twelve. Get thee to bed, Francisco.

FRANCISCO
For this relief much thanks. 'Tis bitter cold,
And I am sick at heart.

BARNARDO
Have you had quiet guard?

A look between them. Both heard the noise. FRANCISCO avoids the issue.

> FRANCISCO
> *Not a mouse stirring.*

Another look. Neither wants to lose the company of the other. Eventually,

> BARNARDO
> *Well, good night.*
> *If you do meet Horatio and Marcellus,*
> *The rivals of my watch, bid them make haste.*

CRACK! They start at another sharp noise. Weapons up like quicksilver. These men are terrified. Then, more in hope than anything else,

> FRANCISCO
> *I think I hear them. Stand! Who's there?*

A comforting voice rings out of the darkness, some distance away.

> HORATIO O/S
> *Friends to this ground.*

We see HORATIO and MARCELLUS approaching in the background.

> MARCELLUS O/S
> *And liegemen to the Dane.*

Huge relief once more. FRANCISCO in a hurry, bids his farewell to BARNARDO, before heading towards the new arrivals.

> FRANCISCO
> *Give you good night.*

Exterior / SENTRY POST APPROACH Night

He reaches the stalwart, kindly MARCELLUS, who is somewhat taken aback by the eagerness of the soldier to return to barracks. What happened?

> MARCELLUS
> *O farewell, honest soldier. Who hath relieved you?*

> FRANCISCO (grimly)
> *Barnardo has my place. Give you good night.*

He nods to HORATIO, before rushing off towards the lights of the Sentries' mess. MARCELLUS decides to hold his ground and calls into the night.

> MARCELLUS
> *Holla, Barnardo!*

> BARNARDO O/S
> *Say what, is Horatio there?*

HORATIO, a natural scholar, not soldier, is the calmest of them all. He decides to be ironic about the bitter cold.

> HORATIO
> *A piece of him.*

He gives the fretful MARCELLUS a gentle pat on the shoulder and smiles as they move off.

Exterior / SENTRY POST Night

    BARNARDO (warmly, relieved)
    Welcome, Horatio. Welcome, good Marcellus.
    MARCELLUS
    What, has this thing appeared again tonight?
    BARNARDO
    I have seen nothing.
So far, MARCELLUS shares BARNARDO's keen apprehension.

    MARCELLUS
    Horatio says 'tis but our fantasy,
    And will not let belief take hold of him
    Touching this dreaded sight twice seen of us.
    Therefore I have entreated him along
    With us to watch the minutes of this night,
    That if again this apparition come
    He may approve our eyes and speak to it.
HORATIO, shuffling and stamping against the cold, is still
faintly amused.

    HORATIO
    Tush, tush, 'twill not appear.
BARNARDO leads them over to a brazier on the other side of
the sentry post, where there are some munition boxes.

    BARNARDO
                     Sit down a while,
    And let us once again assail your ears,
    That are so fortified against our story,
    What we two nights have seen.
HORATIO feigns 'Here we go again ...'

    HORATIO
                     Well, sit we down,
    And let us hear Barnardo speak of this.
But there is no shaking these men with irony. BARNARDO recalls
the terrible events of last night with a stillness and possession that
compel HORATIO's attention.

    BARNARDO
    Last night of all,
As he continues, we see their point of view. A mystical and disturbing
night sky.

    BARNARDO V/O
    When yond same star that's westward from the pole
    Had made his course t'illume that part of heaven
    Where now it burns,
We have been aware of the wind picking up speed through this last
dialogue. We see BARNARDO's gaze drift away in the direction of

what is now a fierce, icy blast. He has to fight to be heard above the ominous rush.

BARNARDO
Marcellus and myself,
The bell then beating one –

Then, almost as one, the three men throw back their heads to look high in the air. We see the terror on their faces at the size and height of this ... thing. But it all happens in an instant, before MARCELLUS yanks them from this spot and yells savagely.

MARCELLUS
Peace, break thee off. Look where it comes again.

Exterior / MAIN COURTYARD Night

The statue come to life! They run for their lives! We are way above them in the night air. THE GHOST's POV as the Camera rushes from a great height, swooping down on the retreating figures racing across the snow. We almost reach them, but no! Just in time they fling themselves behind a pillar.

Exterior / COURTYARD Night

They speak in a terrified, whispered rush, with their halberds raised, and ready to die.

BARNARDO
In the same figure like the King that's dead.

MARCELLUS
Thou art a scholar. Speak to it, Horatio.

BARNARDO
Looks it not like the King? Mark it, Horatio.

HORATIO
Most like. It harrows me with fear and wonder.

A fierce wind still blasts them each time they turn to look at it, and as we see their faces emerge from behind the pillar to gaze up at the great mass.

BARNARDO
It would be spoke to.

MARCELLUS
Speak to it, Horatio.

Exterior / MAIN COURTYARD Night

HORATIO, tentatively from their hiding place. He begins, nervously.

HORATIO (to The Ghost)
What art thou that usurps't this time of night,
Together with that fair and warlike form
In which the majesty of buried Denmark
Did sometimes march? By heaven, I charge thee speak.

We look down on him from THE GHOST's POV.

MARCELLUS
It is offended.

Our high POV retreats and the little figures grow smaller and smaller.

BARNARDO
    See, it stalks away.

HORATIO (to the Ghost)
Stay, speak, speak,

We quickly glimpse the image of THE GHOST.

HORATIO (continuing)
    I charge thee speak.

THE GHOST disappears. The new silence is intense. The palace has not awoken. This visitation was just for them. A kind of sanity returns.

MARCELLUS
'Tis gone, and will not answer.

HORATIO's legs start to buckle. The two men catch him, grateful for something practical to do.

BARNARDO
How now, Horatio? You tremble and look pale.
Is not this something more than fantasy?
What think you on't?

HORATIO
Before my God, I might not this believe
Without the sensible and true avouch
Of mine own eyes.

MARCELLUS
    Is it not like the King?

HORATIO recovers with some help from BARNARDO's hip flask.

HORATIO
As thou art to thyself.
Such was the very armour he had on
When he th' ambitious Norway combated.
So frowned he once when in an angry parle
He smote the sledded Polacks on the ice.
'Tis strange.

HORATIO takes a large swig from Barnardo's hip flask.

MARCELLUS
Thus twice before, and jump at this dead hour,
With martial stalk hath he gone by our watch.

HORATIO
In what particular thought to work I know not,
But in the gross and scope of my opinion
This bodes some strange eruption to our state.

Temporarily recovered. They attempt to walk in order to make the blood flow again. The conversation is building in intensity, as the post-hysteria relief subsides.

Exterior / COLONNADE WALK Night

We track with them as they walk past various doors.

MARCELLUS

Good now, look here, and tell me, he that knows,
Why this same strict and most observant watch
So nightly toils the subject of the land,

MARCELLUS is now heated and angry. He stops at one of the doors
and pulls back a small spy flap. HORATIO looks. We see his POV.
An arms factory in high production.

MARCELLUS (continuing)

And why such daily cast of brazen cannon,
And foreign mart for implements of war,
Why such impress of shipwrights, whose sore task
Does not divide the Sunday from the week:
What might be toward that this sweaty haste
Doth make the night joint-labourer with the day,
Who is't that can inform me?

HORATIO is grateful to be diverted from his ghostly fears by
MARCELLUS's obvious and genuine anguish about the fate of his
country. He explains the background to this warlike state with
obvious authority and passionate interest. He leads them off along
the colonnade.

HORATIO

                              That can I –
At least the whisper goes so: our last King,
Whose image even but now appeared to us,
Was as you know by Fortinbras of Norway,
Thereto pricked on by a most emulate pride,
Dared to the combat; in which our valiant Hamlet –
For so this side of our known world esteemed him –
Did slay this Fortinbras,

HORATIO fully into his stride now is getting carried away with
detail. MARCELLUS and BARNARDO exchange looks.

HORATIO (continuing)

                              Who by a sealed compact,
Well ratified by law and heraldry,
Did forfeit with his life all those his lands
Which he stood seized of to the conqueror;
Against the which a moiety competent
Was gagèd by our King, which had returned
To the inheritance of Fortinbras
Had he been vanquisher, as, by the same cov'nant
And carriage of the article designed,
His fell to Hamlet.

Exterior / COUNCIL CHAMBER Night (Flashback)

We see but cannot hear the dark, wild young man, as he leans yelling across a table. Placed upon it are military flags and toy soldiers. He is surrounded by frightened advisers, whom he is clearly haranguing. This is a group of surly mercenaries.

HORATIO V/O (continuing)

Now sir, young Fortinbras,
Of unimprovèd mettle hot and full,
Hath in the skirts of Norway here and there
Sharked up a list of landless resolutes
For food and diet to some enterprise
That hath a stomach in't, which is no other –
And it doth well appear unto our state –

The Camera rushes with the crazed FORTINBRAS from his campaign table to a board where we see him rip off and tear up a map of Denmark. This ferocious young man wants revenge.

HORATIO V/O (continuing)

But to recover of us by strong hand
And terms compulsatory those foresaid lands
So by his father lost.

Cut to:

Exterior / COURTYARD Night

Back to real time, around a brazier and in sombre mood. MARCELLUS's fears are well-founded. HORATIO has lost his academic enthusiasm and all three men contemplate the awful reality of imminent war.

HORATIO (continuing)

And this, I take it,
Is the main motive of our preparations,
The source of this our watch, and the chief head
Of this post-haste and rummage in the land.

BARNARDO

I think it be no other but e'en so.
Well may it sort that this portentous figure
Comes armèd through our watch so like the King
That was and is the question of these wars.

HORATIO

A mote it is to trouble the mind's eye.
In the most high and palmy state of Rome,
A little ere the mightiest Julius fell,
The graves stood tenantless and the sheeted dead
Did squeak and gibber in the Roman streets;
And even the like precurse of feared events,
As harbingers preceding still the fates
And prologue to the omen coming on,

Have heaven and earth together demonstrated
Unto our climatures and countrymen.
As stars with trains of fire. And dews of blood,
Disasters in the sun; and the moist star,
Upon whose influence Neptune's empire stands,
Was sick almost to doomsday with eclipse.

We look up. THE GHOST has returned!

Cut to:

Exterior / MAIN COURTYARD Night

HORATIO
But soft, behold − lo where it comes again!
I'll cross it though it blast me.
Stay, illusion.

Again the Camera provides THE GHOST's POV. We are high above
HORATIO and tracking back as he tentatively moves towards us.
With each of his steps, we (THE GHOST) retreat. He talks to it as if
talking to a frightened young person who has a gun trained on him.
BARNARDO and MARCELLUS follow behind, weapons raised.

HORATIO (continuing)
If thou hast any sound or use of voice,
Speak to me.
If there be any good thing to be done
That may to thee do ease and grace to me,
Speak to me.
If thou art privy to thy country's fate
Which happily foreknowing may avoid,
O speak!
Or if thou hast uphoarded in thy life
Extorted treasure in the womb of earth −
For which, they say, you spirits oft walk in death,

The Cock crows.

Speak of it, stay and speak.− Stop it, Marcellus.

MARCELLUS
Shall I strike at it with my partisan?

HORATIO
Do if it will not stand.

All is chaos as MARCELLUS and BARNARDO both throw their
partisans at THE GHOST.

BARNARDO
                    'Tis here.

HORATIO
                            'Tis here.

But too late. We glimpse THE GHOST disappearing.

MARCELLUS
'Tis gone.

Cut to:

Exterior / MONUMENT Night

The Statue of Old Hamlet. Unmoved. Impressive.

MARCELLUS V/O
We do it wrong, being so majestical,
To offer it the show of violence,

Cut to:

Exterior / SENTRY POST Night

Again, thick silence. And shame.

MARCELLUS
For it is as the air invulnerable,
And our vain blows malicious mockery.

The sound of larks begins to cut across the awed silence.

BARNARDO
It was about to speak when the cock crew.

HORATIO
And then it started like a guilty thing
Upon a fearful summons. I have heard
The cock, that is the trumpet to the morn,
Doth with his lofty and shrill-sounding throat
Awake the god of day, and at his warning,
Whether in sea or fire, in earth or air,
Th' extravagant and erring spirit hies
To his confine; and of the truth herein
This present object made probation.

All the men have been changed by this experience. MARCELLUS
picks up on the mystical atmosphere.

Exterior / SENTRY POST Dawn

MARCELLUS
It faded on the crowing of the cock.
Some say that ever 'gainst that season comes
Wherein our Saviour's birth is celebrated
The bird of dawning singeth all night long;
And then, they say, no spirit can walk abroad,
The nights are wholesome; then no planets strike,
No fairy takes, nor witch hath power to charm,
So hallowed and so gracious is the time.

HORATIO
So have I heard and do in part believe it.

We see the dawn sky.

HORATIO (continuing)
But look, the morn in russet mantle clad
Walks o'er the dew of yon high eastward hill.
Break we our watch up, and by my advice
Let us impart what we have seen tonight

Unto young Hamlet; for upon my life,
This spirit, dumb to us, will speak to him.
Do you consent we shall acquaint him with it,
As needful in our loves, fitting our duty?
MARCELLUS
Let's do't, I pray; and I this morning know
Where we shall find him most conveniently.

They move off as, we move towards the Danish Royal Crest, atop the gates. The dawn light starts to appear.

Cut to:

Interior / STATE HALL Day

A glorious procession of the new KING CLAUDIUS and his QUEEN GERTRUDE. We move with them into a packed gathering of smiling Courtiers and Commoners. The men are crisp, sexy. The military cut – all dashing clothes and hair. The women's clothes colourful, gloriously textured, shapely and flesh-revealing.

They walk from the enormous doors through rows of bleachers. It's like the House of Commons. Everyone stands. The guard of honour salutes. CLAUDIUS in full military regalia. Severe, cropped hair, brushed back, standing to attention atop a striking face that bears a crisp beard. GERTRUDE, complete with veil and generous bosom on show, also trim and vigorous. This irresistibly sexy, confident couple reach the throne. They face their AUDIENCE of bright festive colours and supportive faces.

The King begins to speak. Measured, compassionate, intelligent. All listen attentively, particularly the Prime Minister, POLONIUS, his son LAERTES, and his beautiful daughter OPHELIA.

CLAUDIUS
Though yet of Hamlet our dear brother's death
The memory be green, and that it us befitted
To bear our hearts in grief, and our whole Kingdom
To be contracted in one brow of woe,
Yet so far hath discretion fought with nature
That we with wisest sorrow think on him
Together with remembrance of ourselves.

Moist eyes. A man of genuine compassion.

CLAUDIUS (continuing)
Therefore our sometime sister, now our Queen

She, also moved, emotions very close to the surface.

CLAUDIUS (continuing)
Th' imperial jointress of this warlike state,
Have we as 'twere with a defeated joy,
With one auspicious and one dropping eye,
With mirth in funeral and with dirge in marriage,
In equal scale weighing delight and dole,
Taken to wife.

(He kisses her hand.)

> *Nor have we herein barred*
> *Your better wisdoms, which have freely gone*
> *With this affair along. For all, our thanks.*

Slow, then quickening and intense applause. He overrides this
reaction with his clearly genuine gratitude to this court. Now to
business and a serious public policy statement for a worried nation.
MARCELLUS is not alone in his fears.

> CLAUDIUS (continuing)
> *Now follows that you know young Fortinbras,*
> *Holding a weak supposal of our worth,*
> *Or thinking by our late dear brother's death*
> *Our state to be disjoint and out of frame,*
> *Co-leaguèd with the dream of his advantage,*
> *He hath not failed to pester us with message*

An Attendant gives him a paper.

> *Importing the surrender of those lands*
> *Lost by his father, with all bonds of law,*
> *To our most valiant brother.*

He tears up the paper. There is a gasp from the CROWD, then
applause. He's playing them well.

> *So much for him.*

Now, tougher still. He's into Norman Schwarzkopf mode. There will
be no messing with the Danish King. He plays it out confidently to
the gallery, taking another paper.

> CLAUDIUS (continuing)
> *Now for ourself, and for this time of meeting,*
> *Thus much the business is: we have here writ*
> *To Norway, uncle of young Fortinbras –*

Cut to:

Interior / BEDROOM Night (Flashback)

We see the wizened, frightened old man.

> CLAUDIUS V/O
> *Who, impotent and bed-rid, scarcely hears*
> *Of this his nephew's purpose – to suppress*

The face grows dark. We see the surly young FORTINBRAS, tearing
up the map.

> CLAUDIUS V/O
> *His further gait herein, in that the levies,*
> *The lists, and full proportions are all made*
> *Out of his subject;*

Cut to:

Interior / STATE HALL Day (Real time)

> CLAUDIUS
> *and we here dispatch*
> *You, good Cornelius, and you, Voltemand,*

The two wise men, also in military garb move to the throne.

CLAUDIUS

For bearers of this greeting to old Norway,
Giving to you no further personal power
To business with the King more than the scope
Of these dilated articles allow.
Farewell, and let your haste commend your duty.

VOLTEMAND takes the papers.

VOLTEMAND

In that, and all things, will we show our duty.

CLAUDIUS

We doubt it nothing, heartily farewell.

The AUDIENCE applauds. No hysteria this time, but all are quietly impressed by this statesmanship. Time now to turn on the charm with the young aristocrats. Also a good show for the ladies, who crane their necks on the balconies to see which of the bright young things around the throne will be indulged with a public favour.

CLAUDIUS

And now, Laertes, what's the news with you?
You told us of some suit.

A darkly handsome young man steps forward. In the uniform of a cadet.

CLAUDIUS (continuing)

                    What is't, Laertes?
You cannot speak of reason to the Dane
And lose your voice. What wouldst thou beg, Laertes,
That shall not be my offer, not thy asking?
The head is not more native to the heart,
The hand more instrumental to the mouth,
Than is the throne of Denmark to thy father.

He turns to POLONIUS, once again letting the court know how the power structure stands. Then on with a smile.

CLAUDIUS (continuing)

What wouldst thou have, Laertes?

LAERTES (nervous)

                              My dread lord,
Your leave and favour to return to France,

Knowing looks from around the court. The phrase 'sowing wild oats' comes to people's minds. LAERTES responds quickly.

LAERTES

From whence, though willingly I came to Denmark
To show my duty in your coronation,
Yet now I must confess, that duty done,
My thoughts and wishes bend again towards France
And bow them to your gracious leave and pardon.

The King teases it out for a moment.

CLAUDIUS
Have you your father's leave? What says Polonius?
Dad joins in with the gentle ribbing.
POLONIUS
He hath, my lord, wrung from me my slow leave
By laboursome petition and at last
Upon his will I sealed my hard consent.
I do beseech you give him leave to go.
CLAUDIUS steps down to LAERTES.
CLAUDIUS
Take thy fair hour, Laertes. Time be thine,
And thy best graces spend it at thy will.
As the AUDIENCE applauds, the Camera tracks slowly past them and comes to a halt under the right hand balcony. There at the other end of the hall is a black silhouette of a man. We make an abrupt Cut. The humorous applause that has greeted LAERTES's departure is stopped by a big Close-up on CLAUDIUS and his firm tone.
CLAUDIUS (continuing)
But now, my cousin Hamlet, and my son —
We make another an abrupt Cut back to the lonely figure behind the bleachers.
HAMLET
A little more than kin, and less than kind.
CLAUDIUS
How is it that the clouds still hang on you?
From CLAUDIUS's POV we see HAMLET move forward and sit down.
HAMLET
Not so, my lord, I am too much in the sun.
We see reaction on the AUDIENCE's faces. This is embarrassing. The QUEEN moves away from the throne and we see her and her son in profile 2-shot. She attempts intimacy. This should not be public.
GERTRUDE
Good Hamlet, cast thy nighted colour off,
And let thine eye look like a friend on Denmark.
Do not for ever with thy vailèd lids
Seek for thy noble father in the dust.
Thou know'st 'tis common — all that lives must die,
Passing through nature to eternity.
HAMLET
Ay, madam, it is common.
GERTRUDE
                        If it be,
Why seems it so particular with thee?
In his shocked reaction he raises his voice, so that the CROWD can almost hear the hissed reproaches that he shoots at her grief-free demeanour.

HAMLET

Seems, madam? Nay, it is. I know not 'seems'.
'Tis not alone my inky cloak, good mother
Nor customary suits of solemn black,
Nor windy suspiration of forced breath,
No, nor the fruitful river in the eye,
Nor the dejected haviour of the visage,
Together with all forms, moods, shapes of grief
That can denote me truly. These indeed 'seem',
For they are actions that a man might play;
But I have that within which passeth show –
These but the trappings and the suits of woe.

There are whispers now through the CROWD. They're witnessing a
scene that should take place behind closed doors. CLAUDIUS has had
enough. Time for action.

CLAUDIUS

'Tis sweet and commendable in your nature, Hamlet,

He goes towards the Prince bringing in the CROWD with his voice.
This will now be a very public conversation.

CLAUDIUS (continuing)

To give these mourning duties to your father;
But you must know your father lost a father;
That father lost, lost his; and the survivor bound
In filial obligation for some term
To do obsequious sorrow. But to persever
In obstinate condolement is a course
Of impious stubbornness, 'tis unmanly grief,
It shows a will most incorrect to heaven,

As CLAUDIUS gives this rough lecture, he directs his injunctions to
the physically immobile Prince. The great gallery of Courtiers behind,
packed to the rafters. The power and strength of the King's position
chillingly clear.

CLAUDIUS (continuing)

A heart unfortified, a mind impatient,
An understanding simple and unschooled;
For what we know must be, and is as common
As any the most vulgar thing to sense,
Why should we in our peevish opposition
Take it to heart? Fie, 'tis a fault to heaven,
A fault against the dead, a fault to nature,
To reason most absurd, whose common theme
Is death of fathers, and who still hath cried
From the first corpse till he that died today,
'This must be so'.

CLAUDIUS puts his arm around HAMLET. An invasion of intimacy.

CLAUDIUS (continuing)
                                      We pray you throw to earth
This unprevailing woe, and think of us
As of a father; for let the world take note

He drags HAMLET out onto the dais and produces the next
information with a great Churchillian flourish. HAMLET eventually
will be King – CLAUDIUS has nominated him here and now – all is
well. The CROWD respond.

CLAUDIUS (continuing)
You are the most immediate to our throne,

Huge applause from the CROWD.

CLAUDIUS (continuing)
And with no less nobility of love
Than that which dearest father bears his son
Do I impart towards you.

Now, the atmosphere changes.

CLAUDIUS (continuing)
                                      For your intent
In going back to school in Wittenberg,

The great issue comes up. LAERTES, OPHELIA, GERTRUDE all
wanting to see HAMLET take his rightful place.

CLAUDIUS (continuing)
It is most retrograde to our desire,
And we beseech you bend you to remain
Here in the cheer and comfort of our eye,
Our chiefest courtier, cousin, and our son.

Quiet again. The AUDIENCE straining to overhear.

GERTRUDE
Let not thy mother lose her prayers, Hamlet.
I pray thee stay with us, go not to Wittenberg.

We see HAMLET's crushed body language. The sense of a head
bowed. Nevertheless he is a Prince and this is clear in the manner of
his reply.

HAMLET
I shall in all my best obey you, madam.

CLAUDIUS
Why, 'tis a loving and a fair reply.
Be as ourself in Denmark.

                            (To Gertrude) *Madam, come.*

He takes her hand and moves to the front of the Dais. They
effectively mask HAMLET from the Court. Peace is restored. Finally
neither foreign upstarts nor truculent nephews have thrown this
new King off balance, at this formal opening of his new parliament.
He is intimate with her now. Happily letting the Court share their
obvious intoxication with each other.

CLAUDIUS
This gentle and unforced accord of Hamlet
Sits smiling to my heart; in grace whereof,
No jocund health that Denmark drinks today
But the great cannon to the clouds shall tell,
And the King's rouse the heavens shall bruit again,
Re-speaking earthly thunder.

Confetti begins to fall.

CLAUDIUS
Come, away.

Cheers, trumpets. The Royal Couple race out like the hungry
newlyweds they are. The happy CROWD chase them like a drunken
wedding party. The huge hall empties almost by magic. We see the
end doors shut and then we see HAMLET still standing at the throne.
His body collapses, leaning on the arms of the thrones as we hear
him start to speak we move slowly around him

HAMLET
O that this too too solid flesh would melt,
Thaw and resolve itself into a dew,
Or that the Everlasting had not fixed
His canon 'gainst self-slaughter! O God, O God,
How weary, stale, flat, and unprofitable
Seem to me all the uses of this world!
Fie on't, ah fie, fie! 'Tis an unweeded garden
That grows to seed; things rank and gross in nature
Possess it merely. That it should come to this -

The Camera moves with HAMLET down the hall.

HAMLET (continuing)
But two months dead − nay, not so much, not two −
So excellent a King, that was to this
Hyperion to a satyr, so loving to my mother
That he might not beteem the winds of heaven
Visit her face too roughly! Heaven and earth,
Must I remember? Why, she would hang on him
As if increase of appetite had grown
By what it fed on, and yet within a month −
Let me not think on't; frailty, thy name is woman −

He turns to face away from the door.

HAMLET (continuing)
A little month, or ere those shoes were old
With which she followed my poor father's body,
Like Niobe, all tears, why she, even she −
O God, a beast that wants discourse of reason
Would have mourned longer! − married with mine uncle,
My father's brother, but no more like my father
Than I to Hercules, within a month,

Ere yet the salt of most unrighteous tears
Had left the flushing in her gallèd eyes,
She married. O most wicked speed, to post
With such dexterity to incestuous sheets!

He looks back down the almost empty state hall. We see the melancholic profile of a young man in black military cadet uniform, flaxen hair and a single tear trailing down a face more used to smiles.

HAMLET (continuing)
It is not, nor it cannot come to good.
But break, my heart, for I must hold my tongue.

His eyes close as he hears a door open and readies himself for one more invasion of his non-existent privacy; a princely sigh.

HORATIO
Hail to your lordship.

HAMLET
                    I am glad to see thee well.

He makes to leave quickly and go to his room but good manners are part of his character and he looks again. His face changes. He speaks slowly. Not quite believing.

HAMLET (continuing)
Horatio – or I do forget myself.

We track with the three men as they walk quickly towards HAMLET.

HORATIO
The same, my lord, and your poor servant ever.

HAMLET
Sir, my good friend,

A gentle tentative hug. HORATIO allows HAMLET to break the protocol.

HAMLET (continuing)
                    I'll change that name with you.
And what make you from Wittenberg, Horatio? –
Marcellus.

A warm handshake. These two know each other of old.

MARCELLUS
              My good lord.

HAMLET
I am very glad to see you.

And he means it.

                    (to Barnardo) *Good even, sir. –*

A slightly more formal but kind greeting for BARNARDO, before returning to his fascination with HORATIO's sudden appearance.

HAMLET (continuing)
But what in faith make you from Wittenberg?

HORATIO (dodging)
A truant disposition, good my lord.

That is absurd. He's beginning to suspect the real, disappointing truth.
His bitterness starts to return.

> HAMLET
> *I would not have your enemy say so,*
> *Nor shall you do my ear that violence*
> *To make it truster of your own report*
> *Against yourself. I know you are no truant.*
> *But what is your affair in Elsinore?*
> *We'll teach you to drink deep ere you depart.*

> HORATIO
> *My lord, I came to see your father's funeral.*

Oh. Come on.

> HAMLET
> *I prithee do not mock me, fellow-student;*
> *I think it was to see my mother's wedding.*

> HORATIO (squirming)
> *Indeed, my lord, it followed hard upon.*

> HAMLET
> *Thrift, thrift, Horatio. The funeral baked meats*
> *Did coldly furnish forth the marriage tables.*

The bitter humour of the remark is replaced by the genuine hurt he
feels. And the loss.

> HAMLET (continuing)
> *Would I had met my dearest foe in heaven*
> *Ere I had ever seen that day, Horatio.*
> *My father – methinks I see my father.*

The three men look at each other while the Prince experiences this
reverie. Unless, of course, he too ...

> HORATIO
> *Where, my lord?*

HORATIO checks for spies; will he have the courage to tell his grief-
stricken friend?

> HAMLET (still distracted)
> > *In my mind's eye, Horatio.*

> HORATIO
> *I saw him once. He was a goodly King.*

> HAMLET
> *He was a man. Take him for all in all,*
> *I shall not look upon his like again.*

This has been a moment of such gentleness and quiet pain that
HORATIO and the others can hardly bear it. He has to jump in.

> HORATIO
> *My lord, I think I saw him yesternight.*

> HAMLET
> *Saw?*

We track into Close shot on the two of them as the import of the remark sinks in. He really is serious.

> HAMLET
> *Who?*

> HORATIO (urgent whisper)
> *My lord, the King your father.*

> HAMLET
> *The King my father?*

> HORATIO
> *Season your admiration for a while*
> *With an attent ear till I may deliver*
> *Upon the witness of these gentlemen,*
> *This marvel to you.*

> HAMLET
> *For God's love let me hear!*

HAMLET pulls himself together enough to bring the three men out of the State Hall and into his apartments. They enter through a mirrored door close to the throne dais. The door slams shut.

Interior / HAMLET'S APARTMENT Day

The four men stand close together in the dark doorway.

> HORATIO
> *Two nights together had these gentlemen,*
> *Marcellus and Barnardo, on their watch,*
> *In the dead waste and middle of the night,*
> *Been thus encountered. A figure like your father,*
> *Armed at all points exactly, cap-à-pie,*
> *Appears before them, and with solemn march*
> *Goes slow and stately by them. Thrice he walked*

HAMLET's astonished reaction is met with nods from the two other men. It did happen.

> HORATIO (continuing)
> *By their oppressed and fear-surprisèd eyes*
> *Within his truncheon's length, whilst they distilled*
> *Almost to jelly with the act of fear,*
> *Stand dumb and speak not to him. This to me*
> *In dreadful secrecy impart they did,*
> *And I with them the third night kept the watch,*
> *Where, as they had delivered, both in time,*
> *Form of the thing, each word made true and good,*
> *The apparition comes. I knew your father;*
> *These hands are not more like.*

> HAMLET
> *But where was this?*

> MARCELLUS
> *My lord, upon the platform where we watched.*

HAMLET almost aggressive in his thirst for the information.

HAMLET
Did you not speak to it?

HORATIO
                    My lord, I did,
But answer made it none; yet once methought
It lifted up it head and did address
Itself to motion like as it would speak,
But even then the morning cock crew loud,
And at the sound it shrunk in haste away
And vanished from our sight.

Even HAMLET cannot resist the black humour of the situation.

HAMLET
                         'Tis very strange.

HORATIO
As I do live, my honoured lord, 'tis true;
And we did think it writ down in our duty
To let you know of it.

HAMLET pours out the words, nervous, highly unsettled.

HAMLET
Indeed, indeed, sirs; but this troubles me.
Hold you the watch tonight?

BARNARDO
                    My lord, we do.

HAMLET
Armed, say you?

This is sinister.

ALL
                 Armed, my lord.

HAMLET
                         From top to toe?

MARCELLUS
My lord, from head to foot.

He tries to catch them out. It can't be true.

HAMLET
                     Then saw you not his face.

HORATIO
O yes, my lord, he wore his beaver up.

But if it was his father, how was he? The pain returns. He is
intensely vulnerable.

HAMLET
What looked he? Frowningly?

HORATIO
A countenance more in sorrow than in anger.

HAMLET

Pale, or red?
HORATIO
Nay, very pale.
HAMLET
And fixed his eyes upon you?
This is beyond comprehension.
HORATIO
Most constantly.
HAMLET (heartfelt)
I would I had been there.
HORATIO
It would have much amazed you.
HAMLET
Very like, very like. Stayed it long?
HORATIO
While one with moderate haste might tell a hundred.
BARNARDO and MARCELLUS
Longer, longer.
HORATIO
Not when I saw't.
One last attempt to test them.
HAMLET
His beard was grizzled, no?
HORATIO
It was as I have seen it in his life
A sable silvered.
A deep breath before making the unavoidable decision. He is
struggling to maintain control.
HAMLET
                    I will watch tonight.
Perchance 'twill walk again.
HORATIO
                              I warrant you it will.
HAMLET
If it assume my noble father's person,
I'll speak to it though hell itself should gape
And bid me hold my peace.
We see a practical man of action.
HAMLET (continuing)
                              I pray you all,
If you have hitherto concealed this sight,
Let it be tenable in your silence still,
And whatsomever else shall hap tonight,
Give it an understanding but no tongue.
I will requite your loves. So fare ye well.
They move to go out of the main door, but HAMLET stops them

and leads them a different way.

HAMLET
Upon the platform 'twixt eleven and twelve
I'll visit you.

HORATIO
Our duty to your honour.

HAMLET
Your loves, as mine to you. Farewell.

He opens the door in a bookcase to let them out, which reveals
another exit. He ushers them out and as the door closes he rushes up
the steps of his study library. The shelves are crammed with books,
but he makes for a particular section. He talks quietly to himself, still
trying to control his breathing.

HAMLET
My father's spirit in arms! All is not well.
I doubt some foul play. Would the night were come.
Till then, sit still, my soul. Foul deeds will rise,
Though all the earth o'erwhelm them, to men's eyes.

He goes back to the ancient tome, whipping the pages back. Our
Camera moves down onto the page to reveal a heavily bound treatise
on demons and demonology. We move closer onto the pages. They
stop moving at a grotesque illustration of skeletons and we

Dissolve to:

Exterior / PALACE GROUNDS Day

We pan down the great South Front of the Palace to find a horse and
carriage with luggage being packed aboard. OPHELIA and
ATTENDANT enter the shot and we move with them to LAERTES
checking his luggage. OPHELIA gives him his gloves.

LAERTES
My necessaries are embarqued. Farewell.

The Camera leads them as they move away from the house.

LAERTES
And sister, as the winds give benefit
And convoy is assistant, do not sleep
But let me hear from you.

OPHELIA
                    Do you doubt that?

As they walk with their arms around each other, they are very, some
might say unnaturally, close.

LAERTES
For Hamlet, and the trifling of his favour,
Hold it a fashion and a toy in blood,
A violet in the youth of primy nature,
Forward not permanent, sweet not lasting,
The perfume and suppliance of a minute,
No more.

OPHELIA

     No more but so?

LAERTES

          Think it no more.

This last exchange has been lighthearted, but the young man is determined to make a serious point.

LAERTES (continuing)

For nature crescent does not grow alone
In thews and bulk, but as his temple waxes
The inward service of the mind and soul
Grows wide withal. Perhaps he loves you now,
And now no soil nor cautel doth besmirch
The virtue of his will;

She knows she is being lectured. She begins to defend herself. He's having none of it.

LAERTES (continuing)

          but you must fear,
His greatness weighed, his will is not his own,
For he himself is subject to his birth.
He may not, as unvalued persons do,
Carve for himself, for on his choice depends
The sanity and health of the whole state;
And therefore must his choice be circumscribed
Unto the voice and yielding of that body
Whereof he is the head.

This is becoming impossible. She tries to interrupt again. Or at least tease him. They twinkle at each other but still he goes on.

LAERTES (continuing)

          Then if he says he loves you,
It fits your wisdom so far to believe it
As he in his particular act and place
May give his saying deed, which is no further
Than the main voice of Denmark goes withal.

They enter the Palace's wondrous Water Gardens. Now we see the real seriousness of his intent. He really does love his sister. She is touched by his concern. And his genuine fear.

LAERTES (continuing)

Then weigh what loss your honour may sustain
If with too credent ear you list his songs,
Or lose your heart, or your chaste treasure open
To his unmastered importunity.
Fear it, Ophelia, fear it, my dear sister,
And keep within the rear of your affection,
Out of the shot and danger of desire.

They continue their walk and we take in the enormous spectacle of Elsinore's rolling gardens and lakes and sheer vastness. But now he's become pompous. A little too much his father's son, and she's started to get irritated.

LAERTES (continuing)
The chariest maid is prodigal enough
If she unmask her beauty to the moon.
Virtue itself scapes not calumnious strokes.

In the background we see HAMLET, a lone black figure, watching fencers in white at practice.

LAERTES (continuing)
The canker galls the infants of the spring
Too oft before their buttons be disclosed,
And in the morn and liquid dew of youth
Contagious blastments are most imminent.

They watch HAMLET, at fencing practice, shaking hands, 'being good' with people. Not being alone or his normal self.

LAERTES turns to OPHELIA

LAERTES
Be wary then; best safety lies in fear;
Youth to itself rebels, though none else near.

OPHELIA
I shall th' effect of this good lesson keep
As watchman to my heart;

Genuine. Real. But she's not letting him off the hook.

OPHELIA (continuing)
                              but, good my brother,
Do not, as some ungracious pastors do,
Show me the steep and thorny way to heaven
Whilst like a puffed and reckless libertine
Himself the primrose path of dalliance treads
And recks not his own rede.

He know he's been caught. A big smile and a kiss on the lips.

LAERTES
                              O fear me not.
I stay too long.

POLONIUS V/O
Yet here, Laertes?

LAERTES (continuing)
                              But here my father comes.

Oh dear. This could be trouble.

LAERTES (continuing)
A double blessing is a double grace;
Occasion smiles upon a second leave.

POLONIUS approaches. He walks very quickly. He cuts a dapper figure. His greying hair we suspect is tinted. The expanding waist, corseted in. A vain, brilliant man. One not consigned to doddering and waffling. Unless it suits him.

POLONIUS
Yet here, Laertes? Aboard, aboard, for shame!
The wind sits in the shoulder of your sail,
And you are stayed for. There – my blessing with thee,
He kisses him on the cheek. As we

Dissolve to:

Interior / CHAPEL Day

The POLONIUS family sit, holding hands, as the organ plays softly in
the background.

POLONIUS
And these few precepts in thy memory
See thou character.
Give thy thoughts no tongue,
Nor any unproportioned thought his act.
Be thou familiar but by no means vulgar.
The friends thou hast, and their adoption tried,
Grapple them to thy soul with 'hoops of steel',
But do not dull thy palm with entertainment
Of each new-hatched, unfledged comrade. Beware
Of entrance to a quarrel, but being in,
Bear't that th'opposèd may beware of thee.
Give every man thine ear but few thy voice.
Take each man's censure, but reserve thy judgement.
Costly thy habit as thy purse can buy,
POLONIUS pats LAERTES's cravat, OPHELIA smiles.

POLONIUS (continuing)
But not expressed in fancy; rich not gaudy;
For the apparel oft proclaims the man,
And they in France of the best rank and station
Are of all most select and generous chief in that.
Neither a borrower nor a lender be,
For loan oft loses both itself and friend,
And borrowing dulls the edge of husbandry.
This above all –
POLONIUS turns LAERTES's head to face him. He speaks quietly and
with great love.

POLONIUS (continuing)
        to thine own self be true,
And it must follow, as the night the day,
Thou canst not then be false to any man.
The young man struggles to remain composed.

POLONIUS (continuing)
Farewell – my blessing season this in thee.
POLONIUS kisses his son on the forehead.

LAERTES
Most humbly do I take my leave, my lord.

POLONIUS
The time invites you. Go; your servants tend.

POLONIUS tries to bluff it out. Apparently offhand. He moves away.
Brother and sister take a tiny moment together. Highly charged.

LAERTES
Farewell, Ophelia, and remember well
What I have said to you.

OPHELIA
      'Tis in my memory locked,
And you yourself shall keep the key of it.

They kiss affectionately.

LAERTES
Farewell.

LAERTES stands and moves briskly out of the chapel. POLONIUS and
OPHELIA watch him go and then POLONIUS, very deliberately, closes
the gates to the chapel. She is alarmed. POLONIUS's tone is quiet,
but menacing.

POLONIUS
What is't, Ophelia, he hath said to you?

OPHELIA (frightened)
So please you, something touching the Lord Hamlet.

POLONIUS
Marry, well bethought.

He moves her away from the gates, and they walk slowly towards
the confessional.

POLONIUS (continuing)
'Tis told me he hath very oft of late
Given private time to you, and you yourself
Have of your audience been most free and bounteous.
If it be so —

The quiet threat is unmistakable.

POLONIUS (continuing)
    as so 'tis put on me,
And that in way of caution — I must tell you
You do not understand yourself so clearly
As it behoves my daughter and your honour.
What is between you? Give me up the truth.

He pushes her into the confessional.

OPHELIA (rising panic)
He hath, my lord, of late made many tenders
Of his affection to me.

POLONIUS
Affection, pooh! You speak like a green girl
Unsifted in such perilous circumstance.
Do you believe his 'tenders' as you call them?

She, utterly panicked and embarrassed.

OPHELIA
I do not know, my lord, what I should think.

Flash cut to:

Interior / BEDROOM Night

Close on HAMLET and OPHELIA as they make tender love.

Cut to:

Interior / CHAPEL Day

POLONIUS (continuing)
Marry, I'll teach you: think yourself a baby
That you have ta'en his tenders for true pay,
Which are not sterling.

Flash cut to:

Interior / BEDROOM Night

HAMLET and OPHELIA both naked, in her bedroom. They touch lightly, beautifully.

POLONIUS V/O (continuing)
Tender yourself more dearly,

Cut to:

Interior / CHAPEL Day

POLONIUS (continuing)
Or – not to crack the wind of the poor phrase,
Running it thus – you'll tender me a fool.

She is near to tears now. Awkward and unhappy.

OPHELIA
My lord, he hath importuned me with love
In honourable fashion –

She tries to stand but he pushes back again.

POLONIUS (contemptuous)
Ay, 'fashion' you may call it. Go to, go to.
More spirited now. Starts to give as good as she gets.

OPHELIA
And hath given countenance to his speech, my lord,
With almost all the holy vows of heaven.

He explodes.

POLONIUS
Ay, springes to catch woodcocks.

This man knows about forbidden love.

POLONIUS (continuing)
I do know

Flash cut to:

Interior / BEDROOM Night

HAMLET and OPHELIA as they make love.

POLONIUS V/O (continuing)
When the blood burns how prodigal the soul
Lends the tongue vows.

Interior / CHAPEL Day

POLONIUS (continuing)
> *These blazes, daughter,*
> *Giving more light than heat, extinct in both*
> *Even in their promise as it is a-making,*
> *You must not take for fire.*

He recovers slightly from his outburst.

POLONIUS (continuing)
> *From this time, daughter,*
> *Be somewhat scanter of your maiden presence.*
> *Set your entreatments at a higher rate*
> *Than a command to parley.*

He realizes he has gone too far and tries to be more sympathetic.

POLONIUS (continuing)
> *For Lord Hamlet,*
> *Believe so much in him, that he is young,*
> *And with a larger tether may he walk*
> *Than may be given you.*

He goes still further.

POLONIUS (continuing)
> *In few, Ophelia,*
> *Do not believe his vows, for they are brokers,*
> *Not of the dye which their investments show,*
> *But mere implorators of unholy suits,*
> *Breathing like sanctified and pious bawds*
> *The better to beguile. This is for all –*
> *I would not, in plain terms, from this time forth*
> *Have you so slander any moment leisure*
> *As to give words or talk with the Lord Hamlet.*
> *Look to't, I charge you. Come your ways.*

He leaves.

Flash cut to:

Interior / BEDROOM Night

HAMLET and OPHELIA lying together in bed, entwined. HAMLET
asleep, OPHELIA tenderly and gently kisses his head.

OPHELIA V/O
> *I shall obey, my lord.*

Cut to:

Interior / CHAPEL Day

OPHELIA closes her eyes in despair.

Cut to:

Interior / ARMOURY Night

HAMLET leads HORATIO and MARCELLUS through the Armoury.
Nerves are fragile. Nothing but jumpy small talk.

HAMLET
The air bites shrewdly, it is very cold.

HORATIO
It is a nipping and an eager air.

HAMLET
What hour now?

HORATIO
                    I think it lacks of twelve.

MARCELLUS
No, it is struck.

HORATIO
                    Indeed? I heard it not. Then it draws near the season
Wherein the spirit held his wont to walk.

Crash! An enormous explosion goes off. After a moment's panic it
becomes clear that it is a ceremonial cannon (albeit, bloody close).
They move over to look out of the door towards the Palace.

HORATIO
What does this mean, my lord?

HAMLET (contemptuous)
The King doth wake tonight and takes his rouse,

                                              Cut to:

Interior / PALACE Night

We track with CLAUDIUS and GERTRUDE from his apartments,
through carousing courtiers egging them on, drinking as they go,
and end with a ritualistic sweep into her chambers and onto the
bridal bed.

HAMLET V/O
Keeps wassail, and the swagg'ring upspring reels;
And as he drains his draughts of Rhenish down
The kettle-drum and trumpet thus bray out
The triumph of his pledge.

HORATIO V/O
Is it a custom?

HAMLET V/O
                    Ay, marry is't,
But to my mind, though I am native here
And to the manner born, it is a custom
More honoured in the breach than the observance.
This heavy-headed revel east and west

                                              Cut to:

Interior / WEAPONS ROOM Night

HAMLET (continuing)
Makes us traduced and taxed of other nations
They clepe us drunkards, and with swinish phrase
Soil our addition; and indeed it takes
From our achievements, though performed at height,

> *The pith and marrow of our attribute,*

He begins to ruminate.

HAMLET (continuing)
> *So, oft it chances in particular men*

They move off along the corridor.

HAMLET (continuing)
> *That for some vicious mole of nature in them,*
> *As in their birth, wherein they are not guilty*
> *Since nature cannot choose his origin,*

He is talking as if he were asking questions of himself.

HAMLET (continuing)
> *By their o'ergrowth of some complexion,*
> *Oft breaking down the pales and forts of reason,*
> *Or by some habit, that too much o'erleavens*
> *The form of plausive manners — that these men,*
> *Carrying, I say, the stamp of one defect,*
> *Being Nature's livery or Fortune's star,*
> *His virtues else, be they as pure as grace,*
> *As infinite as man may undergo,*
> *Shall in the general censure take corruption*
> *From that particular fault.*

He leads them off.

Cut to:

Exterior / PALACE GATES Night

HAMLET (continuing)
> *The dram of evil*
> *Doth all the noble substance over-daub*
> *To his own scandal.*

Suddenly, THE GHOST appears.

HORATIO
> *Look my lord, it comes.*
> *It beckons you to go away with it*
> *As if it some impartment did desire*
> *To you alone.*

THE GHOST signals, pleading, attempting to speak. A pitiable noise.

MARCELLUS (to Hamlet)
> *Look with what courteous action*
> *It waves you to a more removèd ground.*
> *But do not go with it.*

HAMLET struggles to get away from them.

HORATIO (to Hamlet)
> *No, by no means.*

HAMLET
> *It will not speak. Then will I follow it.*

HORATIO
> *Do not, my lord.*

There is a terrifying look in HAMLET's eye now. A man with, as he thinks, nothing to lose.

HAMLET

Why, what should be the fear?
I do not set my life at a pin's fee,
And for my soul, what can it do to that,
Being a thing immortal as itself?

Another great, unearthly yell. Even sadder.

HAMLET (continuing)
It waves me forth again. I'll follow it.

He goes through the gate. The men follow him, now desperate to restrain him.

HORATIO
What if it tempt you toward the flood, my lord,
Or to the dreadful summit of the cliff
That beetles o'er his base into the sea,
And there assume some other horrible form
Which might deprive your sovereignty of reason
And draw you into madness? Think of it.
The very place puts toys of desperation,
Without more motive, into every brain
That looks so many fathoms to the sea
And hears it roar beneath.

Close as he is to HAMLET, the words have not had an effect. HAMLET has eyes for one thing.

HAMLET
It wafts me still.

(To The Ghost) *Go on, I'll follow thee.*

Almost violent now.

MARCELLUS
You shall not go, my lord.

HAMLET

Hold off your hands.

HORATIO
Be ruled. You shall not go.

HAMLET

My fate cries out.
And makes each petty artery in this body
As hardy as the Nemean lion's nerve.
Still am I called. Unhand me, gentlemen.

HAMLET makes one great physical effort to escape this pinioning. He savagely pulls out his sword and trains it on them. He will not be stopped.

HAMLET (continuing)
By heav'n, I'll make a ghost of him that lets me.
I say, away!

(To The Ghost) *Go on, I'll follow thee.*

HAMLET chases off into the woods. The two men remain, shaken to the core.

HORATIO
He waxes desperate with imagination.

MARCELLUS
Let's follow. 'Tis not fit thus to obey him.

HORATIO
Have after. To what issue will this come?

MARCELLUS
Something is rotten in the state of Denmark.

HORATIO
Heaven will direct it.

MARCELLUS
Nay, let's follow him.

Exterior / WOODS Night

We pan and track with HAMLET as he runs through a wood exploding with terror.

HAMLET V/O
Angels and ministers of grace defend us!
Be thou a spirit of health or goblin damned,
Bring with thee airs from heaven or blasts from hell,
Be thy intents wicked or charitable,
Thou com'st in such a questionable shape
That I will speak to thee.

On and on through the wood we race with our Camera. Explosions through the trees, cracks in the ground, the very earth itself shaking, but still no GHOST.

HAMLET V/O (continuing)
I'll call thee Hamlet,
King, father, royal Dane. O answer me!
Let me not burst in ignorance,

Flash cuts of his dead father sear through his mind as his urgent thoughts continue in voice over.

HAMLET V/O (continuing)
but tell
Why thy canonized bones, hearsèd in death,
Have burst their cerements, why the sepulchre
Wherein we saw thee quietly enurned
Hath oped his ponderous and marble jaws
To cast thee up again. What may this mean,
That thou, dead corpse, again in complete steel,
Revisits thus the glimpses of the moon,
Making night hideous, and we fools of nature
So horridly to shake our disposition

> *With thoughts beyond the reaches of our souls?*
> *Say, why is this? Wherefore? What should we do?*
> *Where wilt thou lead me? Speak. I'll go no further.*

Silence at last. We pan around the wood as Hamlet's eerie POV.
THE GHOST's agonized voice cuts through the darkness like a knife.

> THE GHOST O/S
> *Mark me.*
> HAMLET V/O
> *I will.*

Still no sign of this 'thing'. Suspense building. HAMLET's nervous
eyes betray the mounting dread.

> THE GHOST O/S
> > *My hour is almost come*
> *When I to sulph'rous and tormenting flames*
> *Must render up myself.*
> HAMLET V/O
> > *Alas, poor Ghost!*

The response is stern.

> THE GHOST O/S
> *Pity me not, but lend thy serious hearing*
> *To what I shall unfold.*
> HAMLET V/O
> > *Speak, I am bound to hear.*
> THE GHOST
> *So art thou to revenge when thou shalt hear.*
> HAMLET
> *What?*

HAMLET wheels around in surprise as the voice comes from yet
another part of the wood. **Crash**. A great hand grasps his neck and
with some force throws him against a tree. We move in now on the
looming figure that has finally revealed itself. The light comes up
on a face of distressing pallor, lit as if from within by two piercing
blue eyes.

> THE GHOST
> > *I am thy father's spirit,*
> *Doomed for a certain term to walk the night,*
> *And for the day confined to fast in fires,*
> *Till the foul crimes done in my days of nature*
> *Are burnt and purged away. But that I am forbid*
> *To tell the secrets of my prison-house,*

He looks to the ground, where we track across the floor. It cracks
open to reveal an ominous gateway to hell. Agonized voices from
beyond pierce the night's dull ear.

> THE GHOST (continuing)
> *I could a tale unfold whose lightest word*
> *Would harrow up thy soul, freeze thy young blood,*

Make thy two eyes like stars start from their spheres,
Thy knotted and combinèd locks to part,
And each particular hair to stand on end
Like quills upon the fretful porcupine.
But this eternal blazon must not be
To ears of flesh and blood.

THE GHOST becomes quietly impassioned.

THE GHOST (continuing)
                                        List, Hamlet, list, O list!
If thou didst ever thy dear father love –

HAMLET
O God!

HAMLET now gets to his knees, moving nearer THE GHOST.

We cut to:

Close on THE GHOST's mouth.

THE GHOST
Revenge his foul and most unnatural murder.

Cut to:

An ear receiving poison.

HAMLET
Murder?

Cut to:

The skin of the ear expanding.
HAMLET seems overcome.

THE GHOST
Murder

Cut to:

Blood, pus, awfulness.

THE GHOST (continuing)
          most foul, as in the best it is,
But this most foul, strange, and unnatural.

HAMLET tries to rally his father, with his resolution.

HAMLET
Haste me to know it, that I with wings as swift
As meditation or the thoughts of love
May sweep to my revenge.

THE GHOST
                              I find thee apt,
And duller shouldst thou be than the fat weed
That roots itself in ease on Lethe wharf,
Wouldst thou not stir in this. Now, Hamlet, hear.

Cut to:

Exterior / ORCHARD Day (Flashback)
OLD HAMLET asleep in his wintry orchard.

THE GHOST V/O
'Tis given out that, sleeping in mine orchard,

A serpent stung me. So the whole ear of Denmark
Is by a forgèd process of my death
Rankly abused.

Cut to:

Exterior / WOODS Night (Real time)

THE GHOST (continuing)
>   *But know, thou noble youth,*
The serpent that did sting thy father's life
Now wears his crown.

HAMLET
O my prophetic soul! My uncle?

Cut to:

The man himself. CLAUDIUS. Smug – self-satisfied. Eyes on the
QUEEN.

THE GHOST
Ay, that incestuous, that adulterate beast,

Cut to:

Interior / STATE HALL CORRIDOR Day

We see the Royal party in a curling competition, HAMLET throws a
disc. OLD HAMLET instructs. He takes HAMLET off and GERTRUDE
watches.

THE GHOST V/O (continuing)
With witchcraft of his wit, with traitorous gifts –
O wicked wit and gifts, that have the power
So to seduce! – won to his shameful lust
The will of my most seeming-virtuous queen.

Cut to:

Exterior / WOODS Night (Real time)

THE GHOST almost in tears now, very much less ghostly and very
much more human.

THE GHOST (continuing)
O Hamlet, what a falling-off was there! –
From me, whose love was of that dignity

Cut to:

Interior / STATE HALL CORRIDOR Day (Flashback)

CLAUDIUS moves to GERTRUDE and she throws a disc, they
embrace and GERTRUDE joins her men. CLAUDIUS watches her as
POLONIUS joins him.

THE GHOST V/O
That it went hand-in-hand even with the vow
I made to her in marriage, and to decline
Upon a wretch whose natural gifts were poor
To those of mine.
But virtue, as it never will be moved,
Though lewdness court it in a shape of heaven,
So lust, though to a radiant angel linked,

Will sate itself in a celestial bed,
And prey on garbage.

Cut to:

Exterior / WOODS Night (Real time)
Panic in THE GHOST's voice.

> THE GHOST (continuing)
> *But soft, methinks I scent the morning's air.*
> *Brief let me be.*

Cut to:

Exterior / ORCHARD Day (Flashback)
Camera moves slowly back to reveal the sleeping peaceful monarch resting under a tree.

> THE GHOST V/O (continuing)
> *Sleeping within mine orchard,*
> *My custom always in the afternoon,*

A figure walks towards OLD HAMLET.

> *Upon my secure hour thy uncle stole*
> *With juice of cursèd hebenon in a vial,*

Very Close Shot of the poison entering the ear.

> *And in the porches of mine ear did pour*
> *The leperous distilment, whose effect*
> *Holds such an enmity with blood of man*
> *That swift as quicksilver*

A Jump-cut rhythm of the King's convulsions. Fluid and blood bubbling out of the ear. Skin blistering in an instant. Fingers contracting arthritically. Writhing on the ground in agony.

> THE GHOST V/O (continuing)
> *It courses through*
> *The natural gates and alleys of the body,*
> *And with a sudden vigour it doth posset*
> *And curd, like eager droppings into milk,*
> *The thin and wholesome blood. So did it mine;*
> *And a most instant tetter barked about,*
> *Most lazar-like, with vile and loathsome crust,*
> *All my smooth body.*

CLAUDIUS moves away, removing his footprints as he goes.
He stops, watches OLD HAMLET the last time and then runs off.

> THE GHOST V/O (continuing)
> *Thus was I, sleeping, by a brother's hand*
> *Of life, of crown, of queen at once dispatched,*
> *Cut off even in the blossoms of my sin,*
> *Unhouseled, dis-appointed, unaneled,*
> *No reck'ning made, but sent to my account*
> *With all my imperfections on my head.*

We are now Close on the distorted face, a picture of pain

Exterior / WOODS Night (Real time)

>THE GHOST (continuing)
>*O horrible, O horrible, most horrible!*

The two faces close together now.

>THE GHOST (continuing)
>*If thou hast nature in thee, bear it not.*
>*Let not the royal bed of Denmark be*
>*A couch for luxury and damned incest.*
>*But howsoever thou pursuest this act,*

He is especially gentle now. Regretful, compassionate.

>THE GHOST (continuing)
>*Taint not thy mind, nor let thy soul contrive*
>*Against thy mother aught. Leave her to heaven,*
>*And to those thorns that in her bosom lodge*
>*To prick and sting her.*

The sounds of the dawn intrude ominously.

>THE GHOST (continuing)
>   *Fare thee well at once.*
>*The glow-worm shows the matin to be near,*
>*And 'gins to pale his uneffectual fire.*
>*Adieu, adieu, Hamlet. Remember me.*

The Camera tracks away from THE GHOST. From HAMLET. Their hands reach for each other. HAMLET makes a desperate clutch for his father's hand but as the fingers curl around the ghostly armour, it ... vanishes.

>HAMLET
>*O all you host of heaven!*

He looks to the sky, then falls flat on to the ground. His head close to the soil.

>HAMLET (continuing)
>   *O earth! What else?*
>*And shall I couple hell?*

He feels for where his father was. He is in agony.

>HAMLET (continuing)
>   *O fie! Hold, hold, my heart,*
>*And you, my sinews, grow not instant old,*
>*But bear me stiffly up. Remember thee?*
>*Ay, thou poor ghost, whiles memory holds a seat*
>*In this distracted globe. Remember thee?*

Almost laughing now with the hysterical grief. He is aware of wanting to speak to the earth.

>HAMLET (continuing)
>*Yea, from the table of my memory*
>*I'll wipe away all trivial fond records,*
>*All saws of books, all forms, all pressures past,*

That youth and observation copied there,
And thy commandment all alone shall live
Within the book and volume of my brain
Unmixed with baser matter. Yes,

He gets up onto his knees.

    HAMLET (continuing)

                            by heaven.

    O most pernicious woman!
    O villain, villain, Smiling, damnèd villain!
    My tables, meet it is I set it down
    That one may smile and smile and be a villain.
    At least I'm sure it may be so in Denmark.

(he writes)

    So, uncle, there you are. Now to my word:
    It is 'Adieu, adieu, remember me'.
    I have sworn't.

The dawn almost upon us and HAMLET is sobering up fast. The sounds of cries from MARCELLUS and HORATIO ring through the grey wood.

    HORATIO and MARCELLUS O/S
    My lord, my lord!

We cut to the two men and track with them for a beat.

    MARCELLUS (calling)
    Lord Hamlet.

    HORATIO
    Heaven secure him.

Cut to a Close shot of HAMLET as he stands up – holding his sword in front of him. A still, mystic moment.

    HAMLET
    So be it.

He runs off towards them. Meets them on the way, they change direction to follow him. He seems, quite frankly, mad.

    HORATIO (calling)
    Illo, ho, ho, my lord!

    HAMLET
    Hillo, ho, ho, boy; come, bird, come.

    MARCELLUS
    How is't, my lord?

    HORATIO (to Hamlet)
    What news, my lord?

    HAMLET
    O wonderful!

He is all inscrutable smiles and naughtiness, hiding behind trees and avoiding everything.

    HORATIO
    Good my lord, tell it.

HAMLET

No, you'll reveal it.

HORATIO

Not I, my lord, by heaven.

MARCELLUS

Nor I, my lord.

Will he or won't he?

HAMLET

How say you then, would heart of man once think it?
But you'll be secret?

HORATIO

Ay, by heav'n, my lord.

The mad enigma continues.

HAMLET

There's never a villain dwelling in all Denmark
But he's an arrant knave.

His friends are too tired and frightened for all this.

HORATIO

There needs no ghost, my lord, come from the grave
To tell us this.

HAMLET

Why, right, you are in the right.
And so without more circumstance at all
I hold it fit that we shake hands and part,
You as your business and desires shall point you —
For every man hath business and desire,
Such as it is — and for mine own poor part,
Look you, I'll go pray.

HORATIO

These are but wild and whirling words, my lord.

HAMLET

I am sorry they offend you heartily
Yes, faith, heartily.

He really is appalled to have offended. He just doesn't know what
to do.

HORATIO

There's no offence, my lord.

HAMLET

Yes by Saint Patrick but there is, Horatio,

Urgent now, real. But the necessary secrecy has started already.

HAMLET (continuing)

And much offence, too. Touching this vision here,
It is an honest ghost, that let me tell you.
For your desire to know what is between us,
O'ermaster't as you may.

He turns to MARCELLUS too.

40

And now, good friends,
As you are friends, scholars, and soldiers,
Give me one poor request.

HORATIO

      What is't, my lord? We will.

HAMLET
Never make known what you have seen tonight.

HORATIO
My lord, we will not.

Not good enough.

HAMLET

     Nay, but swear't.

HORATIO
In faith, my lord, not I.

MARCELLUS
Nor I, my lord, not I.

HAMLET
Upon my sword.

He is deadly serious.

MARCELLUS

    We have sworn, my lord, already.

This man is dangerous.

HAMLET
Indeed, upon my sword, indeed.

THE GHOST O/S
Swear!

Without warning the ground under HORATIO's foot splits apart,
smoke rising from the depths.

 Everyone appalled. HAMLET's hysteria mounts.

HAMLET
Ah ha, boy, sayst thou so? Art thou there, truepenny?
Come on. You hear this fellow in the cellarage.
Consent to swear.

HORATIO

    Propose the oath, my lord.

HAMLET
Never to speak of this that you have seen.
Swear by my sword.

They hear the chilling noise afar off. The earth explodes.

THE GHOST O/S
Swear.

HAMLET
Hic et ubique? Then we'll shift our ground. –
Come hither, gentlemen,

They move off in the direction of THE GHOST's voice.

HAMLET (continuing)
And lay your hands again upon my sword.
Never to speak of this that you have heard,
Swear by my sword.

The earth explodes as

THE GHOST O/S
Swear.

The trees around them are starting to move.

HAMLET (continuing)
Well said, old mole. Canst work i'th' earth so fast?

The trees still shaking. The earth smouldering.

HAMLET (continuing)
A worthy pioneer. – Once more remove, good friends.

They move again to another part of the woods. The ground moving under their feet, the trees aquiver. Smoke spurting out behind them as they run through the woods.

HORATIO
O day and night, but this is wondrous strange.

HAMLET
And therefore as a stranger give it welcome.
There are more things in heaven and earth, Horatio,
Than are dreamt of in our philosophy. But come,

He leads them off again. He brings them to their knees amid the earth-moving chaos. Raises his sword aloft.

HAMLET (continuing)
Here as before, never, so help you mercy,
How strange or odd soe'er I bear myself –
As I perchance hereafter shall think meet
To put an antic disposition on –
That you at such time seeing me never shall,
With arms encumbered thus, or with this headshake,
Or by pronouncing of some doubtful phrase
As 'Well, we know' or 'We could an' if we would',
Or 'If we list to speak', or 'There be, an' if they might',
Or such ambiguous giving out, to note
That you know aught of me – this not to do,
So grace and mercy at your most need help you, swear.

Laying the sword on the ground.

THE GHOST O/S
Swear.

They place their hands on the sword and swear. At last, all is quiet. HAMLET speaks in quiet, heartfelt tones. Kindness itself to his two friends.

HAMLET
Rest, rest, perturbèd spirit. – So, gentlemen,
With all my love I do commend me to you,

And what so poor a man as Hamlet is
May do t'express his love and friending to you,
God willing, shall not lack. Let us go in together,
And still your fingers on your lips, I pray.
The time is out of joint. O cursèd spite
That ever I was born to set it right!
Nay, come, let's go together.

Dissolve to:

Exterior / PALACE Night

Meantime the seat of power appears to sleep, but some people are still at work.

Dissolve to:

Interior / POLONIUS'S ROOM Night

The room is dark but we see the foxy face of REYNALDO. Debauched of look, drinking and smoking. In the background we see a prostitute, work over, frightened to move from the bed. POLONIUS, shirt partly undone, corset visible, crosses the room still doing up his trousers, pulling up braces. Completely unembarrassed by the situation. He takes his time, goes to a desk, throws a packet to his pimp.

> POLONIUS
> *Give him this money and these notes, Reynaldo.*

REYNALDO does not move. His attitude barely civil. These men have a deal, that's all.

> REYNALDO
> *I will, my lord.*

POLONIUS is over-polite with him. Heavily ironic. There is a perverse pleasure to be had from this low-life sparring match.

> POLONIUS
> *You shall do marv'lous wisely, good Reynaldo,*
> *Before you visit him, to make inquire*
> *Of his behaviour.*

REYNALDO all feigned humility and 'but of course'-ness.

> REYNALDO
> *My lord, I did intend it.*

POLONIUS continues the cruel patronage. A certain relish, but he wants this thing done. He pours himself a drink.

> POLONIUS
> *Marry, well said, very well said. Look you, sir,*
> *Enquire me first what Danskers are in Paris,*
> *And how, and who, what means, and where they keep,*
> *What company, at what expense; and finding*
> *By this encompassment and drift of question*
> *That they do know my son, come you more nearer*
> *Than your particular demands will touch it.*
> *Take you, as 'twere, some distant knowledge of him,*

43

As thus: 'I know his father and his friends,
And in part him' – do you mark this, Reynaldo?
REYNALDO
Ay, very well, my lord.
POLONIUS
'And in part him, but', you may say, 'not well,
But if't be he I mean, he's very wild,
Addicted so and so'; and there put on him
What forgeries you please – marry, none so rank
As may dishonour him,

A cynical smile between them. What have these men done in the
past? They reek of corruption.

POLONIUS (continuing)
      take heed of that –
But, sir, such wanton, wild, and usual slips
As are companions noted and most known
To youth and liberty.
REYNALDO
    As gaming, my lord?
POLONIUS
Ay, or drinking, fencing, swearing,
Quarrelling, drabbing –

He remembers the girl in the bed, almost as an afterthought. Clicks
his fingers for her to go.

POLONIUS (continuing)
     you may go so far.

As she is passing REYNALDO, he grabs her, signalling for her to keep
her mouth shut. He enjoys the irony of the situation.

REYNALDO
My lord, that would dishonour him.

REYNALDO brutally pushes her away. She leaves through a secret
door in the wall.

POLONIUS
Faith, no, as you may season it in the charge.
You must not put another scandal on him,
That he is open to incontinency –
That's not my meaning –
But breathe his faults so quaintly
That they may seem the taints of liberty,
(he crosses to sit down)
The flash and outbreak of a fiery mind,
A savageness in unreclaimèd blood.
Of general assault.
REYNALDO
    But, my good lord –

POLONIUS

Wherefore should you do this?

He wants to hear REYNALDO's poisonous irony.

REYNALDO

Ay, my lord.

I would know that.

POLONIUS very happy now. Physically satisfied, relishing his smoke and drink he expands on his theory of information gathering.

POLONIUS

Marry, sir, here's my drift,
And I believe it is a fetch of warrant.
You laying these slight sullies on my son,
As 'twere a thing a little soiled i'th' working,
Mark you, your party in converse, him you would sound,
Having ever seen in the prenominate crimes
The youth you breathe of guilty, be assured
He closes with you in this consequence:
'Good sir', or so, or 'friend', or 'gentleman',
According to the phrase and the addition
Of man and country.

REYNALDO

Very good, my lord.

POLONIUS has started to lose interest himself. More interested in the effects of sex and substance.

POLONIUS

And then, sir, does he this – he does – what was I about to say?
By the mass, I was about to say something. Where did I leave?

REYNALDO repeats with relish and contempt. Almost an impersonation. He manages to stay this side of getting a smack in the face.

REYNALDO

At 'closes in the consequence', at 'friend,
Or so', and 'gentleman'.

POLONIUS

At 'closes in the consequence'- ay, marry,
He closes with you thus: 'I know the gentleman,
I saw him yesterday'- or t'other day,
Or then, or then -'with such and such, and, as you say,
There was a gaming, there o'ertook in's rouse,
There falling out at tennis', or perchance
'I saw him enter such a house of sale',
Videlicet, a brothel, or so forth. See you now,

He enjoys over-elaborating this to a man who has no need of such instruction. He talks gently, kindly, as if to a bad, stupid child.

POLONIUS (continuing)

Your bait of falsehood takes this carp of truth;

And thus do we of wisdom and of reach
With windlasses and with assays of bias
By indirections find directions out.
So, by my former lecture and advice,
Shall you my son. You have me, have you not?
REYNALDO
My lord, I have.
POLONIUS
                    God be with you. Fare ye well.
REYNALDO stands up, picks up the money and crosses the room.
REYNALDO
Good my lord.
Another beat. A look.
POLONIUS
Observe his inclination in yourself.
These two men, like mafiosi, very wary of each other. Neither is one
on whom you turn your back.
REYNALDO
I shall, my lord
Then, very gently, almost feminine.
POLONIUS
                    And let him ply his music.
This raises a smile.
REYNALDO
  Well, my lord.
He exits through another hidden door.
POLONIUS
Farewell.
As it closes OPHELIA rushes through yet another hidden door.
POLONIUS starts up and goes to her. She is very, very distressed.
POLONIUS (continuing)
            How now, Ophelia, what's the matter?
OPHELIA
Alas, my lord, I have been so affrighted.
POLONIUS
With what, i'th'name of God?
OPHELIA
My lord, as I was sewing in my chamber,
Lord Hamlet, with his doublet all unbraced,
No hat upon his head, his stockings fouled,
Ungartered, and down-gyvèd to his ankle,
Pale as his shirt, his knees knocking each other,
And with a look so piteous in purport
As if he had been loosèd out of hell
To speak of horrors, he comes before me.

POLONIUS
Mad for thy love?

She thinks probably yes. But not in a way she can remotely
understand. And now there is no one to talk to except her father.
Her concern is for HAMLET as much as herself.

OPHELIA
                        My lord, I do not know,
But truly I do fear it.

POLONIUS
                        What said he?

OPHELIA
He took me by the wrist and held me hard,
Then goes he to the length of all his arm,
And with his other hand thus o'er his brow
He falls to such perusal of my face
As 'a would draw it. Long stayed he so.
At last, a little shaking of mine arm,
And thrice his head thus waving up and down,
He raised a sigh so piteous and profound
That it did seem to shatter all his bulk
And end his being. That done, he lets me go,
And, with his head over his shoulder turned,
He seemed to find his way without his eyes,
For out o'doors he went without their help,
And to the last bended their light on me.

POLONIUS moves over to her at the door.

POLONIUS
Come, go with me. I will go seek the King.
This is the very ecstasy of love,
Whose violent property fordoes itself
And leads the will to desperate undertakings
As oft as any passion under heaven
That does afflict our natures.

He had no idea this was so serious. He's also relieved to be back in
his daughter's attention. Apparently. He holds her and is tender with
her. Kisses and squeezes. She is agonized over her own reaction and
now about whether she's done the right thing.

POLONIUS (continuing)
                        I am sorry —
What, have you given him any hard words of late?

This is too much. She explodes with righteous indignation.

OPHELIA
No, my good lord, but as you did command
I did repel his letters and denied
His access to me.

OPHELIA rushes over to the bed and curls up on it. POLONIUS, now tremendously understanding.

POLONIUS

That hath made him mad.
I am sorry that with better heed and judgement
I had not quoted him. I feared he did but trifle
And meant to wreck thee. But beshrew my jealousy!
By heaven, it is as proper to our age
To cast beyond ourselves in our opinions
As it is common for the younger sort
To lack discretion.

He sits on the bed next to her, gently stroking her hair.

POLONIUS (continuing)

Come, go we to the King.
This must be known, which, being kept close, might move
More grief to hide than hate to utter love. Come.

Dissolve to:

Exterior / PALACE Day

Elsinore, serene and majestic. What could disturb its peaceful state?

Dissolve to:

Interior / QUEEN'S APARTMENTS Day

A Wide shot of the palatial bedroom. ROSENCRANTZ and
GUILDENSTERN are waiting. The KING, slightly dishevelled, crosses
over to them, doing up the buttons on his tunic. In the background
the ATTENDANTS are making up the marital bed. GERTRUDE and
CLAUDIUS have not been discussing the weather! During the first part
of the scene they are being dressed, combed and spruced, the room is
being tidied.

CLAUDIUS

Welcome, dear Rosencrantz and Guildenstern.
Moreover that we much did long to see you,
The need we have to use you did provoke
Our hasty sending. Something have you heard
Of Hamlet's transformation – so I call it,
Since not th' exterior nor the inward man
Resembles that it was. What it should be,
More than his father's death, that thus hath put him
So much from th' understanding of himself,
I cannot dream of. I entreat you both

He moves away to sit on the bed. An ATTENDANT brings
CLAUDIUS a drink.

CLAUDIUS (continuing)

That, being of so young days brought up with him,
And since so neighboured to his youth and humour,
That you vouchsafe your rest here in our court
Some little time, so by your companies
To draw him on to pleasures, and to gather,

So much as from occasions you may glean,
Whether aught to us unknown afflicts him thus
That, opened, lies within our remedy.

The QUEEN emerges, still dressing. She takes them by the hand.
Woos them. They are both weak-kneed with desire for her.

GERTRUDE
Good gentlemen, he hath much talked of you,
And sure I am, two men there is not living
To whom he more adheres. If it will please you
To show us so much gentry and good will
As to expend your time with us a while
For the supply and profit of our hope,
Your visitation shall receive such thanks
As fits a King's remembrance.

GERTRUDE and CLAUDIUS lead them out of the room.
ROSENCRANTZ, slightly more prone to justifications, starts timidly.

ROSENCRANTZ
                    Both your majesties
Might, by the sovereign power you have of us,
Put your dread pleasures more into command
Than to entreaty.

GUILDENSTERN knows when they're on to a winner. Besides they
have no choice. Quickly.

GUILDENSTERN
                    But we both obey,
And here give up ourselves in the full bent
To lay our service freely at your feet
To be commanded.

Right. Now on with business. The KING, far less able to disguise
his indifference to the pair, leads the way out.

CLAUDIUS
Thanks, Rosencrantz and gentle Guildenstern.

Interior / CORRIDOR Day

Now they are in the main corridor on the way to the State Hall
and work. Attended by a retinue. Very efficient, brisk.

GERTRUDE
Thanks, Guildenstern and gentle Rosencrantz.
And I beseech you instantly to visit
My too-much changèd son. —

She sends them off down a side corridor.

GERTRUDE (continuing)
                    Go, some of ye,
And bring the gentlemen where Hamlet is.

The two men hardly know what's happening to them as they are
almost bundled away. The 'audience' is over.

GUILDENSTERN
Heavens make our presence and our practices
Pleasant and helpful to him.
GERTRUDE
Ay, amen.

The Royal Party still moving. No time wasted. Like a shadow
POLONIUS emerges from another door to join the progress. It feels
like a team of spin doctors, media advisers, and security experts
briefing the President on the way to a White House press conference.
Still the Camera keeps moving.

POLONIUS (confidentially)
Th' ambassadors from Norway, my good lord,
Are joyfully return'd.
CLAUDIUS
Thou still hast been the father of good news.

They have reached the main door.

Interior / STATE HALL Day

We see a fencing practice occupying the State Hall. Arranged in
symmetrical patterns. All dressed in white, it's like an Olympic
opening ceremony. The moves are viciously elegant. The fencers
file out as the Royal Group moves through without pause.

POLONIUS
Have I, my lord? Assure you, my good liege,
I hold my duty as I hold my soul,
Both to my God and to my gracious King.
And I do think –

We continue to track with them down the hall.

POLONIUS (continuing)
                 or else this brain of mine
Hunts not the trail of policy so sure
As it hath used to do – that I have found
The very cause of Hamlet's lunacy.

A brief pause. An intimate moment.

CLAUDIUS
O speak of that, that do I long to hear!

The Prime Minister even more confidential. Conscious of his power
as King-maker over CLAUDIUS.

POLONIUS
Give first admittance to th' ambassadors.
My news shall be the fruit to that great feast.

A look that says CLAUDIUS knows he's being 'handled'.

CLAUDIUS
Thyself do grace to them, and bring them in.

POLONIUS moves off and CLAUDIUS goes back to GERTRUDE.
He whispers.

CLAUDIUS (continuing)
He tells me, my sweet queen, that he hath found
The head and source of all your son's distemper.

She barely looks at him. Preoccupied, ready for work.

GERTRUDE
I doubt it is no other but the main
His father's death and our o'er-hasty marriage.

CLAUDIUS
Well, we shall sift him.

They have now reached the thrones and take their places, glamorous as ever. From another hidden door, POLONIUS leads VOLTEMAND and CORNELIUS over to the throne.

CLAUDIUS (continuing)
     Welcome, my good friends.
Say, Voltemand, what from our brother Norway?

VOLTEMAND
Most fair return of greetings and desires.

           Cut to:

Interior / WOODS Night (Flashback)

YOUNG FORTINBRAS on horseback, with his men.

VOLTEMAND V/O
Upon our first he sent out to suppress
His nephew's levies, which to him appeared

           Cut to:

Interior / COUNCIL ROOM Night (Flashback)

OLD NORWAY reading the news of FORTINBRAS's misdemeanours.

VOLTEMAND V/O (continuing)
To be a preparation 'gainst the Polack;
But better looked into, he truly found

           Cut to:

Exterior / ELSINORE Night (Flashback)

Yes. This is what the Norwegian Prince wants.

VOLTEMAND V/O (continuing)
It was against your highness;

           Cut to:

Interior / COUNCIL ROOM Night (Flashback)

OLD NORWAY turns and we see the young troublemaker FORTINBRAS, head bowed. He suddenly receives a crashing blow from the old man.

VOLTEMAND V/O (continuing)
        whereat grieved
That so his sickness, age, and impotence
Was falsely borne in hand, sends out arrests
On Fortinbras, which he, in brief, obeys,
Receives rebuke from Norway,

We see FORTINBRAS on his knees asking for forgiveness and

eventually the old man does so and hugs him. Now he gives him written permission to approach Poland, not Denmark.

VOLTEMAND V/O (continuing)
                              and, in fine,
Makes vow before his uncle never more
To give th' essay of arms against your majesty;
Whereon old Norway, overcome with joy,
Gives him three thousand crowns in annual fee
And his commission to employ those soldiers
So levied as before, against the Polack,

                                              Cut to:

Interior / STATE HALL Day (Real time)

VOLTEMAND (continuing)
With an entreaty herein further shown,
(he gives Claudius a letter)
    That it might please you to give quiet pass
    Through your dominions for his enterprise
    On such regards of safety and allowance
    As therein are set down.
CLAUDIUS (impressed)
                              It likes us well,
And at our more considered time we'll read,
Answer, and think upon this business.
Meantime we thank you for your well-took labour.
Go to your rest;
VOLTEMAND and CORNELIUS turn and walk away. CLAUDIUS stands.

CLAUDIUS (continuing)
                        at night we'll feast together.
Most welcome home.
The ambassadors leave. GERTRUDE stands up.

POLONIUS
                    This business is well ended.
My liege and madam,
They move off, away from the thrones.

                                              Cut to:

Interior / ANTE STATE ROOM Day

This is clearly a top-secret discussion and ought to be urgent. But POLONIUS knows he has them in his thrall. Documents are being signed.

POLONIUS (continuing)
                        to expostulate
What majesty should be, what duty is,
Why day is day, night night, and time is time,
Were nothing but to waste night, day, and time.
Therefore, since brevity is the soul of wit,

And tediousness the limbs and outward flourishes,
I will be brief.

The signing is over. ATTENDANTS leave. CLAUDIUS and
GERTRUDE are very pissed off with this waffling. POLONIUS
changes the tone, leaning forwards onto the desk and adds brutally.

> POLONIUS (continuing)
> *Your noble son is mad –*

Close on their reactions. But wait, there's more.

> POLONIUS (continuing)
> *'Mad' call I it, for to define true madness,*
> *What is't but to be nothing else but mad?*

He remains cold, sinister.

> POLONIUS (continuing)
> *But let that go.*

The Queen replies through gritted teeth.

> GERTRUDE
> *More matter with less art.*

He won't be put off by a woman, least of all an adulterous wife and
insensitive mother.

> POLONIUS
> *Madam, I swear I use no art at all.*
> *That he is mad, 'tis true; 'tis true 'tis pity;*
> *And pity 'tis 'tis true – a foolish figure,*
> *But farewell it, for I will use no art.*

They exchange looks. She has no choice but to listen to this man who
momentarily has them in his power. He stands up.

> POLONIUS (continuing)
> *Mad let us grant him, then; and now remains*
> *That we find out the cause of this effect –*
> *Or rather say 'the cause of this defect',*
> *For this effect defective comes by cause.*
> *Thus it remains, and the remainder thus.*

He is pushing his luck now. To the limit.

> POLONIUS (continuing)
> *Perpend.*

He walks over to a hidden door and calls.

> POLONIUS
> *Ophelia.*

The door opens and OPHELIA comes out, she hands a letter to
POLONIUS and he brings her over to the desk.

> POLONIUS
> *I have a daughter – have whilst she is mine –*
> *Who in her duty and obedience, mark,*
> *Hath given me this. Now gather and surmise.*

He hands the letter to OPHELIA. With enormous difficulty she
begins to read.

OPHELIA

'To the celestial and my soul's idol,
The most beautified Ophelia.'

POLONIUS

That's an ill phrase, a vile phrase, 'beautified'
is a vile phrase. But you shall hear –

His daughter now almost on the point of breakdown.

OPHELIA

'these in her excellent white bosom, these'.

This is too much for OPHELIA and she runs from the room.

GERTRUDE

Came this from Hamlet to her?

POLONIUS

Good madam, stay a while. I will be faithful.

Cut to:

Interior / OPHELIA'S BEDROOM Day (Flashback)

HAMLET, undressed, and OPHELIA, in her nightgown, are sitting at
the piano.

HAMLET

   'Doubt thou the stars are fire,
      Doubt that the sun doth move,
   Doubt truth to be a liar,
      But never, never,
   But never doubt I love.'

They smile and kiss. He has to go.

HAMLET

'O dear Ophelia, I am ill at these numbers. I have not art to reckon
my groans. But that I love thee best, O most best, believe it. Adieu.'

He's almost gone, she won't let him go.

HAMLET (continuing)

'Thine evermore,

He has one final kiss and leaves, she watches him go.

We cut to:

Interior / ANTE STATE ROOM Day

CLAUDIUS and GERTRUDE a little more relaxed but still suspicious
of POLONIUS's leery triumph.

POLONIUS

'most dear lady, whilst this
     machine is to him,
        Hamlet.'

This in obedience hath my daughter showed me,
And more above hath his solicitings,
As they fell out by time, by means, and place,
All given to mine ear.

CLAUDIUS

        But how hath she

Receiv'd his love?

POLONIUS

     What do you think of me?

CLAUDIUS

As of a man faithful and honourable.

POLONIUS

I would fain prove so. But what might you think,
When I had seen this hot love on the wing,
As I perceived it − I must tell you that −
Before my daughter told me, what might you,
Or my dear majesty your queen here, think,
If I had played the desk or table-book,
Or given my heart a winking mute and dumb,
Or looked upon this love with idle sight −
What might you think? No, I went round to work,
And my young mistress thus I did bespeak:
'Lord Hamlet is a prince out of thy star.
This must not be'.

The QUEEN finds this hard to believe.

POLONIUS (continuing)

     And then I precepts gave her,
That she should lock herself from his resort,
Admit no messengers, receive no tokens;
Which done, she took the fruits of my advice,
And he, repulsèd − a short tale to make −
Fell into a sadness, then into a fast,
Thence to a watch, thence into a weakness,
Thence to a lightness, and, by this declension,
Into the madness wherein now he raves,
And all we wail for.

The pair of them are strangely vulnerable. Guilt-ridden,
desperately hopeful.

CLAUDIUS (to Gertrude)

     Do you think 'tis this?

Genuinely at a loss.

GERTRUDE

It may be; very like.

POLONIUS

Hath there been such a time − I'd fain know that −
That I have positively said ''Tis so'
When it proved otherwise?

If so, he is reluctant to admit it. Ditto GERTRUDE.

CLAUDIUS

     Not that I know.

POLONIUS (pointing to his head and shoulder)
Take this from this if this be otherwise.

If circumstances lead me I will find
Where truth is hid, though it were hid indeed
Within the centre.

CLAUDIUS stands up.

CLAUDIUS
                                How may we try it further?

POLONIUS joins him.

POLONIUS
You know sometimes he walks four hours together
Here in the lobby.

GERTRUDE (standing up)
                                So he does indeed.

POLONIUS
At such a time I'll loose my daughter to him.
Be you and I behind an arras then.
Mark the encounter. If he love her not,
And be not from his reason fall'n thereon,
Let me be no assistant for a state,
But keep a farm and carters.

Entrapment for the heir to the throne.

CLAUDIUS
                                We will try it.

Suddenly GERTRUDE sees a figure appear on the gallery above the chapel.

GERTRUDE
But look where sadly the poor wretch comes reading.

POLONIUS
Away, I do beseech you both away.
I'll board him presently. O give me leave.

                                                      Cut to:

Interior / GALLERY Day

POLONIUS heading up the stairs

POLONIUS
How does my good Lord Hamlet?

Boo! A great skull appears around the pillar. It is HAMLET wearing a grotesque commedia dell'arte mask. He takes the mask off, and attempts a zany dismissal. Eyes bulging.

HAMLET
Well, God-a-mercy.

He leads off, through a door and onto the state hall gallery.
POLONIUS follows.

Interior / UPPER GALLERY Day

They walk along the Upper Gallery. POLONIUS rushes to keep up with him. HAMLET is constantly on the look-out for other spies. Paranoia intense.

POLONIUS
Do you know me, my lord?

HAMLET
Excellent well. You are a fishmonger.

POLONIUS
Not I, my lord.

HAMLET
Then I would you were so honest a man.

POLONIUS
Honest, my lord?

HAMLET
Ay sir. To be honest, as this world goes, is to be one man picked out of ten thousand.

POLONIUS
That's very true, my lord.

HAMLET
For if the sun breed maggots in a dead dog, being a god kissing carrion —

HAMLET (continuing)
   Have you a daughter?

POLONIUS
I have, my lord.

He steps and looks at him. Here comes something significant.

HAMLET
Let her not walk i'th' sun. Conception is a blessing, but as your daughter may conceive — Friend, look to't.

He walks on. POLONIUS turns and talks to Camera.

POLONIUS
How say you by that? Still harping on my daughter. Yet he knew me not at first; he said I was a fishmonger. He is far gone, far gone. And truly in my youth I suffered much extremity for love, very near this. I'll speak to him again.

He chases down the gallery after him.

POLONIUS
— What do you read, my lord?

HAMLET
Words, words, words.

POLONIUS
What is the matter, my lord?

HAMLET
Between who?

POLONIUS
I mean the matter you read, my lord.

Time to get rid of him, with bitter irony and some proper madness — the antic disposition. He enjoys the chance to be cruel to this man.

HAMLET

Slanders, sir; for the satirical rogue says here that old men have grey beards, that their faces are wrinkled, their eyes purging thick amber and plum-tree gum, and that they have a plentiful lack of wit, together with most weak hams. All which, sir, though I most powerfully and potently believe, yet I hold it not honesty to have it thus set down; for you yourself, sir, shall grow old as I am – if, like a crab, you could go backward.

POLONIUS (aside)

Though this be madness, yet there is method in't –

They have reached a door at the end of the Upper Gallery.

POLONIUS

Will you walk out of the air, my lord?

HAMLET

Into my grave?

POLONIUS

Indeed, that's out of the air –

HAMLET goes.

POLONIUS (continuing)

How pregnant sometimes his replies are! A happiness that often madness hits on, which reason and sanity could not so prosperously be delivered of. I will take my leave of him, and suddenly contrive the means of meeting between him and my daughter.

POLONIUS exits, in pursuit of the Prince.

Cut to:

Exterior / RAILWAY PADDOCK Day

We find POLONIUS, finally catching up with HAMLET, annoyed now.

POLONIUS

– My lord, I will take my leave of you.

HAMLET turns and faces him. He cannot resist this one.

HAMLET

You cannot, sir, take from me anything that I will more willingly part withal –

Nor can he resist the slide into suicidal despair.

HAMLET (continuing)

except my life, except my life, except my life.

POLONIUS (going)

Fare you well, my lord.

We Cut to a horizon through which a charming miniature train now starts to choo, choo. ROSENCRANTZ and GUILDENSTERN hanging from it. POLONIUS moves off towards the train. HAMLET enraged with himself for having let POLONIUS get to him.

HAMLET

These tedious old fools!

POLONIUS calls to the steaming caterpillar.

POLONIUS
You go to seek the Lord Hamlet. There he is.

Two of the KING'S ATTENDANTS approach POLONIUS and they all move back towards the house. We see the childishly excited faces of ROSENCRANTZ and GUILDENSTERN, who make their re-entrance into HAMLET's life precariously perched aboard a primitive miniature steam train – a toy of the new King.

ROSENCRANTZ
God save you, sir.

GUILDENSTERN (to Polonius)
Mine honoured lord.

HAMLET approaches them amazed.

ROSENCRANTZ (to Hamlet)
My most dear lord.

They get off the train as HAMLET approaches.

HAMLET
My excellent good friends. How dost thou,
Guildenstern? (shaking hands)
    Ah, Rosencrantz,
Good lads, how do ye both?

ROSENCRANTZ
As the indifferent children of the earth.

They were instructed to draw him on to pastimes.

GUILDENSTERN
Happy in that we are not over-happy,
On Fortune's cap we are not the very button.

HAMLET plays the bantering game, but determined to extract real information.

HAMLET
Nor the soles of her shoe?

ROSENCRANTZ
Neither, my lord.

HAMLET
Then you live about her waist, or in the middle of her favour?

GUILDENSTERN
Faith, her privates we.

He indulges this weak, bawdy banter. They are clearly very nervous.

HAMLET
In the secret parts of Fortune? O, most true, she is a strumpet.
What news?

A tiny beat. They hadn't banked on him being quite so inquisitive so soon. Isn't he supposed to be mad?

ROSENCRANTZ
None, my lord, but that the world's grown honest.

Not good enough.

HAMLET

Then is doomsday near. But your news is not true. Let me question
more in particular. What have you, my good friends, deserved at the
hands of Fortune that she sends you to prison hither?

A note of genuine alarm in GUILDENSTERN's voice. After all, the
Danish crown is not secure.

GUILDENSTERN

Prison, my lord?

HAMLET

Denmark's a prison.

Oh. Metaphors. Thank Christ for that.

ROSENCRANTZ

Then is the world one.

His genuine melancholy returns.

HAMLET

A goodly one, in which there are many confines,
wards, and dungeons, Denmark being one o'th' worst.

Oh come on. Cheer up. We're your friends.

ROSENCRANTZ

We think not so, my lord.

Oh really. The disappointment grows.

HAMLET

Why, then 'tis none to you, for there is nothing either good or bad
but thinking makes it so. To me it is a prison.

He starts to walk away from the little railway line towards the palace,
they have to run to catch him up.

ROSENCRANTZ

Why, then your ambition makes it one; 'tis too narrow for your mind

HAMLET speaks the first phrase with a weariness so intense it's as if
he's been wounded.

HAMLET

O God, I could be bounded in a nutshell and count myself a
King of infinite space, were it not that I have bad dreams.

Oh no you don't. We've got you sussed. We're just as clever,
for all your little enigmas.

GUILDENSTERN

Which dreams indeed are ambition; for the very substance
of the ambitious is merely the shadow of a dream.

He puts the ball back. Work that one out.

HAMLET

A dream itself is but a shadow.

But we're still on your side, remember.

ROSENCRANTZ

Truly, and I hold ambition of so airy and light a quality that it is
but a shadow's shadow.

HAMLET
Then are our beggars bodies, and our monarchs and outstretched
heroes the beggars' shadows.

He has had enough. Let's get rid of them. He starts to run.

HAMLET (continuing)
Shall we to th' court? For, by my fay, I cannot reason.

No, they mean business, following him at a run.

ROSENCRANTZ and GUILDENSTERN
We'll wait upon you.

He stops with his back to them in the gateway.

HAMLET
No such matter. I will not sort you with the rest
of my servants, for, to speak to you like an honest
man, I am most dreadfully attended.

He turns to face them. Let's try again. Banter out of the way now.
The pleading is heartfelt.

HAMLET (continuing)
But in the beaten way of friendship, what make you at Elsinore?

A beat. A look between the two of them. A little shiftier now.

ROSENCRANTZ
To visit you, my lord, no other occasion.

HAMLET
Beggar that I am, I am even poor in thanks but
I thank you;

He steps up the pressure now. Resentment building.

HAMLET (continuing)
            and sure, dear friends, my thanks are too dear a
halfpenny. Were you not sent for? Is it your own inclining? Is it a
free visitation? Come, deal justly with me. Come, come. Nay, speak.

GUILDENSTERN
What should we say, my lord?

HAMLET (fiercely)
Anything but to th' purpose. You were sent for, and there is a kind
of confession in your looks, which your modesties have not craft
enough to colour.

Heavy with sarcasm.

HAMLET (continuing)
I know the good King and Queen have sent for you.

ROSENCRANTZ (innocent)
To what end, my lord?

HAMLET (sinister)
That you must teach me.

One last chance for whatever there was of their friendship to endure.

HAMLET (continuing)
But let me conjure you by the rights of our fellowship, by the
consonancy of our youth, by the obligation of our ever-preserved love,

*and by what more dear a better proposer could charge you withal, be
even and direct with me whether you were sent for or no.*

They are paralysed with guilt and fear.

ROSENCRANTZ (to Guildenstern)
What say you?

HAMLET (swiftly)
*Nay then, I have an eye of you − if you love me,
hold not off.*

GUILDENSTERN (ashamed)
My lord, we were sent for.

All HAMLET's spleen seems to disappear. He just needed to know.
With the knowledge that his paranoia is not without foundation he
seems to relax. He has led them now to −

Exterior / COLONNADE Day

They climb the steps to the colonnade.

HAMLET
*I will tell you why. So shall my anticipation prevent your discovery,
and your secrecy to the King and Queen moult no feather.*

He seems quite simply like a child who has become lost. He talks
quietly and without self-pity. His melancholy seems almost serene.

HAMLET (continuing)
*I have of late − but wherefore I know not − lost all my mirth, forgone
all custom of exercise; and indeed it goes so heavily with my
disposition that this goodly frame, the earth, seems to me a sterile
promontory.*

He looks out to a glorious blue sky.

HAMLET (continuing)
*This most excellent canopy the air, look you, this brave o'erhanging
firmament, this majestical roof fretted with golden fire − why, it
appears no other thing to me but a foul and pestilent congregation
of vapours.*

He turns to his two 'friends' and still manages to be naively
enthusiastic. Inspired for a moment and inspiring to hear.

HAMLET (continuing)
*What a piece of work is a man! How noble in reason, how infinite in
faculty, in form and moving how express and admirable, in action
how like an angel, in apprehension how like a god − the beauty of
the world, the paragon of animals! And yet*

The crushing weight of his situation comes home once more.

HAMLET (continuing)
to me what is this quintessence of dust? Man delights not me −

He sees them smile and turns on them sharply.

HAMLET (continuing)
no, nor woman neither, though by your smiling you seem to say so.

ROSENCRANTZ
My lord, there was no such stuff in my thoughts.
HAMLET
Why did you laugh, then, when I said 'Man delights not me'?
ROSENCRANTZ
*To think, my lord, if you delight not in man, what lenten
entertainment the players shall receive from you. We coted them on
the way, and hither are they coming to offer you service.*
HAMLET
*He that plays the King shall be welcome; his majesty shall have
tribute of me. The adventurous Knight shall use his foil and target,
the Lover shall not sigh gratis, the Humorous Man shall end his part
in peace, the Clown shall make those laugh whose lungs are tickle
o'th'sear, and the Lady shall say her mind freely, or the blank verse
shall halt for't. What players are they?*

The two 'friends' are now delighted that they've finally struck the
right note.

ROSENCRANTZ
*Even those you were wont to take delight in, the tragedians of
the city.*

Terrific. They start to make a bee-line back to the Palace. HAMLET
now his true self, completely intrigued by the news. He talks at
a gallop.

HAMLET
*How chances it they travel? Their residence, both in reputation
and profit, was better both ways.*
ROSENCRANTZ
I think their inhibition comes by the means of the 'late innovation'.

HAMLET is now transformed into a gossipy theatrical.

HAMLET
*Do they hold the same estimation they did when
I was in the city? Are they so followed?*

This is fun. ROSENCRANTZ starts to camp it up.

ROSENCRANTZ
No, indeed, they are not.

At last we see how they might have been friends. At least on a
superficial level.

HAMLET
How comes it? Do they grow rusty?

ROSENCRANTZ very pleased with his inside knowledge.

ROSENCRANTZ
*Nay, their endeavour keeps in the wonted pace. But there is, sir, an
eyrie of children, little eyases, that cry out on the top of question and
are most tyrannically clapped for't.*

He pulls out a newspaper to prove his point.

ROSENCRANTZ (continuing)
These are now the fashion, and so berattle the common stages — so
they call them — that many wearing rapiers are afraid of goose-quills,
and dare scarce come thither.

HAMLET seizes the paper and scans the article. He is shocked.

HAMLET
What, are they children? Who maintains 'em? How are they escoted?
Will they pursue the quality no longer than they can sing? Will they
not say afterwards, if they should grow themselves to common players
— as it is most like, if their means are not better — their writers do
them wrong to make them exclaim against their own succession?

ROSENCRANTZ
Faith, there has been much to-do on both sides, and the nation holds
it no sin to tarre them to controversy. There was for a while no
money bid for argument unless the poet and the player went to cuffs
in the question.

HAMLET (genuinely baffled)
                    Is't possible?

GUILDENSTERN
O, there has been much throwing about of brains.

HAMLET
Do the boys carry it away?

ROSENCRANTZ
Ay, that they do, my lord, Hercules and his load too.

Having seemed that he was 'with' them, it's now clear that HAMLET
very much retains his own mind.

HAMLET
It is not very strange; for mine uncle is King of Denmark, and
those that would make mouths at him while my father lived give
twenty, forty, fifty, an hundred ducats apiece for his picture in little.
'Sblood, there is something in this more than natural, if philosophy
could find it out.

They run off towards the Palace.

                                                  Cut to:

Interior / STATE HALL GALLERY Day

GUILDENSTERN, a little discomfited by these last remarks follows
HAMLET onto the balcony above the state hall.

GUILDENSTERN
There are the players.

HAMLET gazes down onto the floor of the hall to this motley troupe
who look like the 'Crummles' from *Nicholas Nickleby* — a real family
affair. Tatty grand. He turns to his pals, beaming.

HAMLET
Gentlemen, you are welcome to Elsinore. Your hands, come then.
Th' appurtenance of welcome is fashion and ceremony. Let me
comply with you in this garb, lest my extent to the players — which,

I tell you, must show fairly outward – should more appear like
entertainment than yours.

He pulls them close to him, whispers.

> You are welcome. But my uncle-father and aunt-mother are deceived.
> GUILDENSTERN (uneasily)
> In what, my dear lord?
> HAMLET
> I am but mad north-north-west; when the wind is southerly, I know
> a hawk from a handsaw.

POLONIUS appears on the other side of the gallery.

> POLONIUS
> Well be with you, gentlemen.

HAMLET is speeding with excitement. He turns and walks way from
the smug Prime Minister. POLONIUS tries to keep up with him from
the other end of the balcony.

> HAMLET (aside)
> Hark you, Guildenstern, and you too – at each ear a hearer – that
> great baby you see there is not yet out of his swaddling-clouts.
> ROSENCRANTZ (aside)
> Haply he's the second time come to them, for they say an old man
> is twice a child.
> HAMLET (aside)
> I will prophesy he comes to tell me of the players.

(he speaks loudly)

> Mark it. – You say right, sir, o' Monday
> morning, 'twas then indeed.

POLONIUS calls to them.

> POLONIUS
> My lord, I have news to tell you.
> HAMLET
> My lord, I have news to tell you. When Roscius was
> an actor in Rome –

POLONIUS will obviously now have to deal with a raving idiot.

> POLONIUS
> The actors are come hither, my lord.
> HAMLET
> Buzz, buzz.
> POLONIUS
> Upon mine honour-
> HAMLET
> Then came each actor on his ass.
> POLONIUS
> The best actors in the world,

He indicates the group below, who have now noticed HAMLET's
presence.

POLONIUS (continuing)
either for tragedy, comedy, history, pastoral, pastoral-comical,
historical-pastoral, tragical-historical, tragical-comical-historical-
pastoral, scene individable or poem unlimited. Seneca cannot be too
heavy, nor Plautus too light. For the law of writ and the liberty,
these are the only men.

HAMLET
O Jephthah, judge of Israel, what a treasure hadst thou!

POLONIUS
What a treasure had he, my lord?

HAMLET (mock-sinister)
Why,

> *'One fair daughter and no more,*
> *The which he lovèd passing well'*

POLONIUS (to Camera)
Still on my daughter.

HAMLET
Am I not i'th' right, old Jephthah?

POLONIUS still desperate to crack HAMLET's mad 'code'.

POLONIUS
If you call me Jephthah, my lord, I have a
daughter that I love passing well.

HAMLET (harsh)
Nay, that follows not

POLONIUS (irritated)
What follows then, my lord?

HAMLET
Why

> *'As by lot, God wot',*

and then you know

> *'It came to pass*
> *As most like it was' –*

the first row of the pious chanson will show you more, for look where
my abridgement comes.

He rushes down the stairs towards the players. Whirls about them
with genuine glee. The Camera glides with him, capturing the joy.

HAMLET (continuing)
You're welcome, masters, welcome all. – I am glad to
see thee well. – Welcome, good friends.

He goes first to the leader of the troupe.

HAMLET (continuing)
O, my old friend! Thy face is valanced since I saw thee last. Com'st
thou to beard me in Denmark?

Then to the child actress, whom he picks up in his arms.

HAMLET (continuing)
What, my young lady and mistress.

He checks out her footwear.

HAMLET (continuing)
By'r Lady, your ladyship is nearer heaven than when I saw you last by the altitude of a chopine. Pray God your voice, like a piece of uncurrent gold, be not cracked within the ring.

He obviously knows them all intimately and likes them.

HAMLET (continuing)
Masters, you are all welcome.

He walks them up the State Hall to the throne area. He and the FIRST PLAYER stand on the platform.

HAMLET (continuing)
We'll e'en to't like French falconers, fly at anything we see. We'll have a speech straight. Come, give us a taste of your quality. Come, a passionate speech.

They're all terribly excited. This, although unusual, looks as if it will be a good gig.

FIRST PLAYER
What speech, my good lord?

HAMLET thinks very specifically about this. He's aware, as always, of being watched, not just by the actors but by POLONIUS, attendants, etc. Still, his enthusiasm is unbridled.

HAMLET
I heard thee speak me a speech once, but it was never acted, or, if it was, not above once; for the play, I remember, pleased not the million.

The Players know about that kind of reaction.

HAMLET (continuing)
'Twas caviare to the general.

He throws a look at POLONIUS oblivious.

HAMLET (continuing)
But it was — as I received it, and others whose judgements in such matters cried in the top of mine — an excellent play, well digested in the scenes, set down with as much modesty as cunning.

He really is getting into his stride now and we see a real aficionado of drama.

HAMLET (continuing)
I remember one said there was no sallets in the lines to make the matter savoury, nor no matter in the phrase which might indict the author of affectation, but called it an honest method, as wholesome as sweet, and by very much more handsome than fine.

Once again we see the eyes sparkle.

HAMLET (continuing)
One speech in it I chiefly loved, 'twas Aeneas' tale to Dido, and thereabout of it especially where he speaks of Priam's slaughter. If it live in your memory, begin at this line — let me see, let me see:

HAMLET begins slowly, modestly, aware of his audience.

HAMLET (continuing)
'The rugged Pyrrhus, like th' Hyrcanian beast' –
'tis not so.

FIRST PLAYER
    It begins with Pyrrhus.

He is quietly possessed, the delivery assured. He loves the language, savours the sounds.

HAMLET
    It begins with Pyrrhus –
'The rugged Pyrrhus, he whose sable arms,
Black as his purpose, did the night resemble
When he lay couchèd in the ominous horse,
Hath now this dread and black complexion smeared
With heraldry more dismal. Head to foot
Now is he total gules, horridly tricked
With blood of fathers, mothers, daughters, sons,
Baked and impasted with the parching streets,
That lend a tyrranous and damnèd light
To their lord's murder. Roasted in wrath and fire.
And thus o'er-sizèd with coagulate gore,
With eyes like carbuncles the hellish Pyrrhus
Old grandsire Priam seeks.'

A beat as the CROWD take the moment. This was good.

HAMLET (continuing)
So, proceed you.

Spontaneous applause.

POLONIUS cannot resist the chance to patronize.

POLONIUS
Fore God, my lord, well spoken, with good accent and
good discretion.

A look between them that almost interrupts. But Dr Theatre is at work and immediately the FIRST PLAYER goes into action.

FIRST PLAYER
    'Anon he finds him,

                                                  Cut to:

Exterior / TROY Night

OLD PRIAM, battling in blood and gore to stay alive.

FIRST PLAYER V/O (continuing)
Striking too short at Greeks. His antique sword,
Rebellious to his arm, lies where it falls,
Repugnant to command. Unequal match,
Pyrrhus at Priam drives, in rage strikes wide;

We see the action in violent, gory detail, amid the smoke and flames.

                                                  Cut to:

Interior / STATE HALL Day

For appalled reactions.

FIRST PLAYER (continuing)
But with the whiff and wind of his fell sword
Th' unnervèd father falls. Then senseless Ilium,
Seeming to feel his blow, with flaming top
Stoops to his base, and with a hideous crash
Takes prisoner Pyrrhus' ear. For lo, his sword,
Which was declining on the milky head
Of reverend Priam, seemed i' th' air to stick.
So, as a painted tyrant, Pyrrhus stood,
And, like a neutral to his will and matter,
Did nothing.

The Player has them enthralled. He is in tremendous form.

FIRST PLAYER (continuing)
But as we often see against some storm
A silence in the heavens, the rack stand still,
The bold winds speechless, and the orb below
As hush as death, anon the dreadful thunder
Doth rend the region: so, after Pyrrhus' pause,
A rousèd vengeance sets him new a-work;
And never did the Cyclops' hammers fall
On Mars his armour, forged for proof eterne,
With less remorse

Cut to:

Exterior / TROY Night

We see PRIAM dying.

FIRST PLAYER V/O (continuing)
                    than Pyrrhus' bleeding sword
Now falls on Priam.

Cut to:

Interior / STATE HALL Day

FIRST PLAYER (continuing)
Out, out, thou strumpet Fortune! All you gods,
In general synod, take away her power,
Break all the spokes and fellies from her wheel,
And bowl the round nave down the hill of heaven,
As low as to the fiends!'

POLONIUS
This is too long.

HAMLET barely keeps control.

HAMLET
It shall to the barber's, with your beard.
(to First Player)
Prithee, say on. He's for a jig or a tale of bawdry, or he sleeps.
Say on, come to Hecuba.

FIRST PLAYER
'But who, O who had seen the mobbled queen'–

HAMLET had forgotten about this part of the tragedy.

> HAMLET
> *'The mobbled queen'?*
>
> POLONIUS
> *That's good; 'mobbled queen' is good.*

HAMLET, and all, shoot him a look.

> FIRST PLAYER
> *'Run barefoot up and down, threat'ning the flames*
> *With bisson rheum; a clout upon that head*
> *Where late the diadem stood, and for a robe,*
> *About her lank and all o'er-teemèd loins,*

Cut to:

Exterior / TROY Night

To find the distracted and hysterical HECUBA running among
the debris.

> FIRST PLAYER V/O (continuing)
> *A blanket in th' alarm of fear caught up –*
> *Who this had seen, with tongue in venom steeped,*
> *'Gainst Fortune's state would reason have pronounced.*

We track into her face as she sees the savage murder of her husband.
She opens her mouth to scream. No sound emerges. Just empty,
aching grief.

> FIRST PLAYER V/O (continuing)
> *But if the gods themselves did see her then,*
> *When she saw Pyrrhus make malicious sport*
> *In mincing with his sword her husband's limbs,*
> *The instant burst of clamour that she made,*
> *Unless things mortal move them not at all,*
> *Would have made milch the burning eyes of heaven,*

Cut to:

Interior / STATE HALL Day

We cut back to the face of the Player who is profoundly moved
by her plight. So are they all.

> FIRST PLAYER (continuing)
> *And passion in the gods.'*
>
> POLONIUS (genuinely amazed)
> *Look whe'er he has not turned his colour, and has tears in's eyes.*
> (to the First Player) *Prithee, no more.*

Applause.

> HAMLET (to First Player)
> *'Tis well. I'll have thee speak out the rest soon.*
> (To Polonius)
> *Good my lord, will you see the players well bestowed? Do ye hear? –*
> *let them be well used, for they are the abstracts and brief chronicles of*
> *the time. After your death you were better have a bad epitaph than*
> *their ill report while you live.*

POLONIUS
My lord, I will use them according to their desert.

HAMLET (furious)
God's bodykins, man, much better. Use every man after his desert,
and who should scape whipping?

A passionate plea for kindness.

HAMLET (continuing)
Use them after your own honour and dignity – the less they deserve,
the more merit is in your bounty. Take them in.

POLONIUS
Come, sirs.

HAMLET (to the players)
Follow him, friends. We'll hear a play tomorrow.

As they leave, he takes aside the FIRST PLAYER. Whispers.

HAMLET
Dost thou hear me, old friend? Can you play the Murder
of Gonzago?

FIRST PLAYER
Ay, my lord.

HAMLET
We'll ha't tomorrow night.

He is about to go but once more HAMLET stops him.

HAMLET (continuing)
You could for a need study a speech of some dozen or sixteen lines
which I would set down and insert in't, could you not?

FIRST PLAYER
Ay, my lord.

HAMLET
Very well. Follow that lord, and

His evenness of temper has returned. Enough to make him instruct
the Player not to emulate his treatment of the Prime Minister.

HAMLET (continuing)
                              look you mock him not.

He walks down the Hall with HORATIO and the ever-clinging
ROSENCRANTZ and GUILDENSTERN.

HAMLET (continuing)
My good friends, I'll leave you till night. You are
welcome to Elsinore.

Reluctantly, they bow and go.

ROSENCRANTZ
Good my lord.

HAMLET
Ay, so. God b' wi' ye.

He is at the door of his apartments, which he enters in a rush and
snaps shut.

Interior / HAMLET'S APARTMENTS Day

    HAMLET
                    Now I am alone.

He says it with intense relief. Moves slowly into the room.

    HAMLET (continuing)
    O, what a rogue and peasant slave am I!
    Is it not monstrous that this player here,
    But in a fiction, in a dream of passion,
    Could force his soul so to his own conceit
    That from her working all his visage wanned,
    Tears in his eyes, distraction in's aspect,
    A broken voice, and his whole function suiting
    With forms to his conceit? And all for nothing.
    For Hecuba!

He asks the question with genuine astonishment. He moves away
through the apartment now, pacing.

    HAMLET (continuing)
    What's Hecuba to him, or he to Hecuba,
    That he should weep for her? What would he do
    Had he the motive and the cue for passion
    That I have?

He opens the doors of a beautiful model theatre.

    HAMLET (continuing)
    He would drown the stage with tears,
    And cleave the general ear with horrid speech,
    Make mad the guilty and appal the free,
    Confound the ignorant, and amaze indeed
    The very faculty of eyes and ears. Yet I,
    A dull and muddy-mettled rascal, peak
    Like John-a-dreams, unpregnant of my cause,
    And can say nothing – no, not for a King
    Upon whose property and most dear life
    A damned defeat was made.

He moves across to the wardrobe.

    HAMLET (continuing)
                  Am I a coward?
    Who calls me villain, breaks my pate across,
    Plucks off my beard and blows it in my face,
    Tweaks me by th' nose, gives me the lie i'th' throat
    As deep as to the lungs? Who does me this?
    Ha? 'Swounds, I should take it;

Enraged now, he smashes bottles and furniture.

    HAMLET (continuing)
                  for it cannot be
    But I am pigeon-livered and lack gall
    To make oppression bitter, or ere this

I should ha' fatted all the region kites
With this slave's offal. Bloody, bawdy villain!

He leans back against the wardrobe.

HAMLET (continuing)
Remorseless, treacherous, lecherous, kindless villain!
O, vengeance! –

He rushes to the window, eager to shout it to the heavens.

HAMLET (continuing)
Why, what an ass am I? This is most brave,
That I, the son of a dear father murdered,
Prompted to my revenge by heaven and hell,
Must, like a whore, unpack my heart with words
And fall a-cursing like a very drab,
A scullion! Fie upon't, foh!
About, my brain. I have heard
That guilty creatures sitting at a play
Have by the very cunning of the scene
Been struck so to the soul that presently
They have proclaimed their malefactions;

He drags himself into action and looks again at the model theatre.
Ideas, ideas.

HAMLET (continuing)
For murder, though it have no tongue, will speak
With most miraculous organ. I'll have these players
Play something like the murder of my father
Before mine uncle. I'll observe his looks,
I'll tent him to the quick. If he but blench,
I know my course.

The haunted look returns.

HAMLET (continuing)
                    The spirit that I have seen
May be the devil, and the devil hath power
T'assume a pleasing shape; yea, and perhaps,
Out of my weakness and my melancholy –
As he is very potent with such spirits –
Abuses me to damn me. I'll have grounds
More relative than this.

He sinks behind the theatre so that his face is level with the stage.
Yes! That's it.

HAMLET (continuing)
                    The play's the thing
Wherein I'll catch the conscience of the King.

We move closer in on the tiny stage where the figure of the King
stands over the trapdoor, which HAMLET releases with a violent
snap! The Model King is dispatched to 'the other place' as

Interior / STATE HALL Night

The doors open to reveal the real CLAUDIUS at the head of the royal group, no longer stage models, but alive. It's another furtive meeting. The tension in this court is building. CLAUDIUS, GERTRUDE, POLONIUS, ROSENCRANTZ and GUILDENSTERN. All picking up on CLAUDIUS's barely concealed impatience with the two men's work.

CLAUDIUS
And can you by no drift of conference
Get from him why he puts on this confusion,
Grating so harshly all his days of quiet
With turbulent and dangerous lunacy?

ROSENCRANTZ (placatory)
He does confess he feels himself distracted,
But from what cause he will by no means speak.

All right. It's not their fault. But GUILDENSTERN decides to twist the knife.

GUILDENSTERN
Nor do we find him forward to be sounded,
But with a crafty madness keeps aloof
When we would bring him on to some confession
Of his true state.

Well, give us some details then. Anything.

GERTRUDE
                    Did he receive you well?

ROSENCRANTZ
Most like a gentleman.

GUILDENSTERN
But with much forcing of his disposition.

A little irritation building between the two over-eager school friends.

ROSENCRANTZ
Niggard of question, but of our demands
Most free in his reply.

The QUEEN getting quite firm with them now too.

GERTRUDE
                    Did you assay him
To any pastime?

Ah. A chance to give some good news at last.

ROSENCRANTZ
Madam, it so fell out that certain players
We o'er-raught on the way. Of these we told him,
And there did seem in him a kind of joy
To hear of it. They are about the court,
And, as I think, they have already order
This night to play before him.

POLONIUS knows that this will be the key to it all and wants to get on with it.

POLONIUS

'Tis most true,
And he beseeched me to entreat your majesties
To hear and see the matter.

It really does seem as though this might help.

CLAUDIUS

With all my heart; and it doth much content me
To hear him so inclined.
Good gentlemen, give him a further edge,
And drive his purpose on to these delights.

ROSENCRANTZ

We shall, my lord.

The two men exit faintly relieved. There was more at stake than they realized.

CLAUDIUS (tentatively)

Sweet Gertrude, leave us too,
For we have closely sent for Hamlet hither
That he, as 'twere by accident, may here
Affront Ophelia.

This is news. And faintly distasteful. Rather more spying goes on in this court than in OLD HAMLET's.

CLAUDIUS (continuing)

Her father and myself, lawful espials,
Will so bestow ourselves that, seeing unseen,
We may of their encounter frankly judge,
And gather by him, as he is behaved,
If't be th' affliction of his love or no
That thus he suffers for.

The last remark lingers. It may be something more sinister.
GERTRUDE takes a moment to decide.

GERTRUDE

I shall obey you.

She goes to OPHELIA, who looks more frightened than ever at this strange turn of events.

GERTRUDE (continuing)

And for your part, Ophelia, I do wish
That your good beauties be the happy cause
Of Hamlet's wildness; so shall I hope your virtues
Will bring him to his wonted way again,
To both your honours.

OPHELIA

Madam, I wish it may.

We see GERTRUDE react slightly to the indignity of having to leave them.

POLONIUS
Ophelia, walk you here. –

He moves her over to one of the pillars, giving her a book.

POLONIUS (continuing to the King)
                    Gracious, so please you,
We will bestow ourselves. –

He instructs OPHELIA again.
            Read on this book,
That show of such an exercise may colour
Your loneliness.

            (to The King) *We are oft to blame in this:*
'Tis too much proved that with devotion's visage
And pious action we do sugar o'er
The devil himself.

CLAUDIUS
                    O, 'tis too true.

He turns back into the room while POLONIUS moves away,
watching for Hamlet

CLAUDIUS (continuing)
How smart a lash that speech doth give my conscience.
The harlot's cheek, beautied with plast'ring art,
Is not more ugly to the thing that helps it
Than is my deed to my most painted word.
O heavy burden!

POLONIUS
I hear him coming. Let's withdraw, my lord.

They rush off, watched by OPHELIA. POLONIUS bundles CLAUDIUS
into a room as –

Interior / STATE HALL Day

HAMLET emerges from a door at the throne end of the Hall.
OPHELIA hides behind a pillar as HAMLET walks slowly down the
side of the Hall. He is directly under the Gallery. As he passes each
of the mirrored doors, he casts a look at them, gradually slowing
down until he stops directly in front of the mirrored door behind
which CLAUDIUS and POLONIUS wait.

  All the passionate bravado of the previous scene is gone. All the
reacting, all the emotion, all the certainty about what to do. Now
the play has been set up and the awful spectre of what he might
prove, and therefore have to do, is very real. There is nothing
indulgent or mildly ruminative in this most famous moment. Here is
a man faced with the prospect of murder or his own death. He faces
both as absolute realities and it is the most quiet and terrifying dread
he has ever known. He looks directly into the mirror.

Interior / ANTE-ROOM Day

With great care we see POLONIUS pull back a panel to reveal a two-way mirror on their side of the door. Now CLAUDIUS and HAMLET are face to face but the latter is unaware. We Cut between the two.

> HAMLET
>
> *To be, or not to be, that is the question:*
> *Whether 'tis nobler in the mind to suffer*
> *The slings and arrows of outrageous fortune,*
> *Or to take arms against a sea of troubles,*
> *And, by opposing, end them. To die, to sleep —*
> *No more, and by a sleep to say we end*
> *The heartache and the thousand natural shocks*
> *That flesh is heir to — 'tis a consummation*
> *Devoutly to be wished. To die, to sleep.*
> *To sleep, perchance to dream. Ay, there's the rub,*

HAMLET moves into the mirror, really asking the question of himself.

> HAMLET (continuing)
>
> *For in that sleep of death what dreams may come*
> *When we have shuffled off this mortal coil*
> *Must give us pause. There's the respect*
> *That makes calamity of so long life,*

HAMLET seems to spell out the whips and scorns as if CLAUDIUS was personally responsible.

> HAMLET (continuing)
>
> *For who would bear the whips and scorns of time,*
> *Th' oppressor's wrong, the proud man's contumely,*
> *The pangs of disprized love, the law's delay,*
> *The insolence of office, and the spurns*
> *That patient merit of th' unworthy takes,*
> *When he himself might his quietus make*
> *With a bare bodkin?*

He whips out a dagger with the swiftness of a trained soldier. He points it for a moment at the mirror/CLAUDIUS, his face very close to the glass.

> HAMLET (continuing)
>
>   *Who would fardels bear,*
> *To grunt and sweat under a weary life,*
> *But that the dread of something after death,*
> *The undiscovered country from whose bourn*
> *No traveller returns, puzzles the will,*
> *And makes us rather bear those ills we have*
> *Than fly to others that we know not of?*
> *Thus conscience doth make cowards of us all,*
> *And thus the native hue of resolution*

Is sicklied o'er with the pale cast of thought,
And enterprises of great pith and moment
With this regard their currents turn awry,
And lose the name of action.

OPHELIA moves out from her hiding place, into the hall and
HAMLET turns to see her.

    HAMLET (continuing)

                Soft you, now,

    The fair Ophelia! –
He walks towards her.

    HAMLET (continuing)

            Nymph, in thy orisons?
They stand facing each other for a moment.

                              Cut to:

Interior / HALL STAIRS Day

    HAMLET
    Be all my sins remembered?

    OPHELIA

               Good my lord,
    How does your honour for this many a day?
It's a huge relief to see her. But this is a very formal greeting. Strange,
even despite recent events.

    HAMLET
    I humbly thank you; well, well, well.
He moves to her and they embrace and kiss, a moment of bliss but
then she breaks away. She is still cool, trying to hold herself together.

    OPHELIA
    My lord, I have remembrances of yours
    That I have longèd long to redeliver.
She hands him a package of his love letters and poems.

    OPHELIA (continuing)
    I pray you now receive them.
This is not like her. Or if it is, he won't play this adolescent game.
He is petulant.

    HAMLET
    No, not I, I never gave you aught.
Starting to have more of a conversation with him now, instead of
worrying about the listeners. She lowers her voice, she is annoyed
and hurt by him in her own right. She wants him to know the
truth of her feelings. Not what she's been told to do.

    OPHELIA
    My honoured lord, you know right well you did,
    And with them words of so sweet breath compos'd
    As made the things more rich.
She tries to be hard.

OPHELIA (continuing)

Their perfume lost,
Take these again; for to the noble mind
Rich gifts wax poor when givers prove unkind.
There, my lord.

He lashes out at the letters, sending them flying from her hand across the hall.

HAMLET
Ha, ha? Are you honest?

OPHELIA

My lord.

Come on.

HAMLET
Are you fair?

OPHELIA
What means your lordship?

Oh, really.

HAMLET
That if you be honest and fair, your honesty should admit no
discourse to your beauty.

She tries to give as good as she gets but she is still brittle, on her dignity, and never unaware of being watched.

OPHELIA
Could beauty, my lord, have better commerce
than with honesty?

He replies fiercely and with a heart–rending disillusion.

HAMLET
Ay, truly, for the power of beauty will sooner transform honesty
from what it is to a bawd than the force of honesty can translate
beauty into his likeness. This was sometime a paradox, but now
the time gives it proof.

Don't you **realize** what was between us?

HAMLET (continuing)

I did love you once.

I don't know any more. I hoped so. I hope so.

OPHELIA
Indeed, my lord, you made me believe so.

He seems to understand her confusion and berates himself. She is right. He **is** unworthy. He ought to end it now.

HAMLET
You should not have believed me, for virtue cannot so inoculate our
old stock but we shall relish of it. I loved you not.

Ah, the truth at last.

OPHELIA
I was the more deceived.

But of course it isn't the truth. It's much more complex than that. He can't tell her why it has ended, of his terrible personal situation, but he can warn someone he loves to beware of CLAUDIUS, POLONIUS, and even him, a man unworthy of her love. He wants her to be safe. To escape.

> HAMLET
> *Get thee to a nunnery. Why wouldst thou be a breeder of sinners?*
> *I am myself indifferent honest, but yet I could accuse me of such*
> *things that it were better my mother had not borne me. I am very*
> *proud, revengeful, ambitious, with more offences at my beck than*
> *I have thoughts to put them in, imagination to give them shape,*
> *or time to act them in. What should such fellows as I do crawling*
> *between earth and heaven? We are arrant knaves, all. Believe none*
> *of us. Go thy ways to a nunnery.*

A tiny noise! She glances across the room. And then it dawns.
The Hall is empty. As never before. It's a trap. She has been unable to be purely honest – almost an impossibility with her – surely she is not part of a trap? Not her ... not her ...

> HAMLET (continuing)
> *Where's your father?*

The most agonizing decision of her young life.

> OPHELIA
> *At home, my lord.*

And with that phrase their love is dead. We seem to see both their hearts break before us. Both their hearts and, apparently, his mind.

> HAMLET
> *Let the doors be shut upon him, that he may*
> *play the fool nowhere but in's own house. Farewell.*

We are Close on her agonized face.

> OPHELIA
> *O help him, you sweet heavens!*

He explodes with fury. He picks her up by the arm with great force. He then starts to drag her down the opposite side of the Hall to the spying pair. As he does so he flings open each mirrored door. We track with them and see many pairs of HAMLETs and OPHELIAs as the inner and outer mirrors add visual chaos to the already savage race around the Hall.

> HAMLET
> *If thou dost marry, I'll give thee this plague for thy dowry: be thou*
> *as chaste as ice, as pure as snow, thou shalt not escape calumny. Get*
> *thee to a nunnery, go, farewell. Or if thou wilt needs marry, marry a*
> *fool; for wise men know well enough what monsters you make of*
> *them. To a nunnery, go, and quickly, too. Farewell.*

He has run off for a moment, leaving her sobbing.

> OPHELIA
> *Heavenly powers, restore him.*

He rushes back to her and drags her to the other side of the hall.

HAMLET

I have heard of your paintings, too, well enough.

God hath given you one face,

He flings her around like a rag doll.

HAMLET (continuing)

         and you make yourselves another.

You jig, you amble, and you lisp, and nickname God's creatures,

He shoves her hard against the mirrored door behind which her father stands.

           Cut to:

Interior / ANTE-ROOM Day

POLONIUS inside is appalled. CLAUDIUS stops him opening the door.

HAMLET (continuing)

and make your wantonness your ignorance.

All passion almost spent. We see from inside the two faces against the mirror. Hers contorted against the glass.

HAMLET (continuing)

Go to, I'll no more on't. It hath made me mad.

I say we will have no more marriages. Those that are married already — all but one — shall live. The rest shall keep as they are.

He flings open the door and drags OPHELIA into the room and pushes her to the floor. He catches sight of one of the hidden doors just before it snaps shut!

Interior / ANTE-ROOM Day

He moves back to OPHELIA. He speaks quietly to her now. Their heads very close together. It's over.

HAMLET (continuing)

To a nunnery, go.

Hamlet goes back into the State Hall and away.

OPHELIA stays where he has pushed her, wrecked in every sense.

OPHELIA

O what a noble mind is here o'erthrown!

The courtier's, soldier's, scholar's eye, tongue, sword,

Th' expectancy and rose of the fair state,

The glass of fashion and the mould of form,

Th' observed of all observers, quite, quite, down!

She is in a state of utter shock.

OPHELIA (continuing)

And I, of ladies most deject and wretched,

That sucked the honey of his music vows,

Now see that noble and most sovereign reason

Like sweet bells jangled out of tune and harsh;

That unmatched form and feature of blown youth

Blasted with ecstasy. O woe is me,

T' have seen what I have seen, see what I see!

From the other hidden door enter CLAUDIUS and POLONIUS. The
national crisis steps up a gear. This man is dangerous. POLONIUS
goes to the prostrate OPHELIA and cradles her in his arms. He is
severely shaken.

CLAUDIUS

Love? His affections do not that way tend,
Nor what he spake, though it lacked form a little,
Was not like madness. There's something in his soul
O'er which his melancholy sits on brood,
And I do doubt the hatch and the disclose
Will be some danger; which to prevent
I have in quick determination
Thus set it down: he shall with speed to England
For the demand of our neglected tribute.

He calms down a little after this outburst. Rationalizes.

CLAUDIUS (continuing)

Haply the seas and countries different,
With variable objects, shall expel
This something-settled matter in his heart,
Whereon his brains still beating puts him thus
From fashion of himself. What think you on't?

POLONIUS (strangely quiet)

It shall do well. But yet do I believe
The origin and commencement of this grief
Sprung from neglected love.

He continues to stroke her head like a parent singing a lullaby to
a baby.

POLONIUS (continuing)

                    How now, Ophelia?
You need not tell us what Lord Hamlet said;
We heard it all.

He quietly offers the following advice.

POLONIUS (continuing)

               My lord, do as you please,
But, if you hold it fit, after the play
Let his queen mother all alone entreat him
To show his griefs. Let her be round with him,
And I'll be placed, so please you, in the ear
Of all their conference. If she find him not,
To England send him, or confine him where
Your wisdom best shall think.

CLAUDIUS

                  It shall be so.
Madness in great ones must not unwatch'd go.

He closes his eyes for a moment, behind him we see the father's and
daughter's silent distress.

Exterior / MONUMENT Day

HORATIO, reading a newspaper detailing YOUNG FORTINBRAS's ongoing incursions across Northern Europe. The proximity of war is clear in his worried face. He folds up the paper and moves off back towards the Palace.

Interior / STATE HALL STAIRS–THEATRE Night

The stairs' end of the State Hall has been transformed into a theatre, based to some extent on the Elizabethan model – no doubt to HAMLET's instructions. The re-decoration is still taking place across this scene.

   Curtains across the Gallery and Inner Stage. Chairs being taken up to the Bridge Gallery, where the Royal Box will be. Bleachers being rolled in underneath to create the auditorium. We see the magic of theatre happening before our very eyes. HAMLET loves it and we constantly move with him through the scene. His advice is urgent. Very firm, lives are at stake. A very bossy writer, director. He enters with the actor who will play LUCIANUS. They walk around the Gallery of the State Hall.

> HAMLET
>
> *Speak the speech, I pray you, as I pronounced it to you – trippingly on the tongue; but if you mouth it, as many of your players do, I had as lief the town-crier had spoke my lines. Nor do not saw the air too much with your hand,*

He is demonstrating with his hand.

> HAMLET (continuing)
>
> *thus, but use all gently; for in the very torrent, tempest, and as I may say the whirlwind of your passion, you must acquire and beget a temperance that may give it smoothness.*

He pauses in the doorway to his apartments to see HORATIO inside, signalling to him that it's time to get ready.

> HAMLET (continuing)
>
> *O, it offends me to the soul to hear a robustious, periwig-pated fellow tear a passion to tatters, to very rags, to split the ears of the groundlings, who for the most part are capable of nothing but inexplicable dumb shows and noise. I would have such a fellow whipped for o'erdoing Termagant. It out-Herods Herod. Pray you avoid it.*
>
> LUCIANUS
>
> *I warrant your honour.*

HAMLET the worrier is never far away.

A couple of the other actors join the conversation.

> HAMLET
>
> *Be not too tame, neither; but let your own discretion be your tutor. Suit the action to the word, the word to the action, with this*

special observance:

Hugely important point. If this doesn't happen, he may not obtain the proof of murder.

HAMLET (continuing)
> *That you o'erstep not the modesty of nature.*
> *For anything so overdone is from the purpose of playing, whose end,*
> *both at the first and now, was and is to hold as 'twere the mirror up*
> *to nature, to show virtue her own feature, scorn her own image, and*
> *the very age and body of the time his form and pressure. Now this*
> *overdone, or come tardy off, though it make the unskilful laugh,*
> *cannot but make the judicious grieve;*

And make my task even harder.

HAMLET (continuing)
> *The censure of the which one must in your allowance o'erweigh a*
> *whole theatre of others.*

They join the rest of the company, who sit amongst their props and costumes in last-minute preparation.

HAMLET (continuing)
> *O, there be players that I have seen play, and heard others praise,*
> *and that highly, not to speak it profanely, that neither having the*
> *accent of Christians nor the gait of Christian, pagan, nor man,*
> *have so strutted and bellowed that I have thought some of nature's*
> *journeymen had made men, and not made them well, they*
> *imitated humanity so abominably.*

FIRST PLAYER (rather smug)
> *I hope we have reformed that indifferently with us, sir.*

HAMLET
> *O, reform it altogther. And let those that play*
> *your clowns speak no more than is set down*
> *for them;*

He picks out the obvious cheeky chappie. He's not joking.

HAMLET (continuing)
> *for there be of them that will themselves laugh to set on*
> *some quantity of barren spectators to laugh too, though in the mean*
> *time some necessary question of the play be then to be considered.*
> *That's villainous, and shows a most pitiful ambition in the fool*
> *that uses it. Go make you ready.*

HAMLET walks away and into POLONIUS.

HAMLET (continuing)
> *How now, my lord? Will the King hear this piece of work?*

POLONIUS (guarded)
> *And the Queen too, and that presently.*

Well then, get on with it!

HAMLET
> *Bid the players make haste.*

ROSENCRANTZ and GUILDENSTERN join them.

HAMLET (continuing)
Will you two help to hasten them?

ROSENCRANTZ and GUILDENSTERN
We will, my lord.

HAMLET disappears before they have a chance to finish their bow.

Cut to:

Interior / HAMLET'S APARTMENTS Night

HORATIO is waiting in the apartment as HAMLET comes in to surprise him, entering from, yes, another hidden door.

HAMLET
What ho, Horatio!

HORATIO
Here, sweet lord, at your service.

HAMLET
Horatio, thou art e'en as just a man
As e'er my conversation coped withal.

HORATIO, embarrassed and slightly thrown by the intimacy,

HORATIO
O my dear lord –

HAMLET
                    Nay, do not think I flatter;

He will go on. He moves away, putting on his waistcoat.

HAMLET (continuing)
For what advancement may I hope from thee
That no revenue hast but thy good spirits
To feed and clothe thee?

There is a knock at the door, HAMLET goes over to greet a cadet.

HAMLET (continuing)
                    Why should the poor be flattered?
No, let the candied tongue lick absurd pomp,
And crook the pregnant hinges of the knee
Where thrift may follow fawning.

He leads HORATIO over to the desk and HORATIO sits down.

HAMLET (continuing)
                    Dost thou hear? –
Since my dear soul was mistress of her choice
And could of men distinguish, her election
Hath sealed thee for herself; for thou hast been
As one in suff'ring all that suffers nothing,
A man that fortune's buffets and rewards
Has ta'en with equal thanks;

HAMLET means this compliment. Very tender.

HAMLET (continuing)
                    and blest are those
Whose blood and judgement are so well commingled
That they are not a pipe for Fortune's finger

85

To sound what stop she please. Give me that man
That is not passion's slave, and I will wear him
In my heart's core, ay, in my heart of heart,
As I do thee.

A beat.

> HAMLET (continuing)
> > *Something too much of this.*
> *There is a play tonight before the King.*
> *One scene of it comes near the circumstance*
> *Which I have told thee of my father's death.*
> *I prithee, when thou seest that act afoot,*
> *Even with the very comment of thy soul*
> *Observe my uncle. If his occulted guilt*
> *Do not itself unkennel in one speech,*
> *It is a damnèd ghost that we have seen,*
> *And my imaginations are as foul*
> *As Vulcan's stithy.*

This is a truly grim thought.

> HAMLET (continuing)
> > *Give him heedful note,*
> *For I mine eyes will rivet to his face,*
> *And after, we will both our judgements join*
> *In censure of his seeming.*

> HORATIO
> > *Well, my lord.*
> *If he steal aught the whilst this play is playing*
> *And scape detecting,*

He flourishes the glasses.

> HORATIO (continuing)
> > *I will pay the theft.*

> HAMLET
> *They are coming to the play. I must be idle.*
> *Get you a place.*

> > > > **Cut to:**

Interior / STATE HALL–THEATRE Night

The far end of the State Hall is unrecognizable. An elegant Court Theatre is in its place with drapes and raked seating, candles and servants with programmes.

Close on CLAUDIUS and GERTRUDE who kiss and then feign embarrassment at being 'caught out' but the moment is delicious for all. Applause, they smile and sit down as do the rest of the AUDIENCE.

HORATIO takes up the position for his spying, seeing CLAUDIUS and GERTRUDE settling into their chairs.

HAMLET now appears to huge applause. Is he in the play?

CLAUDIUS
How fares our cousin Hamlet?

HAMLET
Excellent, i' faith, of the chameleon's dish. I eat
the air, promise-crammed. You cannot feed capons so.

CLAUDIUS
I have nothing with this answer, Hamlet.
These words are not mine.

HAMLET
No, nor mine now.

POLONIUS enters the auditorium. HAMLET rushes down to drag
POLONIUS on stage, playing to the Gallery as warm-up man.
They play this like a double-act. Quickly with lots of AUDIENCE
reactions.

HAMLET (to Polonius)
    My lord, you played once i' th' university, you say.

POLONIUS
That I did, my lord, and was accounted a good actor.

HAMLET
And what did you enact?

POLONIUS
I did enact Julius Caesar. I was killed i'th' Capitol. Brutus
killed me.

HAMLET (mock heroic)
    It was a brute part of him to kill so capital a calf there.-

Boom Boom. Applause. Then urgently to ROSENCRANTZ and
GUILDENSTERN who are coming from 'backstage'.

HAMLET
Be the players ready?

ROSENCRANTZ
Ay, my lord, they stay upon your patience.

They move off towards their seats. We cut backstage to see the
PLAYERS doing their last-minute preparations. HAMLET makes his
way up the stairs to take his place beside OPHELIA. GERTRUDE
calls to him before he sits down.

GERTRUDE
Come hither, my good Hamlet. Sit by me.

HAMLET
No, good mother, here's metal more attractive.

POLONIUS has now moved up into position in the Royal Box
behind them. He whispers to them.

POLONIUS (aside)
    O ho, do you mark that?

We are Close on HAMLET and OPHELIA. His voice a little too loud
for comfort. Courtiers pretending not to hear.

HAMLET (to Ophelia)
Lady, shall I lie in your lap?
Desperate to maintain her dignity.

OPHELIA
No, my lord.

HAMLET
I mean my head upon your lap?

OPHELIA
Ay, my lord.

HAMLET (goading)
Do you think I meant country matters?
Quite firm with him now.

OPHELIA
I think nothing, my lord.

HAMLET
That's a fair thought to lie between maids' legs.
She's becoming exasperated.

OPHELIA
What is, my lord?

HAMLET
No thing.

OPHELIA
You are merry, my lord.

HAMLET
Who, I?

OPHELIA
Ay, my lord.

HAMLET
O God, your only jig-maker!
He ups the volume.

HAMLET (continuing)
*What should a man do but be merry? For look you how cheerfully
my mother looks, and my father died within's two hours.*
The auditorium falls completely silent. Reactions all round. At such
a moment, she can only feel profoundly sorry for him. She whispers
gently.

OPHELIA
Nay, 'tis twice two months, my lord.
He will not let it go. Not even in public.

HAMLET
*So long? Nay then, let the devil wear black, for
I'll have a suit of sables. O heavens, die two months ago and not
forgotten yet! Then there's hope a great man's memory may outlive
his life half a year. But, by'r lady, a must build churches then, or
else shall a suffer not thinking on, with the hobby-horse, whose
epitaph is 'For O, for O, the hobby-horse is forgot.'*

He is interrupted by the ACTORS coming onto the stage. This is **not** what he'd planned. A Dumb Show. This kind of diversion is useless. Already he senses the attention of the AUDIENCE wandering. Already the King and Queen are in conversation, ignoring it. After all it is not the play. Typical bloody actors!

THE DUMB SHOW
The King lies down. The Queen, seeing him asleep, leaves him. A man enters, takes off his crown, kisses it, and pours poison in the King's ears, and exits. The Queen returns, finds the King dead, and makes passionate action. The poisoner comes in again, seeming to lament with her. The poisoner woos the Queen. She seems loath and unwilling a while, but in the end accepts his love.

There is mild applause from the few who tore themselves away from their drinks and sweets long enough to take it in.

During the Dumb Show HAMLET and OPHELIA are discussing it.

OPHELIA
What means this, my lord?

HAMLET (annoyed)
Marry, this miching malicho. It means mischief.

OPHELIA beginning to relax a little. At least this is a diversion. At least they're sitting together.

OPHELIA
Belike this show imports the argument of the play.

One of the actors appears.

HAMLET
*We shall know all by this fellow. The players
cannot keep counsel, they'll tell all.*

Rather excited.

OPHELIA
Will he tell us what this show meant?

HAMLET (vicious shut-up)
*Ay, or any show that you will show him: be not you
ashamed to show, he'll not shame to tell you what it means.*

OPHELIA
You are naught, you are naught. I'll mark the play.

PROLOGUE
*For us and for our tragedy
Here stooping to your clemency,
We beg your hearing patiently.*

Even the introduction is crap. Why can't they just get on with HAMLET's bit of the play? He heckles aggressively.

HAMLET
Is this a prologue, or the posy of a ring?

The AUDIENCE turn around shocked at what they hear.

OPHELIA (understanding)
'Tis brief, my lord.

HAMLET
As woman's love.

Bloody hell. Everyone knows who that's meant for. The AUDIENCE, especially the Royal Couple, are completely focused on the play.

The PLAYER KING sits down in a chair. The PLAYER QUEEN now enters, she kneels down beside the KING.

PLAYER KING
Full thirty times hath Phoebus' cart gone round
Neptune's salt wash and Tellus' orbèd ground,
And thirty dozen moons with borrowed sheen
About the world have times twelve thirties been
Since love our hearts and Hymen did our hands
Unite commutual in most sacred bands.

PLAYER QUEEN
So many journeys may the sun and moon
Make us again count o'er ere love be done.
But woe is me, you are so sick of late,
So far from cheer and from your former state,
That I distrust you. Yet, though I distrust,
Discomfort you my lord it nothing must.
For women's fear and love holds quantity,
In neither aught, or in extremity.
Now what my love is, proof hath made you know,
And as my love is sized, my fear is so.
Where love is great, the littlest doubts are fear;
Where little fears grow great, great love grows there.

HAMLET watches them both, now the ACTRESS, now GERTRUDE.

PLAYER KING
Faith, I must leave thee, love, and shortly too.
My operant powers their functions leave to do,
And thou shalt live in this fair world behind,
Honoured, beloved; and haply one as kind
For husband shalt thou –

PLAYER QUEEN
                    O, confound the rest!
Such love must needs be treason in my breast.
In second husband let me be accurst;
None wed the second but who killed the first.

HAMLET now really caught up in the play.

HAMLET
That's wormwood, wormwood.

PLAYER QUEEN
The instances that second marriage move
Are base respects of thrift, but none of love.

> *A second time I kill my husband dead*
> *When second husband kisses me in bed.*

More head turning and tutting in the AUDIENCE. This is too much.
The ACTOR continues very naturalistic.

> PLAYER KING
> *I do believe you think what now you speak;*
> *But what we do determine oft we break.*
> *Purpose is but the slave to memory,*
> *Of violent birth but poor validity,*
> *Which now like fruit unripe sticks on the tree,*
> *But falls unshaken when they mellow be.*
> *Most necessary 'tis that we forget*
> *To pay ourselves what to ourselves is debt.*
> *What to ourselves in passion we propose,*
> *The passion ending, doth the purpose lose.*

POLONIUS also has something to learn from HAMLET's play.

> PLAYER KING (continuing)
> *The violence of either grief or joy*
> *Their own enactures with themselves destroy.*
> *Where joy most revels, grief doth most lament;.*

GERTRUDE knows this only too well.

> PLAYER KING (continuing)
> *Grief joys, joy grieves, on slender accident.*
> *This world is not for aye, nor 'tis not strange*
> *That even our loves should with our fortunes change;*

A special meaning for OPHELIA.

> PLAYER KING (continuing)
> *For 'tis a question left us yet to prove*
> *Whether love lead fortune or else fortune love.*
> *The great man down, you mark his favourite flies;*

CLAUDIUS sneaks a look to GERTRUDE on this.

> PLAYER KING (continuing)
> *Poor men advanced make friends of enemies.*
> *And hitherto doth love on fortune tend,*
> *For who not needs shall never lack a friend,*
> *And who in want a hollow friend doth try*
> *Directly seasons him his enemy.*
> *But orderly to end where I begun,*
> *Our wills and fates do so contrary run*
> *That our devices still are overthrown;*
> *Our thoughts are ours, their ends none of our own.*
> *So think thou wilt no second husband wed;*
> *But die thy thoughts when thy first lord is dead*
> PLAYER QUEEN (impassioned)
> *Nor earth to me give food, nor heaven light,*
> *Sport and repose lock from me day and night,*

To desperation turn my trust and hope,
An anchor's cheer in prison be my scope,
Each opposite that blanks the face of joy
Meet what I would have well and it destroy,
Both here and hence pursue me lasting strife
If, once a widow, ever I be wife.

We see GERTRUDE, fuming.

HAMLET
If she should break it now!

PLAYER KING (to Player Queen)
                     'Tis deeply sworn.

Sweet, leave me here a while.
My spirits grow dull, and fain I would beguile
The tedious day with sleep.

PLAYER QUEEN
                     Sleep rock thy brain.
And never come mischance between us twain.

PLAYER QUEEN exits. PLAYER KING sleeps. HAMLET takes the
stage.

HAMLET (to Gertrude)
Madam, how like you this play?

GERTRUDE
The lady doth protest too much, methinks.

HAMLET
O, but she'll keep her word.

CLAUDIUS leans forward. The Court turn around. There's more
drama here than there was in the play.

CLAUDIUS (abrupt)
Have you heard the argument? Is there no offence in't?

HAMLET
No, no, they do but jest, poison in jest. No offence i' th' world.

CLAUDIUS
What do you call the play?

HAMLET (sharp)
The Mousetrap.

Then he rattles on at speed, gleefully. Rushing up the steps towards
the Royal Box.

HAMLET (continuing)
                   Marry, how? Tropically. This play is the image of a
murder done in Vienna – Gonzago is the Duke's name, his wife
Baptista. You shall see anon. 'Tis a knavish piece of work; but what
o' that? Your Majesty, and we that have free souls, it touches us not.
Let the galled jade wince, our withers are unwrung.

Enter Lucianus.

This is one Lucianus, nephew to the King.

HORATIO, looking through the glasses, takes them from the stage and trains them on the KING. OPHELIA tries to re-establish contact.

OPHELIA
You are as good as a chorus, my lord.

HAMLET (brutally)
I could interpret between you and your love if I
could see the puppets dallying.

She's a little more confident now. She will stand up to him.

OPHELIA
You are keen, my lord, you are keen.

HAMLET
It would cost you a groaning to take off mine edge.

A lot of disdainful tutting at that. It really isn't seemly.

OPHELIA
Still better, and worse

HAMLET
So you mis-take your husbands.

HAMLET (moving down to the stage)
Begin, murderer. Pox, leave thy damnable faces and begin.
Come: 'the croaking raven doth bellow for revenge'.

HAMLET now on the stage, the AUDIENCE certain something is amiss. Threat is in the air.

LUCIANUS
Thoughts black, hands apt, drugs fit, and time agreeing,
Confederate season, else no creature seeing;
Thou mixture rank of midnight weeds collected,
With Hecate's ban thrice blasted, thrice infected,
Thy natural magic and dire property
On wholesome life usurp immediately.

HAMLET grabs the poison phial from the actor, and turns on CLAUDIUS.

Through the following we track faster and faster towards HAMLET and the KING. Flash Cuts of the poisoning. The Courtiers reacting. CLAUDIUS's mind reeling. HAMLET possessed.

HAMLET
He poisons him i' th' garden for's estate. His name's Gonzago.
The story is extant, and writ in very choice Italian. You shall
see anon how the murderer gets the love of Gonzago's wife!

The AUDIENCE wheels around to see the KING's reaction. He stands up. The AUDIENCE follows suit.

OPHELIA
The King rises.

HAMLET
What, frighted with false fire?

GERTRUDE (to Claudius)
How fares my lord?

POLONIUS
Give o'er the play.

What will the KING do? A loaded pause.

CLAUDIUS
Give me some light. Away.

COURTIER
Lights, lights, lights!

The KING and his party leave the balcony as candles are brought
to light his way.

  In the theatre there is total pandemonium. A Piccadilly of panic.
HAMLET is ecstatic and most dangerous. He was right. He was right.
He shouts for HORATIO.

HAMLET
Horatio, Horatio!

He runs half way up the stairs and turns and as he speaks HORATIO
appears from the balcony behind him.

HAMLET
Why, let the stricken deer go weep,
The hart ungallèd play,
For some must watch, while some must sleep,
Thus runs the world away.
Would not this, sir, and a forest of feathers, if the rest of
my fortunes turn Turk with me, with two Provençal roses on
my razed shoes, get me a fellowship in a cry of players, sir?

His friend isn't nearly so able to join in.

HORATIO
Half a share.

HAMLET (unabashed)
      A whole one, I.
For thou dost know, O Damon dear,
        This realm dismantled was
Of Jove himself, and now reigns here
        A very, very – peacock.

Then a strained attempt at humour.

HORATIO
You might have rhymed.

HAMLET finally, snaps out of it. He wants the proof from HORATIO.

HAMLET
O good Horatio, I'll take the ghost's word for a
thousand pound. Didst perceive?

HORATIO
Very well, my lord.

HAMLET
Upon the talk of the pois'ning?

HORATIO
I did very well note him.

He still won't commit himself to the horror of what is likely to follow
this 'proof'. There is a moment between them, a distancing moment.
HAMLET has changed. Triumph and blood lust possess him.
HORATIO does not like it. Suddenly HAMLET sees the PLAYERS
coming and instigates a diversionary tactic. ROSENCRANTZ and
GUILDENSTERN close behind them. He is physically restless,
they have to chase him all round the stage.

> HAMLET
> *Ah ha! Come, some music, come, the recorders,*
> *For if the King like not the comedy,*
> *Why then, belike he likes it not, pardie.*
> *Come, some music.*
>
> GUILDENSTERN (firm)
> *Good my lord, vouchsafe me a word with you.*
>
> HAMLET (delighted)
> *Sir, a whole history.*
>
> GUILDENSTERN
> *The King, sir –*
>
> HAMLET (surprised)
> *Ay, sir, what of him?*

GUILDENSTERN tries to match him for sarcasm and understatement.

> GUILDENSTERN
> *Is in his retirement marvellous distempered.*
>
> HAMLET
> *With drink, sir?*

Ta-dah!

> GUILDENSTERN
> *No, my lord, rather with choler.*
>
> HAMLET
> *Your wisdom should show itself more richer to signify this to*
> *his doctor, for for me to put him to his purgation would perhaps*
> *plunge him into far more choler.*
>
> GUILDENSTERN (very annoyed)
> *Good my lord, put your discourse into some frame, and start not so*
> *wildly from my affair.*
>
> HAMLET (mousey)
> *I am tame, sir. Pronounce.*
>
> GUILDENSTERN
> *The Queen your mother, in most great affliction of spirit, hath sent*
> *me to you.*
>
> HAMLET (very polite)
> *You are welcome.*

The thuggish side of GUILDENSTERN's personality very close
to the surface now.

> GUILDENSTERN
> *Nay, good my lord, this courtesy is not of the right breed. If it shall*

please you to make me a wholesome answer, I will do your mother's
commandment; if not, your pardon and my return shall be the end of
my business.

Ooo. A bit narked are we?

HAMLET
Sir, I cannot.

GUILDENSTERN
What, my lord?

HAMLET
Make you a wholesome answer. My wit's
diseased.

Remember ...?

HAMLET (continuing)
    But, sir, such answers as I can make, you
shall command; or rather, as you say, my mother.
Therefore no more, but to the matter. My mother, you say?

ROSENCRANTZ
Then thus she says: your behaviour hath struck her into
amazement and admiration.

HAMLET (very camp)
O wonderful son, that can so astonish a mother! But is there no
sequel at the heels of this mother's admiration impart?

ROSENCRANTZ
She desires to speak with you in her closet ere you go to bed.

HAMLET (sinister)
We shall obey, were she ten times our mother.

A beat. If looks could kill.

HAMLET (continuing)
Have you any further trade with us?

He tries a different tack.

ROSENCRANTZ
My lord, you once did love me.

HAMLET returns the understanding tone.

HAMLET
And do still, by these pickers and stealers.

ROSENCRANTZ
Good my lord, what is your cause of distemper? You do freely
bar the door of your own liberty if you deny your griefs to
your friend.

HAMLET (poisonous irony)
Sir, I lack advancement.

ROSENCRANTZ
How can that be when you have the voice of the King himself
for your succession in Denmark?

HAMLET
Ay, but 'while the grass grows ...' – the proverb is something musty.

One of the actors returns with a recorder.

HAMLET (continuing)
O, the recorder. Let me see one.

To GUILDENSTERN, taking him aside.

HAMLET (continuing)
To withdraw with you, why do you go about to recover the
wind of me as if you would drive me into a toil?

They realize they've gone too far. They want to leave this country
in one piece.

GUILDENSTERN
O my lord, if my duty be too bold, my love
is too unmannerly.

HAMLET
I do not well understand that. Will you play upon this pipe?

He thrusts it in his face.

GUILDENSTERN
My lord, I cannot.

More threateningly.

HAMLET
I pray you.

GUILDENSTERN
Believe me, I cannot.

It might be a dagger.

HAMLET
I do beseech you.

GUILDENSTERN
I know no touch of it, my lord.

He has pinned him in a corner of the stage now. His tone still,
quiet, menacing.

HAMLET
It is as easy as lying. Govern these ventages with
your fingers and thumb, give it breath with your
mouth, and it will discourse most eloquent music.
Look you, these are the stops.

GUILDENSTERN
But these cannot I command to any utterance of harmony.
I have not the skill.

His lips are now an inch away from GUILDENSTERN's ear.
HORATIO watches for any move from ROSENCRANTZ to help.

HAMLET
Why, look you now, how unworthy a thing you make of me.
You would play upon me, you would seem to know my stops,
you would pluck out the heart of my mystery, you would sound me
from my lowest note to the top of my compass; and there is much
music, excellent voice in this little organ, yet cannot you make
it speak.

Then he explodes with passion.

    HAMLET (continuing)
        'Sblood, do you think I am easier to be played on than a
    pipe? Call me what instrument you will, though you can fret me,
    yet you cannot play upon me.
POLONIUS enters the back of the 'auditorium'.

    HAMLET (continuing)
                        God bless you, sir.

    POLONIUS
    My lord, the queen would speak with you, and presently.
HAMLET looks up to an imaginary sky. Happy to mock his alleged
madness with these people who treat him with similar contempt.

    HAMLET
    Do you see yonder cloud that's almost in shape of a camel?

    POLONIUS (barely civil)
    By th' mass, and 'tis: like a camel, indeed.

    HAMLET (provoking)
    Methinks it is like a weasel.

    POLONIUS
    It is backed like a weasel.

    HAMLET (cold-eyed)
    Or like a whale.

    POLONIUS (vicious)
    Very like a whale.

    HAMLET
    Then will I come to my mother by and by.
    They fool me to the top of my bent.
    I will come by and by.

    POLONIUS
    I will say so.

    HAMLET
    'By and by' is easily said.
Exit POLONIUS.

    HAMLET (continuing)
                        Leave me. 'Friends'.
They go. HORATIO waits for a moment, but HAMLET races up the
stairs through a door and out onto the balcony.

                                            Cut to:

Interior / KING'S APARTMENT Night
KING CLAUDIUS marches into the room, taking off his jacket, and
attended by his valets. ROSENCRANTZ and GUILDENSTERN
following. It's as if a war were in expectation.

    CLAUDIUS
    I like him not, nor stands it safe with us
    To let his madness range. Therefore prepare you.
    I your commission will forthwith dispatch,

And he to England shall along with you.
The terms of our estate may not endure
Hazard so dangerous as doth hourly grow
Out of his lunacies.

CLAUDIUS crosses the room and sits at his table.

These men are now terrified. They can't stop themselves
from talking.

GUILDENSTERN
                              We will ourselves provide.
Most holy and religious fear it is
To keep those many many bodies safe
That live and feed upon your majesty.

ROSENCRANTZ
The single and peculiar life is bound
With all the strength and armour of the mind
To keep itself from noyance; but much more
That spirit upon whose weal depends and rests
The lives of many.

He tries to soothe CLAUDIUS. CLAUDIUS drinks. We can see the
burden of responsibility.

ROSENCRANTZ (continuing)
                              The cease of majesty
Dies not alone, but like a gulf doth draw
What's near it with it. It is a massy wheel
Fixed on the summit of the highest mount,
To whose huge spokes ten thousand lesser things
Are mortised and adjoined, which when it falls
Each small annexment, petty consequence,
Attends the boist'rous ruin. Never alone
Did the King sigh, but with a general groan.

His look thanks them.

CLAUDIUS
Arm you, I pray you, to this speedy voyage,
For we will fetters put upon this fear
Which now goes too free-footed.

GUILDENSTERN
                              We will haste us.

POLONIUS comes in and CLAUDIUS moves off.

POLONIUS
My lord.

They leave through one of the secret doors.

Interior / CHAPEL Night

POLONIUS and CLAUDIUS moving down the steps towards
the chapel.

POLONIUS
He's going to his mother's closet.
Behind the arras I'll convey myself
To hear the process. I'll warrant she'll tax him home.
And, as you said – and wisely was it said –
'Tis meet that some more audience than a mother,
Since nature makes them partial, should o'erhear
The speech of vantage. Fare you well, my liege.
I'll call upon you ere you go to bed,
And tell you what I know.
CLAUDIUS
                                    Thanks, dear my lord.
POLONIUS hurries off and CLAUDIUS moves into the chapel.

                                                    Cut to:

Interior-Exterior / BALCONY Night

A new demonic HAMLET smells the midnight air and talks to
Camera. His mood is chilling – unpleasant.

HAMLET
'Tis now the very witching time of night,
When churchyards yawn, and hell itself breathes out
Contagion to this world. Now could I drink hot blood,
And do such bitter business as the day
Would quake to look on. Soft, now to my mother.
He says this with ominous relish.

HAMLET (continuing)
O heart, lose not thy nature! Let not ever
The soul of Nero enter this firm bosom.
Let me be cruel, not unnatural.
I will speak daggers to her, but use none.
My tongue and soul

Interior / BALCONY Night

Whilst HAMLET continues we see CLAUDIUS in the chapel. He
moves to the confessional, checks there is no one there and then
enters the wooden booth, a little drunk and utterly tormented.

HAMLET V/O (continuing)
                        in this be hypocrites –
How in my words somever she be shent,
To give them seals never my soul consent.
CLAUDIUS
O, my offence is rank! It smells to heaven.
It hath the primal eldest curse upon't,
A brother's murder. Pray can I not.
Though inclination be as sharp as will,
My stronger guilt defeats my strong intent,
And like a man to double business bound

I stand in pause where I shall first begin,
And both neglect. What if this cursèd hand
Were thicker than itself with brother's blood,
Is there not rain enough in the sweet heavens
To wash it white as snow? Whereto serves mercy
But to confront the visage of offence?
And what's in prayer but this twofold force,
To be forestallèd ere we come to fall,
Or pardoned being down? Then I'll look up.

He does, but more in hope than anything else.

CLAUDIUS (continuing)
My fault is past – but O, what form of prayer
Can serve my turn? 'Forgive me my foul murder'?
That cannot be, since I am still possessed
Of those effects for which I did the murder –
My crown, mine own ambition, and my queen.

This last said with real tenderness and longing.

CLAUDIUS (continuing)
May one be pardoned and retain th' offence?
In the corrupted currents of this world
Offence's gilded hand may shove by justice,
And oft 'tis seen the wicked prize itself
Buys out the law. But 'tis not so above.
There is no shuffling, there the action lies
In his true nature, and we ourselves compelled
Even to the teeth and forehead of our faults
To give in evidence. What then? What rests?
Try what repentance can. What can it not?
Yet what can it when one cannot repent?
O wretched state, O bosom black as death,
O limèd soul that, struggling to be free,
Art more engaged! Help, angels! Make assay.
Bow, stubborn knees;

He kneels down. His head inches away from the grille. We can hear
his guilty breathing.

CLAUDIUS
                              and heart with strings of steel,

We see, but he does not, a hand on the other side of the grille.

CLAUDIUS (continuing)
Be soft as sinews of the new-born babe.
All may be well.

His eyes close and we move slowly to the other side of the booth
to find HAMLET.

  As the voice/over begins he slowly brings out his dagger.

HAMLET V/O
Now might I do it pat, now he is praying,

And now I'll do't,

He puts the long thin dagger through one of the grille holes and moves it very slowly to a centimetre away from CLAUDIUS's ear. He puts the palm of his hand against the hilt ready to hammer it into CLAUDIUS's skull.

> HAMLET V/O (continuing)
> > *and so he goes to heaven,*
>
> *And so am I revenged.*

And he does! We see the blood spurt before an abrupt **cut** we are back in real time as before – CLAUDIUS is still praying – HAMLET fine-tuning his revenge. Wait, just a minute.

> HAMLET V/O (continuing)
> > *That would be scanned.*
>
> *A villain kills my father, and for that*
> *I, his sole son, do this same villain send*
> *To heaven.*
> *O, this is hire and salary, not revenge!*
> *He took my father grossly,*

Cut to:

Exterior / GARDEN Day (Flashback)

OLD HAMLET in the snow-covered Palace garden, clutching his ear in pain, and collapsing on the floor – dead.

> HAMLET V/O (continuing)
> > *full of bread,*
>
> *With all his crimes broad blown,*

Cut to:

Interior / CHAPEL Night

Close-up on his eyes.

> HAMLET (continuing)
> > *as flush as May;*
>
> *And how his audit stands, who knows save heaven?*
> *But in our circumstance and course of thought*

Cut to:

Exterior / PIT Night

The Entrance to Hell.

> HAMLET V/O (continuing)
> *'Tis heavy with him.*

Cut to:

Interior / CHAPEL Night

CLAUDIUS's eyes closed and praying.

> HAMLET (continuing)
> > *And am I then revenged*
>
> *To take him in the purging of his soul,*
> *When he is fit and seasoned for his passage?*
> *No.*

He lifts the dagger to his head.

HAMLET (continuing)
Up, sword, and know thou a more horrid hint.
We see quick cuts of CLAUDIUS, drinking, arguing with POLONIUS,
in bed with GERTRUDE, kissing GERTRUDE, talking, hiding.
HAMLET V/O
When he is drunk asleep, or in his rage,
Or in th' incestuous pleasure of his bed,
At game, a-swearing, or about some act
That has no relish of salvation in't,
Then trip him that his heels may kick at heaven,
And that his soul may be as damned and black

Cut to:

Exterior / PIT Night
The gates to Hell shut fast.

Cut to:

Interior / CHAPEL Night
HAMLET V/O (continuing)
As hell whereto it goes. My mother stays.
This physic but prolongs thy sickly days.
CLAUDIUS knows there is no absolution, his prayer has not worked.
CLAUDIUS V/O
My words fly up, my thoughts remain below.
Words without thoughts never to heaven go.
He hears a noise and slowly turns to look through the grille.

Cut to:

Interior / GERTRUDE'S APARTMENTS Night
GERTRUDE, ravishing as ever in her nightwear, is joined by an
anxious POLONIUS.
POLONIUS
He will come straight. Look you lay home to him.
Tell him his pranks have been too broad to bear with,
And that your grace hath screened and stood between
Much heat and him. I'll silence me e'en here.
Pray you be round with him.
GERTRUDE
                              I'll warr'nt you. Fear me not.
HAMLET (O/S)
Mother, mother, mother!
GERTRUDE
Withdraw; I hear him coming.
POLONIUS goes behind some of the drapes in which the room
is lavishly and beautifully decked.
  She gathers herself for the interview which should have occurred
three months ago.
  HAMLET enters slowly and deliberately through one of the
hidden doors.

HAMLET
Now, mother, what's the matter?

GERTRUDE
Hamlet, thou hast thy father much offended.

He moves towards her.

HAMLET
Mother, you have my father much offended.

GERTRUDE
Come, come, you answer with an idle tongue.

She is becoming anxious.

HAMLET
Go, go, you question with a wicked tongue.

GERTRUDE
Why, how now, Hamlet?

HAMLET
                        What's the matter now?

By this time she is enraged.

GERTRUDE
Have you forgot me?

HAMLET (vicious)
                    No, by the rood, not so.
You are the Queen, your husband's brother's wife.
And − would it were not so − you are my mother.

GERTRUDE
Nay, then, I'll set those to you that can speak.

She rushes for the door, he grabs her in an instant and pulls her
down onto a chair.

HAMLET
Come, come, and sit you down. You shall not budge.
You go not till I set you up a glass
Where you may see the inmost part of you.

GERTRUDE
What wilt thou do? Thou wilt not murder me?
Help, ho!

POLONIUS (behind the drapes)
            What ho! Help, help, help!

HAMLET looks over his shoulder to see movement behind the
drapes. He is outraged. At last.

HAMLET
How now, a rat?

He rushes across the room and grabs the figure behind the drapes.
He thrusts, and thrusts the dagger into POLONIUS's jacket, which is
quickly drenched in blood.

HAMLET (continuing)
                    Dead for a ducat, dead.

POLONIUS
O, I am slain!

HAMLET steps away and the body falls, pulling the drape down with it onto the floor. The QUEEN incredulous, shocked, crosses over to it.

GERTRUDE (to Hamlet)
O me, what hast thou done?

He can hardly speak. He has killed.

HAMLET
Nay, I know not. Is it the King?

GERTRUDE
O, what a rash and bloody deed is this!

Don't even start.

HAMLET
A bloody deed — almost as bad, good mother,
As kill a king and marry with his brother.

She cannot believe what she has heard.

GERTRUDE
As kill a king?

HAMLET
                    Ay, lady, 'twas my word.

GERTRUDE unwraps the drapes around the bleeding mass on the floor to reveal it is POLONIUS. HAMLET is damned again. His wretchedness is complete.

HAMLET (continuing)
Thou wretched, rash, intruding fool, farewell.
I took thee for thy better. Take thy fortune.
Thou find'st to be too busy is some danger. —
Leave wringing of your hands.

He pulls her up onto her feet and throws her onto the bed.

GERTRUDE watches him in horror as he paces around the bed.

HAMLET (continuing)
                    Peace, sit you down,
And let me wring your heart; for so I shall
If it be made of penetrable stuff,
If damnèd custom have not brassed it so
That it be proof and bulwark against sense.

GERTRUDE (indignant)
What have I done, that thou dar'st wag thy tongue
In noise so rude against me?

He cannot believe her audacity.

HAMLET
                    Such an act
That blurs the grace and blush of modesty,

He moves slowly to her. Talks as if he were a priest about to pronounce eternal damnation.

HAMLET (continuing)
Calls virtue hypocrite, takes off the rose
From the fair forehead of an innocent love
And sets a blister there, makes marriage vows
As false as dicers' oaths – O, such a deed
As from the body of contraction plucks
The very soul, and sweet religion makes
A rhapsody of words. Heaven's face doth glow,
Yea, this solidity and compound mass

He indicates the very world itself, the earth.

HAMLET (continuing)
With tristful visage, as against the doom,
is thought-sick at the act.

GERTRUDE (furious exasperation)
                    Ay me, what act,
That roars so loud and thunders in the index?

For a moment it seems as though he will kill her. He jumps onto the
bed and shows her two miniatures, one of CLAUDIUS, the other of
his Father. He is very close to her.

HAMLET
Look here upon this picture, and on this,

Showing her the portrait of his Father.

HAMLET (continuing)
The counterfeit presentment of two brothers.
See what a grace was seated on this brow –
Hyperion's curls, the front of Jove himself,
An eye like Mars, to threaten and command,
A station like the herald Mercury
New lighted on a heaven-kissing hill;
A combination and a form indeed
Where every god did seem to set his seal
To give the world assurance of a man.
This was your husband.

Now showing her the portrait of CLAUDIUS.

HAMLET (continuing)
            Look you now what follows.
Here is your husband, like a mildewed ear
Blasting his wholesome brother. Have you eyes?
Could you on this fair mountain leave to feed,
And batten on this moor? Ha, have you eyes?
You cannot call it love, for at your age
The heyday in the blood is tame, it's humble,
And waits upon the judgement; and what judgement
Would step from this to this?

He throws her back down on the bed and leaps off to pace the room.

HAMLET (continuing)

                        Sense, sure you have,
Else you could not have motion. But sure that sense
Is apoplexed; for madness would not err,
Nor sense to ecstasy was ne'er so thralled
But it reserved some quantity of choice
To serve in such a difference. What devil was't
That thus hath cozened you at hoodman-blind?
Eyes without feeling, feeling without sight,
Ears without hands or eyes, smelling sans all,
Or but a sickly part of one true sense
Could not so mope. O shame, where is thy blush?
Rebellious hell,
If thou canst mutine in a matron's bones,
To flaming youth let virtue be as wax
And melt in her own fire. Proclaim no shame
When the compulsive ardour gives the charge,
Since frost itself as actively doth burn,
And reason panders will.

She is stricken.

GERTRUDE

                      O, Hamlet, speak no more!
Thou turn'st mine eyes into my very soul,
And there I see such black and grainèd spots
As will not leave their tinct.

HAMLET

                      Nay, but to live
In the sweat of an enseamèd bed,

He leans nearer her.

HAMLET (continuing)
Stew'd in corruption, honeying and making love
Over the nasty sty!

This is too much for flesh and blood.

GERTRUDE

                    O, speak to me no more!
These words like daggers enter in mine ears.
No more, sweet Hamlet.

The fire and brimstone continues.

HAMLET
    A murderer and a villain,
A slave that is not twentieth part the tithe
Of your precedent lord, a vice of kings,
A cutpurse of the empire and the rule,
That from a shelf the precious diadem stole
And put it in his pocket —

GERTRUDE
No more.

HAMLET
A king of shreds and patches –

Suddenly his eyes open wide, the atmosphere has changed. He slowly
pulls away from his mother and we see THE GHOST, with them by
the window. HAMLET moves across the room.

HAMLET (continuing)
Save me and hover o'er me with your wings,
You heavenly guards!
(to The Ghost)
                    What would you, gracious figure?

GERTRUDE sees nothing of the spectre. Only her son responding
with sheer lunacy ... to ... nothing.

GERTRUDE (to herself)
Alas, he's mad.

HAMLET (to The Ghost)
Do you not come your tardy son to chide,
That, lapsed in time and passion, lets go by
Th' important acting of your dread command?
O, say!

THE GHOST replies, firm in his instruction. But the tone is weary
and sad. As if he had expected HAMLET's vacillation.

THE GHOST
        Do not forget. This visitation
Is but to whet thy almost blunted purpose.
But look, amazement on thy mother sits.
O, step between her and her fighting soul.
Conceit in weakest bodies strongest works.
Speak to her, Hamlet.

HAMLET hardly dare look at her, in case his Father disappears
while he does so.

HAMLET
How is it with you, lady?

She is genuinely concerned for him. Perhaps it really is madness.

GERTRUDE
                    Alas, how is't with you,
That you do bend your eye on vacancy,
And with th' incorporal air do hold discourse?

She goes to him, takes his head in her hands, as if realizing for the
first time the extent of his illness.

GERTRUDE (continuing)
Forth at your eyes your spirits wildly peep,
And, as the sleeping soldiers in th' alarm,
Your bedded hair, like life in excrements,
Start up and stand on end.

Very tender now. This is so disturbing to witness.

GERTRUDE (continuing)

O gentle son,
Upon the heat and flame of thy distemper
Sprinkle cool patience! Whereon do you look?

HAMLET

On him, on him. Look you how pale he glares.

And he does. We see all three close. The complete family, now all unable to reach each other and all heartbroken by the frustration of the attempt.

HAMLET (continuing)

His form and cause conjoined, preaching to stones,
Would make them capable.

(to The Ghost)

Do not look upon me
Lest with this piteous action you convert
My stern effects. Then what I have to do
Will want true colour – tears perchance for blood.

GERTRUDE (more practical now)

To whom do you speak this?

HAMLET (agonized)

Do you see nothing there?

GERTRUDE (compassionate)

Nothing at all, yet all that is I see.

HAMLET (incredulous)

Nor did you nothing hear?

GERTRUDE

No, nothing but ourselves.

THE GHOST has started to move away. His expression bleaker and sadder than ever.

HAMLET (desperate)

Why, look you there. Look how it steals away.
My father, in his habit as he lived.
Look where he goes even now out at the portal.

THE GHOST disappears.

Now she feels she knows the truth. She is dealing with a genuine lunatic. She pities him. She is calmer now.

GERTRUDE

This is the very coinage of your brain.
This bodiless creation ecstasy
Is very cunning in.

His manner turns to ice. She won't get away with that tack.

HAMLET

Ecstasy!

He pulls her across the room and down onto the sofa.

HAMLET
My pulse as yours doth temperately keep time,
And makes as healthful music. It is not madness
That I have uttered. Bring me to the test,

Go on, try it.

HAMLET (continuing)
And I the matter will reword, which madness
Would gambol from. Mother,

Don't even think of looking for a way out of facing your guilt.

HAMLET (continuing)
  for love of grace
Lay not that flattering unction to your soul
That not your trespass but my madness speaks.

Who are you trying to kid?

HAMLET (continuing)
It will but skin and film the ulcerous place
Whilst rank corruption, mining all within,
Infects unseen.

You have one choice.

HAMLET (continuing)
   Confess yourself to heaven;
Repent what's past, avoid what is to come,
And do not spread the compost on the weeds
To make them ranker. Forgive me this my virtue,
For in the fatness of these pursy times
Virtue itself of vice must pardon beg,
Yea, curb and woo for leave to do him good.

She looks at him and in some perceptible way she looks into herself.

GERTRUDE
O Hamlet, thou hast cleft my heart in twain!

We know that she means it, and we cannot but feel compassion for
a woman who has undoubtedly paid a heavy price for her actions.
HAMLET is pleased with this tangible shift but has no mercy.
He is gentler now. But that's almost worse.

HAMLET
O, throw away the worser part of it,
And live the purer with the other half!
Good night —

He pauses.

HAMLET (continuing)
   but go not to mine uncle's bed.
Assume a virtue if you have it not.
That monster custom, who all sense doth eat,
Of habits devil, is angel yet in this,
That to the use of actions fair and good
He likewise gives a frock or livery

That aptly is put on. Refrain tonight,
And that shall lend a kind of easiness
To the next abstinence. The next more easy;
For use almost can change the stamp of nature,
And either shame the devil, or throw him out
With wondrous potency. Once more, good night;

At last he concedes something of filial affection.

HAMLET (continuing)
And when you are desirous to be blest,
I'll blessing beg of you.

To the dead POLONIUS.

HAMLET (continuing)
      For this same lord,
I do repent. But heaven hath pleased it so
To punish me with this, and this with me,
That I must be their scourge and minister.
I will bestow him, and will answer well
The death I gave him. So, again, good night.
I must be cruel only to be kind.
Thus bad begins, and worse remains behind.
One word more, good lady.

She is strangely vulnerable. The child almost, to his scolding father.
She seems on the edge of a breakdown. Her voice fragile. The
question, endlessly resonant.

GERTRUDE
What shall I do?

HAMLET
Not this, by no means, that I bid you do:
Let the bloat King tempt you again to bed,
Pinch wanton on your cheek, call you his mouse,

He particularly despises these words as he says them.

HAMLET (continuing)
And let him, for a pair of reechy kisses,
Or paddling in your neck with his damned fingers,
Make you to ravel all this matter out,
That I essentially am not in madness,
But mad in craft. 'Twere good you let him know,
For who that's but a queen, fair, sober, wise,
Would from a paddock, from a bat, a gib,
Such dear concernings hide? Who would do so?

No, let's abandon caution.

HAMLET (continuing)
No, in despite of sense and secrecy,
Unpeg the basket on the house's top,
Let the birds fly, and, like the famous ape,
To try conclusions in the basket creep,

And break your own neck down.

THE QUEEN is still trying to contain her reactions. His effect on her, his madness (whatever form), the awful notion that her new husband killed to have her.

GERTRUDE
Be thou assured, if words be made of breath,
And breath of life, I have no life to breathe
What thou hast said to me.

They now sit side by side, like two lost children.

HAMLET
I must to England, you know that?

GERTRUDE
Alack, I had forgot. 'Tis so concluded on.

HAMLET
There's letters sealed; and my two schoolfellows,
Whom I will trust as I will adders fanged,
They bear the mandate, they must sweep my way
And marshal me to knavery. Let it work;
For 'tis the sport to have the engineer
Hoist with his own petard; and't shall go hard
But I will delve one yard below their mines
And blow them at the moon. O, 'tis most sweet
When in one line two crafts directly meet.
This man shall set me packing.
I'll lug the guts into the neighbour room.
Mother, good night indeed.

They have one last hug and he stands and moves away towards POLONIUS.

HAMLET (continuing)
                    This counsellor
Is now most still, most secret, and most grave,
Who was in life a foolish prating knave. –

He crouches down by the body.

HAMLET
Come, sir, to draw toward an end with you. –

A last look. The last ever?

HAMLET (continuing)
Good night, mother.

He exits with the body. GERTRUDE stands. The strain overwhelming. She sobs.

Cut to:

Interior / CORRIDOR Night

To see CLAUDIUS, ROSENCRANTZ and GUILDENSTERN plus GUARDS, striding along the corridor as GERTRUDE comes out of her apartment.

CLAUDIUS goes straight to his wife.

CLAUDIUS
There's matter in these sighs, these profound heaves,
You must translate. 'Tis fit we understand them.
Where is your son?

GERTRUDE (to ROSENCRANTZ and GUILDENSTERN)
Bestow this place on us a little while.

ROSENCRANTZ and GUILDENSTERN and the ATTENDANTS
move away and CLAUDIUS and GERTRUDE move into the
King's apartments.

Interior / KING'S APARTMENTS Night

We follow them as CLAUDIUS and GERTRUDE face each other.

GERTRUDE (shaking)
Ah, mine own lord, what have I seen tonight!

He touches her, holds her. But she does not respond.

CLAUDIUS (gently but firmly)
What, Gertrude? How does Hamlet?

She talks as if her mind were somewhere else. Which it probably is.

GERTRUDE
Mad as the sea and wind when both contend
Which is the mightier. In his lawless fit,
Behind the arras hearing something stir,
Whips out his rapier, cries 'A rat, a rat!',
And in this brainish apprehension kills
The unseen good old man.

GERTRUDE moves away.

CLAUDIUS (appalled)
                    O heavy deed!
It had been so with us had we been there.

CLAUDIUS moves back into GERTRUDE's apartment to the pool
of blood on the floor and searches behind the arras.

CLAUDIUS (continuing)
His liberty is full of threats to all –
To you yourself, to us, to everyone.

Angry now. Paranoid. He kneels down by the blood.

CLAUDIUS (continuing)
Alas, how shall this bloody deed be answered?
It will be laid to us, whose providence
Should have kept short, restrained, and out of haunt
This mad young man.

Rationalizing at a thousand miles an hour.

CLAUDIUS (continuing)
                    But so much was our love,
We would not understand what was most fit,
But, like the owner of a foul disease,
To keep it from divulging, let it feed

Even on the pith of life.

He snaps at GERTRUDE as she enters her apartments.

CLAUDIUS (continuing)
Where is he gone?

She pulls herself out of her reverie to make some desperate attempt
at a defence of the son she cannot but love.

GERTRUDE
To draw apart the body he hath killed,
O'er whom − his very madness, like some ore
Amongst a mineral of metals base,
Shows itself pure − a weeps for what is done.

He will have none of this. It's action stations. National crisis.
The heir to the throne has killed the Prime Minister.

CLAUDIUS
O Gertrude, come away!
The sun no sooner shall the mountains touch
But we will ship him hence; and this vile deed
We must with all our majesty and skill
Both countenance and excuse.

He moves out into the corridor where ROSENCRANTZ and
GUILDENSTERN stand, aghast.

CLAUDIUS (continuing)
Ho, Guildenstern!
Friends both, go join you with some further aid.
Hamlet in madness hath Polonius slain,

This is all much more than they can deal with.

CLAUDIUS (continuing)
And from his mother's closet hath he dragged him.
Go seek him out, speak fair, and bring the body
Into the chapel. I pray you haste in this.

ROSENCRANTZ and GUILDENSTERN go.

He tries to be gentle again with her as she joins him.

CLAUDIUS (continuing)
Come, Gertrude, we'll call up our wisest friends
And let them know both what we mean to do
And what's untimely done. So envious slander,
Whose whisper o'er the world's diameter,
As level as the cannon to his blank,
Transports his poisoned shot, may miss our name
And hit the woundless air. O, come away!

He pulls her to him, comforting each other.

CLAUDIUS (continuing)
My soul is full of discord and dismay.

                                        Cut to:

Interior / PALACE ROOMS−MONTAGE Night
Soldiers on red alert.

Alarms go off.

The hunt for HAMLET is on!

Cut to:

Interior / PALACE Night

Guards break into OPHELIA's room. She is terrified. Her bed is searched, with her still in it!

Cut to:

Interior / CHAPEL STAIRS Night

HAMLET finishes disposing of POLONIUS's body.

> HAMLET
> *Safely stowed.*
>
> ROSENCRANTZ AND GUILDENSTERN (O/S)
> *Hamlet, Lord Hamlet!*
>
> HAMLET
> *But soft. What noise? Who calls on Hamlet?*

He rushes through and into the adjoining Ante-Room.

Interior / ANTE-ROOM Night

> HAMLET
>
> > *O, here they come.*

Where he is joined by a panting ROSENCRANTZ and GUILDENSTERN. What a surprise.

> ROSENCRANTZ
> *What have you done, my lord, with the dead body?*

They circle each other in the large room. Wary of a quick move.

> HAMLET (cheerful)
> *Compounded it with dust, whereto 'tis kin.*

COURTIERS and SOLDIERS arrive throughout the scene, cornering the Prince. HAMLET leads them around the Hall, through the remains of the theatre.

> ROSENCRANTZ
> *Tell us where 'tis, that we may take it thence*
> *And bear it to the chapel.*

HAMLET fixes him with a particularly contemptuous glare.

> HAMLET
> *Do not believe it.*
>
> ROSENCRANTZ
> *Believe what?*
>
> HAMLET
> *That I can keep your counsel and not mine own. Besides, to be demanded of a sponge — what replication should be made by the son of a king?*

ROSENCRANTZ can barely tolerate this so-called 'wit'.

> ROSENCRANTZ
> *Take you me for a sponge, my lord?*

He talks as if filling him in on a particularly useful piece of information. Meantime the room starting to fill up with other guards, and their dogs.

HAMLET

Ay, sir, that soaks up the King's countenance, his rewards, his authorities. But such officers do the King best service in the end. He keeps them, like an Ape an apple in the corner of his jaw, first mouthed to be last swallowed. When he needs what you have gleaned, it is but squeezing you, and, sponge, you shall be dry again.

With this HAMLET grabs ROSENCRANTZ around the neck, taking him hostage against the growing CROWD.

ROSENCRANTZ

I understand you not, my lord.

HAMLET

I am glad of it. A knavish speech sleeps in a foolish ear.

They start to move in on him.

ROSENCRANTZ

My lord, you must tell us where the body is, and go with us to the King.

HAMLET

The body is with the King, but the King is not with the body. The King is a thing —

HAMLET throws ROSENCRANTZ back to the CROWD.

GUILDENSTERN

A thing, my lord?

HAMLET

Of nothing. Bring me to him.

He appears to go with them willingly. They go towards the stairs as OPHELIA runs down

OPHELIA

My lord!

HAMLET

Hide fox and all after.

HAMLET escapes, ROSENCRANTZ and GUILDENSTERN and the soldiers begin the chase.

Cut to:

Interior / LOWER HALL ROOMS Night

Chaos. Close shots of the dogs, the troops, ROSENCRANTZ and GUILDENSTERN. HAMLET runs through room after room, hidden door after hidden door, we track beside them. Surely he, who knows this spy-infested rabbit warren, can escape?

But no, as he closes the door in his apartment, apparently safe ... a gun barrel trains itself on his head.

Cut to:

Interior / KING'S APARTMENTS Night

CLAUDIUS talks to Camera. Quiet, grim, drinking.

CLAUDIUS
I have sent to seek him, and to find the body.
How dangerous is it that this man goes loose!
Yet must not we put the strong law on him.
He's loved of the distracted multitude,
Who like not in their judgement but their eyes,
And where 'tis so, th' offender's scourge is weighed,
But never the offence. To bear all smooth and even,
This sudden sending him away must seem
Deliberate pause. Diseases desperate grown
By desperate appliance are relieved,
Or not at all.

ROSENCRANTZ comes straight in.

CLAUDIUS (urgent)
            How now,

He stands and crosses over to ROSENCRANTZ.

CLAUDIUS
                    what hath befall'n?

ROSENCRANTZ
Where the dead body is bestowed, my lord,
We cannot get from him.

CLAUDIUS
                    But where is he?

ROSENCRANTZ
Without, my lord, guarded, to know your pleasure.

CLAUDIUS
Bring him before us.

ROSENCRANTZ
Ho, Guildenstern! Bring in my lord.

They drag in a badly shaken HAMLET, spirit intact. HORATIO is dragged through another door.

CLAUDIUS (menacing)
Now, Hamlet, where's Polonius?

HAMLET (deadpan)
At supper.

CLAUDIUS (patient)
At supper? Where?

HAMLET (jolly)
Not where he eats, but where he is eaten. A certain convocation of politic worms are e'en at him. Your worm is your only emperor for diet. We fat all creatures else to fat us, and we fat ourselves for maggots. Your fat King and your lean beggar is but variable service — two dishes, but to one table. That's the end.

CLAUDIUS
Alas, alas!

This last for the company.

HAMLET (still blabbering)
A man may fish with the worm that hath eat of a King, and eat
of the fish that hath fed of that worm.

CLAUDIUS
What dost thou mean by this?

He looks straight at him.

HAMLET
Nothing but to show you how a King may go a progress through
the guts of a beggar.

With this the KING explodes and gives HAMLET a mighty whack.

CLAUDIUS
Where is Polonius?

Pause. The Prince unruffled.

HAMLET
In heaven. Send thither to see. If your messenger find him not there,
seek him i'th'other place yourself. But indeed, if you find him not
this month, you shall nose him as you go up the stairs into the lobby.

CLAUDIUS (to Rosencrantz)
Go seek him there.

HAMLET makes a little cough. ROSENCRANTZ delays.

HAMLET (to Rosencrantz)
He will stay till you come.

Exit ROSENCRANTZ.

CLAUDIUS
Hamlet, this deed of thine, for thine especial safety —
Which we do tender as we dearly grieve
For that which thou hast done — must send thee hence
With fiery quickness. Therefore prepare thyself.
The barque is ready, and the wind at help,
Th' associates tend, and everything is bent
For England.

HAMLET
For England?

CLAUDIUS
Ay, Hamlet.

HAMLET
Good.

CLAUDIUS will not give in to Mr Smart-arse.

CLAUDIUS
So is it if thou knew'st our purposes.

HAMLET
I see a cherub that sees them. But come, for England. Farewell,
dear mother.

And now even CLAUDIUS thinks that perhaps HAMLET is mad.

CLAUDIUS
Thy loving father, Hamlet.

HAMLET (brightly)
My mother. Father and mother is man and wife, man and wife is
one flesh, and so my mother.

This last with real hatred.

HAMLET (continuing)
                    Come, for England.

He turns and is about to leave when HORATIO moves to him.
He looks at his old friend and whispers.

HAMLET
Stay.

With that he is dragged from the room.

CLAUDIUS (to Guildenstern) (shaken)
Follow him at foot. Tempt him with speed aboard.
Delay it not. I'll have him hence tonight.
Away, for everything is sealed and done
That else leans on th' affair. Pray you, make haste.

GUILDENSTERN leaves and CLAUDIUS closes the door. At the
point of collapse.

CLAUDIUS (continuing)
And, England, if my love thou hold'st at aught –
As my great power thereof may give thee sense,
Since yet thy cicatrice looks raw and red
After the Danish sword, and thy free awe
Pays homage to us – thou mayst not coldly set
Our sovereign process, which imports at full,
By letters conjuring to that effect,
The present death of Hamlet.

Almost in tears now.

CLAUDIUS (continuing)
                    Do it, England,
For like the hectic in my blood he rages,
And thou must cure me. Till I know 'tis done,
Howe'er my haps, my joys were ne'er begun.

                                        We cut to:

Interior / CHAPEL Night

The Camera still moving, this time with the body of POLONIUS as
it is carried into the Chapel. OPHELIA being restrained by GUARDS.
A great primal yell and then she flings herself at the body, held back
by the Chapel gates. We move in on her screaming face. A scene
of ugly grief.

                                        Dissolve to:

Interior / PALACE Night

We see a distant Elsinore, we are reminded once again of its massivity,
its loneliness. Still moving, we Dissolve again, to grey misty dawn:

Exterior / PLAIN Day

A low Wide Shot with grass in foreground and misty suggestions of landscape in the far distance. Slowly out of the mist and like a great god comes a chillingly calm FORTINBRAS. After a moment, he is joined by a second RIDER. He speaks with quiet authority, barely looking at his CAPTAIN, watching always.

> FORTINBRAS
> *Go, captain, from me greet the Danish King.*
> *Tell him that by his licence Fortinbras*
> *Craves the conveyance of a promised march*
> *Over his Kingdom. You know the rendezvous.*

The following carries an air of quiet menace.

> FORTINBRAS (continuing)
> *If that his majesty would aught with us,*
> *We shall express our duty in his eye,*
> *And let him know so.*

One look to the CAPTAIN which says, 'Don't even think of making a mistake.'

> CAPTAIN
> *I will do't, my lord.*

Then with surprising gentleness. Almost whispered.

> FORTINBRAS
> *Go softly on.*

FORTINBRAS exits Shot.

We cut back to the Wide Shot to see an awesome number of Soldiers appear through the mist. They seem to go on and on. The CAPTAIN rides across and out of Frame Right.

We pick him up entering Camara Left having cantered up to a hill, from which we can see, moving right to left this vast army. We have Close Shots of 'softly' marching feet, the set expressions, hands on weapons, the commanders on horses. From the hill it's like seeing a massive army of deadly ants, dotting and cutting through the mist with silent, ominous power.

Above the army on the plain, HAMLET, ROSENCRANTZ and GUILDENSTERN appear on a ridge. The CAPTAIN walks his horse up to them.

HAMLET stops him. Polite to strangers as ever.

> HAMLET
> *Good sir, whose powers are these?*

> CAPTAIN
> *They are of Norway, sir.*

> HAMLET
> *How purposed, sir, I pray you?*

> CAPTAIN
> *Against some part of Poland.*

HAMLET

Who commands them, sir?

CAPTAIN

The nephew of Old Norway, Fortinbras.

HAMLET

Goes it against the main of Poland, sir,
Or for some frontier?

Well, there's a question indeed, and this grizzled campaigner feels
he can offer his opinion on the issue to this noblemen so clearly
intrigued by the massive troop movement at a time of so-called peace.

CAPTAIN

Truly to speak, and with no addition,
We go to gain a little patch of ground
That hath in it no profit but the name.
To pay five ducats — five — I would not farm it;
Nor will it yield to Norway or the Pole
A ranker rate should it be sold in fee.

HAMLET is utterly astonished. It simply doesn't make sense.

HAMLET

Why, then the Polack never will defend it.

CAPTAIN

Yes, it is already garrison'd.

The news hits HAMLET like a hammer blow. It is madness.

HAMLET

Two thousand souls and twenty thousand ducats
Will not debate the question of this straw!
This is th' impostume of much wealth and peace,
That inward breaks, and shows no cause without
Why the man dies. I humbly thank you, sir.

The Captain gives him a last look before riding off.

CAPTAIN

God be with you, sir.

ROSENCRANTZ

         Will't please you go, my lord?

HAMLET (sharply)

I'll be with you straight. Go a little before.

The two friends move away. HAMLET stands looking out at the mass
of the travelling army and talks partly to Camera, partly for himself.
The tone is simple, grave. The Camera slowly moves away from him.

HAMLET (continuing)

How all occasions do inform against me,
And spur my dull revenge.

He asks the question directly to us.

HAMLET (continuing)

         What is a man
If his chief good and market of his time

Be but to sleep and feed? A beast, no more.
Sure he that made us with such large discourse,
Looking before and after, gave us not
That capability and godlike reason
To fust in us unused. Now whether it be
Bestial oblivion, or some craven scruple
Of thinking too precisely on th' event –
A thought which, quartered, hath but one part wisdom
And ever three parts coward – I do not know
Why yet I live to say this thing's to do,
Sith I have cause, and will, and strength, and means
To do't. Examples gross as earth exhort me,
Witness this army of such mass and charge,
Led by a delicate and tender prince,
Whose spirit, with divine ambition puffed,
Makes mouths at the invisible event,

HAMLET becomes smaller and smaller in frame as we continue to move away, the ARMY behind him still marching past.

HAMLET (continuing)
Exposing what is mortal and unsure
To all that fortune, death, and danger dare,
Even for an eggshell. Rightly to be great
Is not to stir without great argument,
But greatly to find quarrel in a straw
When honour's at the stake. How stand I then,
That have a father killed, a mother stained,
Excitements of my reason, and my blood,
And let all sleep, while to my shame I see
The immininent death of twenty thousand men
That, for a fantasy and trick of fame,
Go to their graves like beds, fight for a plot
Whereon the numbers cannot try the cause,
Which is not tomb enough and continent
To hide the Slain? O from this time forth

We are higher now. HAMLET raises his arms with a great cry –

HAMLET (continuing)
My thoughts be bloody or be nothing worth.

The huge scream of resolution hangs in the air as we pull further back and see the now tiny figure in the vast landscape, the music reaches its climax and we fade to black.

Intermission

PART TWO

Exterior / ELSINORE Day

A windswept Elsinore looks bleak in the winter light. A huge shadow
is cast across its face. As we hear the grim tones of the King, we see
the images of the tragedy to date.

CLAUDIUS V/O
When sorrows come they come not single spies,
But in battalions

Cut to:

Interior / GERTRUDE'S APARTMENTS Night

We relive POLONIUS's horrific stabbing.

CLAUDIUS V/O (continuing)
First, her father slain;

Cut to:

Interior / CLAUDIUS'S APARTMENTS Night

HAMLET dragged away to England.

CLAUDIUS V/O (continuing)
Next, your son gone, and he most violent author
Of his own just remove;

Cut to:

Interior / STATE HALL Day

A gaggle of gossiping courtiers share dramatic looks.

CLAUDIUS V/O (continuing)
the people muddied,
Thick and unwholesome in their thoughts and whispers
For good Polonius, death;

Cut to:

Interior / CHAPEL Night

The blood-stained body of the Prime Minister bundled away.

CLAUDIUS V/O (continuing)
and we have done but greenly
In hugger-mugger to inter him;
OPHELIA rushes once again to the Chapel gates where the great
yell of distress warns us of the horror to come.

CLAUDIUS V/O (continuing)
poor Ophelia
Divided from herself and her fair judgement,
Without the which we are pictures or mere beasts;

Cut to:

Interior / STATE HALL Day

We see the noble features of young LAERTES, fresh as he was at
the recent wedding.

CLAUDIUS V/O (continuing)
Last, and as much containing as all these,
Her brother is in secret come from France,

Feeds on this wonder, keeps himself in clouds,
And wants not buzzers to infect his ear
With pestilent speeches of his father's death;

Cut to:

Interior / CHAPEL Night

A distraught CLAUDIUS looks to his God for guidance, then paces
the room.

> CLAUDIUS V/O (continuing)
> *Wherein necessity, of matter beggared,*
> *Will nothing stick our persons to arraign*
> *In ear and ear. O my dear Gertrude,this,*
> *Like to a murd'ring-piece, in many places*
> *Gives me superfluous death.*

Cut to:

Interior / OPHELIA'S CELL Day

We look down from above into a padded cell. OPHELIA straitjacketed
runs around the room banging herself at the walls. We tilt up from
the trap door opening, to find three observers, GERTRUDE,
HORATIO and DOCTOR.

Cut to:

Interior / STATE HALL GALLERY Day

> GERTRUDE
> *I will not speak with her.*
> HORATIO (pleading)
> > *She is importunate,*
> *Indeed distract. Her mood will needs be pitied.*
> GERTRUDE
> *What would she have?*
> HORATIO (gently)
> *She speaks much of her father, says she hears*
> *There's tricks i' th' world, and hems, and beats her heart,*
> DOCTOR
> *Spurns enviously at straws, speaks things in doubt*
> *That carry but half sense.*
> HORATIO
> > *Her speech is nothing,*
> *Yet the unshapèd use of it doth move*
> *The hearers to collection.*
> DOCTOR
> > *They aim at it,*
> *And botch the words up fit to their own thoughts,*
> *Which, as her winks and nods and gestures yield them,*
> *Indeed would make one think there might be thought,*
> *Though nothing sure, yet much unhappily.*

GERTRUDE is shattered.

HORATIO
'Twere good she were spoken with, for she may strew
Dangerous conjectures in ill-breeding minds.
GERTRUDE
Let her come in.
HORATIO and the DOCTOR move off. We move in on GERTRUDE.
Close on her troubled face.
GERTRUDE (continuing)
To my sick soul, as sin's true nature is,
Each toy seems prologue to some great amiss.
So full of artless jealousy is guilt,
It spills itself in fearing to be spilt.

Cut to:

Interior / STATE HALL Day
The lower mirrored door to OPHELIA's 'cell' is opened and she now
lies on the floor. She pushes her squashed face along the floor, unable
to get up, still in the straitjacket.
OPHELIA
Where is the beauteous majesty of Denmark?
GERTRUDE walks over to her, kneels down and speaks gently.
GERTRUDE
How now, Ophelia?
OPHELIA turns over onto her back.
OPHELIA (she sings)
How should I your true love know
From another one? –
By his cockle hat and staff,
And his sandal shoon.
The QUEEN tries again.
GERTRUDE
Alas, sweet lady, what imports this song?
OPHELIA
Say you?
OPHELIA makes conscious reference to her predicament with the
jacket. GERTRUDE undoes the strap binding her.
OPHELIA (continuing)
Nay, pray you, mark.
(she sings)
He is dead and gone, lady,
He is dead and gone.
At his head a grass-green turf,
At his heels a stone.
GERTRUDE
Nay, but Ophelia –
The KING enters the Hall.

OPHELIA

Pray you, mark

(she sings)

White his shroud as the mountain snow —

GERTRUDE

Alas, look here, my lord.

The KING walks over to where this wriggling wreck now sits up.

OPHELIA

Larded with sweet flowers,
Which bewept to the grave did — not — go
With true-love showers.

Much moved, he helps her up a little.

CLAUDIUS

How do you, pretty lady?

OPHELIA (brightly now)

Well, God 'ield you. They say the owl was a baker's daughter.
Lord, we know what we are, but know not what we may be.
God be at your table!

CLAUDIUS (to Gertrude)

Conceit upon her father.

He tries to hold her but she wriggles free. Screaming she runs to the other end of the hall. She begins a demented dance. A grotesque ballet.

OPHELIA

Pray you, let's have no words of this, but when
They ask you what it means, say you this.

(she sings)

Tomorrow is Saint Valentine's day,
All in the morning betime,
And I a maid at your window
To be your Valentine.
Then up he rose, and donned his clothes,
And dupped the chamber door;
Let in the maid, that out a maid
Never departed more.

CLAUDIUS

Pretty Ophelia —

OPHELIA

Indeed, la? Without an oath, I'll make an end on't.

She quickly moves back to CLAUDIUS's side. And stands uncomfortably close to him.

OPHELIA (she sings)

By Gis, and by Saint Charity,
Alack, and fie for shame!
Young men will do't if they come to't,

OPHELIA thrusts lewdly at CLAUDIUS then flings herself to the floor.

OPHELIA (continuing)
By Cock, they are to blame.
Quoth she 'Before you tumbled me,
You promised me to wed.'

Cut to:

Interior / OPHELIA'S BEDROOM Day

Flashback to HAMLET and OPHELIA together.

OPHELIA (continuing)
So would I 'a' done, by yonder sun,
An thou hadst not come to my bed.

Cut to:

Interior / STATE HALL Day

OPHELIA crumbles into tears once more.

CLAUDIUS (to Gertrude)
How long hath she been thus?

She starts to get up. Quietly, sensibly. Sorted out.

OPHELIA
I hope all will be well. We must be patient. But I cannot choose
but weep to think they should lay him i' th' cold ground. My
brother shall know of it.

CLAUDIUS tries to restrain her. She breaks away from him and then
starts to run.

OPHELIA (continuing)
Come, my coach! Good night, ladies, good night, sweet ladies,
good night, good night.

She flies through the main doors. HORATIO and the DOCTOR
follow .

CLAUDIUS (to Horatio)
Follow her close. Give her good watch, I pray you.

The door closes. CLAUDIUS and GERTRUDE are alone.

CLAUDIUS (continuing)
O, this is the poison of deep grief! It springs
All from her father's death. And now behold –
O Gertrude, Gertrude.

Cut to:

Interior / PALACE CORRIDOR Day

Many bodies rushing past. Running along the corridors – weapons
in hands.

Cut to:

Interior / STATE HALL Day

A great shout goes up from somewhere in the Palace.

GERTRUDE
Alack, what noise is this?

From one of the hidden doors, a breathless ATTENDANT enters.

CLAUDIUS
Where are my Switzers? Let them guard the door.

(to the Messenger)
What is the matter?
ATTENDANT
                  Save yourself, my lord.
The ocean, overpeering of his list,
Eats not the flats with more impetuous haste
Than young Laertes, in a riotous head,

                                     Cut to:

Interior / CORRIDOR Day

A great tide of rebellion sweeps away everything in its violent wake -
Guards included.

ATTENDANT V/O (continuing)
O'erbears your officers.

Interior / STATE HALL Day

ATTENDANT (continuing)
                    The rabble call him lord,
And, as the world were now but to begin,
Antiquity forgot, custom not known,
The ratifiers and props of every word,
They cry 'Choose we! Laertes shall be King.'
Caps, hands, and tongues applaud it to the clouds,

Interior / PALACE Day

The rebels charge towards the doors, along the corridor.

ATTENDANT V/O (continuing)
'Laertes shall be king, Laertes king.'

                                       Cut to:

Interior / STATE HALL Day

CLAUDIUS and GERTRUDE move away from the doors.

GERTRUDE
How cheerfully on the false trail they cry!
O, this is counter, you false Danish dogs!
CLAUDIUS
The doors are broke.

And with that, they run for the thrones as more ATTENDANTS run
into the hall and we see the Mob smash their way in. From the depths
of the rabble emerges LAERTES.

LAERTES
Where is this King? – Sirs, stand you all without.
FOLLOWERS
No, let's come in.

No, this one is his. He takes command, firmly.

LAERTES
I pray you, give me leave.

FOLLOWERS
We will, we will.

They understand the personal nature of his grief. Reluctantly they go.

LAERTES
I thank you. Keep the door.

The doors close with an ominous crack and LAERTES runs towards
the KING, his sword raised.

LAERTES (continuing)

O thou vile King,

Give me my father.

GERTRUDE intercepts him, placing her body between LAERTES
and the KING.

GERTRUDE

Calmly, good Laertes.

LAERTES
That drop of blood that's calm proclaims me bastard,
Cries cuckold to my father, brands the harlot
Even here between the chaste unsmirchèd brow
of my true mother.

CLAUDIUS

What is the cause, Laertes,
That thy rebellion looks so giant-like? —

He opts for bravado. He will face him out.

CLAUDIUS (continuing)
Let him go, Gertrude. Do not fear our person.
There's such divinity doth hedge a King
That treason can but peep to what it would,
Acts little of his will. Tell me, Laertes,
Why thou art thus incensed.

Even firmer now.

CLAUDIUS (continuing)

Let him go, Gertrude. —

Speak, man.

He will not be tricked. He stays sane.

LAERTES

Where is my father?

CLAUDIUS

Dead.

The QUEEN intercepts quickly, moving to CLAUDIUS.

GERTRUDE
But not by him.

CLAUDIUS

Let him demand his fill.

The 'fearless' persona is working. He knows the shock of the final
knowledge has stopped the young man in his tracks.

LAERTES (struggling)
How came he dead? I'll not be juggled with.
To hell, allegiance! Vows to the blackest devil!
Conscience and grace to the profoundest pit!

He reaches for a dangerous courage.

LAERTES (continuing)
I dare damnation. To this point I stand,
That both the worlds I give to negligence,
Let come what comes. Only I'll be revenged
Most throughly for my father.

CLAUDIUS
                                        Who shall stay you?

LAERTES (venomously)
My will, not all the world;
And for my means, I'll husband them so well
They shall go far with little.

CLAUDIUS
                                        Good Laertes,
If you desire to know the certainty
Of your dear father's death, is't writ in your revenge
That, sweepstake, you will draw both friend and foe,
Winner and loser?

The KING is manipulating this unbalanced young man already. He
can see the confusion of feeling in this grief-struck lad.

LAERTES
None but his enemies.

He remains tough with him.

CLAUDIUS
                                        Will you know them then?

LAERTES
To his good friends thus wide I'll ope my arms,
And, like the kind life-rend'ring pelican,
Repast them with my blood.

CLAUDIUS
                                        Why, now you speak
Like a good child and a true gentleman.

He slowly pushes the sword away from his throat.

CLAUDIUS (continuing)
That I am guiltless of your father's death,
And am most sensibly in grief for it,
It shall as level to your judgement pierce
As day does to your eye.

                                                        Cut to:

Interior / ANTE-ROOM Day

OPHELIA in full flight from her DOCTOR careers down the passage
towards us, turns and flings open the door into the main hall.

HORATIO

Let her come in.

Interior / STATE HALL Day

OPHELIA bursts into the hall and LAERTES turns.

LAERTES

How now, what noise is that?

She almost floats by him, heading for one of the mirrored doors as
we linger on the aggrieved face of her brother.

LAERTES (continuing)

O heat dry up my brains! Tears seven times salt
Burn out the sense and virtue of mine eye!

He kneels down beside her.

LAERTES (continuing)

By heaven, thy madness shall be paid by weight
Till our scale turns the beam. O rose of May,
Dear maid, kind sister, sweet Ophelia!

He touches her face but she continues to make an imaginary wreath.

LAERTES (continuing)

O heavens, is't possible a young maid's wits
Should be as mortal as an old man's life?
Nature is fine in love, and where 'tis fine
It sends some precious instance of itself
After the thing it loves.

OPHELIA (sings)

They bore him barefaced on the bier,
Hey non nony, nony, hey nony,
And on his grave rained many a tear –
Fare you well, my dove.

LAERTES (whispers)

Hadst thou thy wits and didst persuade revenge,
It could not move thus.

OPHELIA

You must sing 'Down, a-down', and you, 'call him a-down-a'.
O, how the wheel becomes it! It is the false steward that stole his
master's daughter.

The young man looks to the others for the truth of this.

LAERTES

This nothing's more than matter.

She pretends to pass out flowers.

OPHELIA

There's rosemary, that's for remembrance. Pray, love, remember.
And there is pansies; that's for thoughts.

LAERTES

A document in madness – thoughts and remembrance fitted.

OPHELIA

There's fennel for you, and columbines. There's rue for you, and here's some for me. We may call it herb o' grace o' Sundays. O, you must wear your rue with a difference. There's a daisy. I would give you some violets, but they withered all when my father died. They say he made a good end.

She starts to sing.

OPHELIA

For bonny sweet Robin is all my joy.

LAERTES

Thought and affliction, passion, hell itself She turns to favour and to prettiness.

She turns away to leans back against the mirror, for all the world like a five-year-old. She sings with utter simplicity.

OPHELIA (sings)

And will a not come again,
And will a not come again?
No, no, he is dead,
Go to thy death-bed,
He never will come again.
His beard as white as snow,
All flaxen was his poll.
He is gone, he is gone,
And we cast away moan.
God 'a' mercy on his soul.
And of all Christian souls, I pray God. God by you.

She stands up and walks into her cell.

LAERTES follows her and looks in.

LAERTES

Do you see this, O God?

The KING arrives as LAERTES is on the point of madness himself.

CLAUDIUS

Laertes, I must commune with your grief,
Or you deny me right. Go but apart,
Make choice of whom your wisest friends you will,
And they shall hear and judge 'twixt you and me.
If by direct or by collateral hand
They find us touched, we will our kingdom give,
Our crown, our life, and all that we call ours,
To you in satisfaction. But if not,
Be you content to lend your patience to us,
And we shall jointly labour with your soul
To give it due content.

The trauma barely lets him speak.

LAERTES

Let this be so.
His means of death, his obscure burial –
No trophy, sword, nor hatchment o'er his bones,
No noble rite nor formal ostentation –
Cry to be heard, as 'twere from heaven to earth,
That I must call't in question.

For a moment he is almost as childlike as his sister.

CLAUDIUS

So you shall;
And where th' offence is, let the great axe fall.
I pray you go with me.

He leads him off. Two GUARDS enter the cell and take OPHELIA away.

We dissolve to:

Exterior / PALACE Day

A vicious snowstorm engulfs the battered Palace.

Dissolve to:

Interior / CORRIDOR–WASH DOWN CELL Day

HORATIO and ATTENDANT on their way to OPHELIA's latest accommodation. HORATIO's interested in OPHELIA but distracted by this news.

HORATIO

What are they that would speak with me?

ATTENDANT

Sailors, sir. They say they have letters for you.

HORATIO opens a spy hole and we see her, being doused down with a hose. He decides reluctantly to leave her for the time being. We Cut to inside the cell where OPHELIA cowers in the corner. The hose-down stops and the GUARD leaves. She holds the haunted look towards the door and then slowly, from under her tongue OPHELIA produces a small key.

Cut to:

Exterior / PALACE COLONNADE Evening

HORATIO and Two ATTENDANTS in the colonnade, fight the vicious wind and whirling snow.

HORATIO

I do not know from what part of the world
I should be greeted if not from Lord Hamlet.

He reaches the SAILORS.

SAILOR

God bless you, sir.

HORATIO

Let him bless thee too.

SAILOR

He shall, sir, an't please him. There's a letter for you, sir. It comes

from th' ambassador that was bound for England — if your name
be Horatio, as I am let to know it is.

He takes the letter and starts to read.

HORATIO (reads)
'Horatio, when thou shalt have overlooked this, give these fellows
some means to the King. they have letters for him.

He moves away from the SAILORS a little to continue. This is
intriguing.

HORATIO (continuing)
'Ere we were two days old at sea, a pirate of very warlike
appointment gave us chase. Finding ourselves too slow of sail,
we put on a compelled valour, and in the grapple I boarded them.
On the instant they got clear of our ship, so I alone became their
prisoner. They have dealt with me like thieves of mercy; but they
knew what they did: I am to do a good turn for them. Let the
King have the letters I have sent, and repair thou to me with as
much haste as thou wouldst fly death. I have words to speak in
thine ear will make thee dumb, yet are they much too light for
the bore of the matter. These good fellows will bring thee where
I am. Rosencrantz and Guildenstern hold their course for England.
Of them I have much to tell thee. Farewell, He that thou knowest
thine, Hamlet.'

He turns back to the SAILORS.

HORATIO
Come, I will give you way for these your letters,
And do't the speedier that you may direct me
To him from whom you brought them.

He leads them towards the Palace.

We dissolve:

Interior / KING'S APARTMENTS Night

The KING pours LAERTES yet another drink. The KING is beginning
to disintegrate, but he is a survivor and, in battle against HAMLET,
LAERTES may be his greatest weapon.

CLAUDIUS
Now must your conscience my acquittance seal,
And you must put me in your heart for friend,
Since you have heard, and with a knowing ear,
That he which hath your noble father slain
Pursued my life.

LAERTES (still cautious)
                        It well appears. But tell me
Why you proceeded not against these feats,
So crimeful and so capital in nature,
As by your safety, wisdom, all things else,
You mainly were stirred up.

CLAUDIUS

                       O, for two special reasons

He strikes the intimate friendly tone now.

CLAUDIUS (continuing)
Which may to you perhaps seem much unsinewed,
And yet to me they're strong. The Queen his mother
Lives almost by his looks; and for myself –
My virtue or my plague, be it either which –

And for a moment he is also vulnerable. Everyone in this Palace
knows about the awful power of love.

CLAUDIUS (continuing)
She's so conjunctive to my life and soul
That, as the star moves not but in his sphere,
I could not but by her.

Then the return of the ultra-realistic politician.

CLAUDIUS (continuing)
                       The other motive
Why to a public count I might not go
Is the great love the general gender bear him,
Who, dipping all his faults in their affection,
Would, like the spring that turneth wood to stone,
Convert his gyves to graces;

Bitter now.

CLAUDIUS (continuing)
                       so that my arrows,
Too slightly timbered for so loud a wind,
Would have reverted to my bow again,
And not where I had aimed them.

None of this changes anything. The terrible facts remain.

LAERTES
And so have I a noble father lost,
A sister driven into desp'rate terms,
Whose worth, if praises may go back again,
Stood challenger, on mount, of all the age
For her perfections. But my revenge will come.

CLAUDIUS
Break not your sleeps for that.

A comforting tap on the shoulder. The KING prowling around
LAERTES's chair, ready to check any new outburst.

CLAUDIUS (continuing)
                       You must not think
That we are made of stuff so flat and dull
That we can let our beard be shook with danger,
And think it pastime. You shortly shall hear more.

CLAUDIUS kneels to be level with LAERTES.

CLAUDIUS (continuing)
I loved your father, and we love ourself.
And that, I hope, will teach you to imagine –

The door opens, an ATTENDANT comes in.

CLAUDIUS (continuing)
How now? What news?

ATTENDANT
                              Letters, my lord, from Hamlet;

The two men exchange glances.

ATTENDANT (continuing)
This to your majesty; this to the Queen.

CLAUDIUS (highly suspicious)
From Hamlet? Who brought them?

ATTENDANT
Sailors, my lord, they say. I saw them not.
They were given me by Claudio. He received them
Of him that brought them.

A moment's hesitation, then.

CLAUDIUS
Laertes, you shall hear them.
(to the attendant)
                              Leave us.

The MESSENGER leaves and closes the door.

CLAUDIUS (reads)
'High and mighty, you shall know I am set naked on your kingdom.
Tomorrow shall I beg leave to see your kingly eyes, when I shall,
first asking your pardon, thereunto recount th' occasions of my
sudden and more strange return.
                              Hamlet.'
What should this mean? Are all the rest come back?
Or is it some abuse, and no such thing?

LAERTES
Know you the hand?

CLAUDIUS
                    'Tis Hamlet's character.
'Naked' – and in a postscript here he says
'Alone'. Can you advise me?

LAERTES
I'm lost in it, my lord. But let him come.
It warms the very sickness in my heart
That I shall live and tell him to his teeth,
'Thus diest thou'.

CLAUDIUS
                    If it be so, Laertes –
As how should it be so, how otherwise? –
Will you be ruled by me?

LAERTES
Ay, my lord, if so you will not o'errule me to a peace.
CLAUDIUS
To thine own peace. If he be now returned,
As checking at his voyage, and that he means
No more to undertake it, I will work him
To an exploit, now ripe in my device,
Under the which he shall not choose but fall;
And for his death no wind of blame shall breathe;
But even his mother shall uncharge the practice
And call it accident.
LAERTES
     My lord, I will be ruled;
The rather if you could devise it so
That I might be the organ.
CLAUDIUS
       It falls right.
You have been talked of since your travels much —
And that in Hamlet's hearing — for a quality
Wherein they say you shine. Your sum of parts
Did not together pluck such envy from him
As did that one; and that, in my regard,
Of the unworthiest siege.
LAERTES
      What part is that, my lord?
CLAUDIUS
A very ribbon in the cap of youth,
Yet needful too; for youth no less becomes
The light and careless livery that it wears
Than settled age his sables and his weeds,
Importing health and graveness. Some two months since
Here was a gentleman of Normandy.
I've seen myself, and served against, the French,
And they can well on horseback; but this gallant
Had witchcraft in't. He grew into his seat,
And to such wondrous doing brought his horse
As had he been incorpsed and demi-natured
With the brave beast. So far he topped my thought
That I in forgery of shapes and tricks
Come short of what he did.
LAERTES
      A Norman was't?
CLAUDIUS
A Norman.
LAERTES
Upon my life, Lamord.

CLAUDIUS

The very same.

LAERTES

I know him well. He is the brooch indeed
And gem, of all the nation.

CLAUDIUS

He made confession of you,
And gave you such a masterly report
For art and exercise in your defence,
And for your rapier most especial,
That he cried out 'twould be a sight indeed
If one could match you. The scrimers of their nation
He swore had neither motion, guard, nor eye,
If you opposed them, sir. This report of his
Did Hamlet so envenom with his envy
That he could nothing do but wish and beg
Your sudden coming o'er to play with him.
Now, out of this –

LAERTES

What out of this, my lord?

The drink has made the young man slower than usual.

CLAUDIUS

Laertes, was your father dear to you?
Or are you like the painting of a sorrow,
A face without a heart?

LAERTES

Why ask you this?

CLAUDIUS

Not that I think you did not love your father,
But that I know love is begun by time,
And that I see, in passages of proof,
Time qualifies the spark and fire of it.
There lives within the very flame of love
A kind of wick or snuff that will abate it;
And nothing is at a like goodness still;
For goodness, growing to a pleurisy,
Dies in his own too-much. That we would do,
We should do when we would; for this 'would' changes,
And hath abatements and delays as many
As there are tongues, are hands, are accidents,
And then this 'should' is like a spendthrift sigh
That hurts by easing. But to the quick of th' ulcer.
Hamlet comes back. What would you undertake
To show yourself in deed your father's son
More than in words?

LAERTES

                    To cut his throat i' th' church.

Even CLAUDIUS pauses at the vehemence of this.

CLAUDIUS

No place indeed should murder sanctuarize.
Revenge should have no bounds. But, good Laertes,
Will you do this? – Keep close within your chamber.
Hamlet returned shall know you are come home.
We'll put on those shall praise your excellence,
And set a double varnish on the fame
The Frenchman gave you; bring you, in fine, together,
And wager on your heads. He, being remiss,
Most generous, and free from all contriving,
Will not peruse the foils; so that with ease,
Or with a little shuffling, you may choose
A sword unbated, and, in a pass of practice,
Requite him for your father.

LAERTES

                    I will do't.

And for that purpose I'll anoint my sword.

He is possessed by the following images.

LAERTES (continuing)

I bought an unction of a mountebank
So mortal that, but dip a knife in it,
Where it draws blood no cataplasm so rare,
Collected from all simples that have virtue
Under the moon, can save the thing from death
That is but scratched withal. I'll touch my point
With this contagion, that if I gall him slightly,
It may be death.

CLAUDIUS

                Let's further think of this;
Weigh what convenience both of time and means
May fit us to our shape. If this should fail,

He's still not convinced he can rely on the volatility of LAERTES's temper.

CLAUDIUS (continuing)

And that our drift look through our bad performance,
'Twere better not essayed. Therefore this project
Should have a back or second that might hold
If this should blast in proof. Soft, let me see.
We'll make a solemn wager on your cunnings …

He thinks for a moment.

CLAUDIUS (continuing)

I ha't! When in your motion you are hot and dry –
As make your bouts more violent to that end –

And that he calls for drink, I'll have prepared him
A chalice for the nonce, whereon but sipping,
If he by chance escape your venomed stuck,
Our purpose may hold there. But stay, what noise?

The QUEEN enters and walks slowly towards LAERTES who stands.

CLAUDIUS (continuing)

                    How now, sweet Queen?

GERTRUDE (quiet, even)
One woe doth tread upon another's heel,
So fast they follow. Your sister's drowned, Laertes.

He can hardly take it in, and yet what more might he expect?

LAERTES
Drowned? O, where?

The Camera moves in to the QUEEN as she tells her tale.

GERTRUDE
There is a willow grows askant the brook
That shows his hoary leaves in the glassy stream.
Therewith fantastic garlands did she make
Of crow-flowers, nettles, daisies, and long purples,
That liberal shepherds give a grosser name,
But our cold maids do dead men's fingers call them.
There on the pendent boughs her crownet weeds
Clamb'ring to hang, an envious sliver broke,
When down the weedy trophies and herself
Fell in the weeping brook.
Her clothes spread wide,
And mermaid-like a while they bore her up;
Which time she chanted snatches of old tunes,
As one incapable of her own distress,
Or like a creature native and endued
Unto that element. But long it could not be
Till that her garments, heavy with their drink,
Pulled the poor wretch from her melodious lay
To muddy death.

He can barely speak.

LAERTES

               Alas, then is she drowned.

GERTRUDE
Drowned, drowned.

LAERTES
Too much of water hast thou, poor Ophelia,
And therefore I forbid my tears.

He cannot stop the downfall.

LAERTES (continuing)

                  But yet
It is our trick; nature her custom holds,

Let shame say what it will. When these are gone,
The woman will be out.

He gathers whatever vestige of pride and sanity he can as CLAUDIUS joins him.

LAERTES (continuing)

Adieu, my lord.
I have a speech of fire that fain would blaze,
But that this folly douts it.

GERTRUDE watches as the young man leaves the room. CLAUDIUS has other things on his mind.

CLAUDIUS

Let's follow, Gertrude.
How much I had to do to calm his rage!
Now fear I this will give it start again;
Therefore let's follow.

She stares after him in disbelief. She will not follow. Never again.

Dissolve to:

Exterior / WILLOW WEIR Day

Close on the drowned OPHELIA as she lies under the surface of the water. A beautiful, ghostly corpse.

Dissolve to:

Exterior / ELSINORE Day

OPHELIA's watery home in foreground and back, away from the lake, the shimmery evening presence of Elsinore.

Dissolve to:

Exterior / GRAVEYARD Night

We track through a graveyard of sorts. But not a royal one. The atmosphere is secret, eerie. The silhouette of two men half in, half out of the ground. It's tough, wet work. Although the rain has stopped it's still not very pleasant. The men are not used to working at this late hour, even at Royal Command.

The FIRST GRAVEDIGGER, a gold medallist at the irony Olympics, and pedant to boot, is engaged in a bizarre ritual of making sure that he will not get his bottom wet, that there will be space for his midnight lunch box and crucially, that he will do less work than his sidekick. Still, for all this the man, who could be any age from forty upwards is rather a jolly old sod. He throws up the first rhetorical ball. Reads from the newspaper. He's going to find a way of enjoying this shitty night's work. He speaks with great precision and clarity. Very dry. He puts his paper down.

FIRST GRAVEDIGGER

Is she to be buried in Christian burial that wilfully seeks her
own salvation?

His friend just wants to get on with the bloody thing and get home. He's already hard at work, whilst the Maestro sits and smokes.

SECOND GRAVEDIGGER
*I tell thee she is, therefore make her grave straight. The coroner
hath sat on her, and finds it Christian burial.*

So shut up.

FIRST GRAVEDIGGER
How can that be unless she drowned herself in her own defence?

Says Judge Ito.

SECOND GRAVEDIGGER
                    Why, 'tis found so.

Read the papers, would you?

FIRST GRAVEDIGGER
*It must be se offendendo, it cannot be else. For here lies the point:
if I drown myself wittingly, it argues an act; and an act hath three
branches: it is to act, to do, and to perform. Argal, she drowned
herself wittingly.*

The SECOND GRAVEDIGGER **not** in the mood for this.

SECOND GRAVEDIGGER
Nay, but hear you, Goodman Delver.

FIRST GRAVEDIGGER (firm)
Give me leave. Here lies the water – good.

He does a series of what he thinks are quite blindingly good mimes
with his hands. These consist mainly of waving them a bit.

FIRST GRAVEDIGGER (continuing)
*Here stands the man – good. If the man go to this water and drown
himself, it is, will he nill he, he goes. Mark you that. But if the
water come to him and drown him, he drowns not himself. Argal,
he that is not guilty of his own death shortens not his own life.*

All right, clever-ish clogs.

SECOND GRAVEDIGGER
But is this law?

Shut your ignorant mouth. Their friendship is based on a kind of
good-hearted contempt.

FIRST GRAVEDIGGER
Ay, marry, is't: coroner's quest law.

SECOND GRAVEDIGGER weighs in with the *National Enquirer* view.

SECOND GRAVEDIGGER
*Will you ha' the truth on't? If this had not been a gentlewoman,
she should have been buried out o' Christian burial.*

Nudge, nudge.

FIRST GRAVEDIGGER
Why, there thou sayst,

Abso-bloody-lutely.

FIRST GRAVEDIGGER (continuing)
                    *and the more pity that great folk should have
count'nance in this world to drown or hang themselves more than
their even Christian.*

I hate the bloody Royals.

FIRST GRAVEDIGGER (continuing)
Come, my spade.

He stands up. A little pride at work now.

FIRST GRAVEDIGGER (continuing)
              There is no ancient gentlemen but gardeners,
ditchers, and gravemakers; they hold up Adam's profession.

SECOND GRAVEDIGGER rather intrigued by this last remark.

SECOND GRAVEDIGGER
                           Was he a gentleman?

FIRST GRAVEDIGGER
He was the first that ever bore arms.

SECOND GRAVEDIGGER
                            Why, he had none.

I.e. coat of arms, get it?

FIRST GRAVEDIGGER
What, art a heathen? How dost thou understand the Scripture?
The Scripture says Adam digged. Could he dig without arms?

Ho, ho. Yes, I know, they get worse. He sits down

FIRST GRAVEDIGGER (continuing)
I'll put another question to thee. If thou answerest me not to
the purpose, confess thyself –

SECOND GRAVEDIGGER
Go to.

You're gonna like this one. Not a lot. But you'll like it.

FIRST GRAVEDIGGER
What is he that builds stronger than either the mason, the
shipwright, or the carpenter?

Very pleased with himself.

SECOND GRAVEDIGGER
The gallows-maker; for that frame outlives a thousand tenants.

FIRST GRAVEDIGGER
I like thy wit well, in good faith.

Yes, I like your wit about as much as I like eating turds.

FIRST GRAVEDIGGER (continuing)
The gallows does well. But how does it well? It does well to those
that do ill. Now thou dost ill to say the gallows is built stronger than
the church; argal, the gallows may do well to thee. To't again, come.

Please.

SECOND GRAVEDIGGER
'Who builds stronger than a mason, a shipwright, or a carpenter?'

FIRST GRAVEDIGGER
Ay, tell me that, and unyoke.

SECOND GRAVEDIGGER
Marry, now I can tell.

Get on with it then, Einstein. I haven't asked you to move

Denmark a bit to the right, have I?

> FIRST GRAVEDIGGER
> *To't.*

Another long pause.

> SECOND GRAVEDIGGER
> *Mass, I cannot tell.*

FIRST GRAVEDIGGER withers him to within an inch of his life.
Then pities him.

> FIRST GRAVEDIGGER
> *Cudgel thy brains no more about it, for your dull ass will not mend*
> *his pace with beating; and when you are asked this question next,*
> *say 'a grave-maker'. The houses that he makes lasts till doomsday.*

Ho-bleeding-ho, yes I know it's not a belter but look what I'm
working with. Go on, push off.

> FIRST GRAVEDIGGER (continuing)
> *Go, get thee to Johan. Fetch me a stoup of liquor.*

SECOND GRAVEDIGGER goes with a grin that rather suggests
he enjoys this treatment from his superior. As he leaves, the
FIRST GRAVEDIGGER climbs down into the grave, ready
finally to start work.

Wide Shot of FIRST GRAVEDIGGER on his own, singing as he
works. Into the foreground come a rougher looking HAMLET,
casually clothed, and HORATIO.

> FIRST GRAVEDIGGER (sings)
> *In youth when I did love, did love,*
> *Methought it was very sweet*
> *To contract-O-the time for-a-my behove,*
> *O methought there-a-was nothing-a-meet.*

They remain far off.

> HAMLET (taken aback)
> *Has this fellow no feeling of his business that he sings at*
> *grave-making?*

> HORATIO (shrugs)
> *Custom hath made it in him a property of easiness.*

> HAMLET (agrees)
> *'Tis e'en so; the hand of little employment hath the daintier sense.*

They walk a little closer to him.

> FIRST GRAVEDIGGER (sings)
> *But age with his stealing steps*
> *Hath caught me in his clutch,*
> *And hath shipped me intil the land,*
> *As if I had never been such.*

We watch in close detail the filthy skulls and the treatment they
receive at the hands of the Jack Benny of Denmark.

> HAMLET
> *That skull had a tongue in it and could sing once. How the knave*

jowls it to th' ground as if 'twere Cain's jawbone, that did the first
murder! This might be the pate of a politician which this ass now
o'er reaches, one that would circumvent God, might it not?

HORATIO

It might, my lord.

HAMLET getting rather carried away with the notion of maggot-
strewn lords.

HAMLET

Or of a courtier, which could say 'Good morrow, sweet lord.
How dost thou, sweet lord?' this might be my Lord Such-a-one,
that praised my Lord Such-a- one's horse when he meant to beg it,
might it not?

HORATIO

Ay, my lord.

This is making terrific sense to the new unromantic HAMLET.
The Killer. The man who must die.

HAMLET

Why, even so, and now my Lady Worm's, chapless, and knocked
about the mazard with a sexton's spade. Here's fine revolution,
an we had the trick to see't. Did these bones cost no more the
breeding but to play at loggats with 'em?

And then the thought overpowers him.

HAMLET (continuing)
Mine ache to think on't.

FIRST GRAVEDIGGER (sings)
A pickaxe and a spade, a spade,
For and a shrouding-sheet;
O, a pit of clay for to be made
For such a guest is meet.

HAMLET

There's another.

If there were any more of these bloody things he could set up a
skull shop.

HAMLET (continuing)
Why might not that be the skull of a lawyer?
Where be his quiddits now, his quillets, his cases, his tenures, and
his tricks? Why does he suffer this rude knave now to knock him
about the sconce with a dirty shovel, and will not tell him of his
action of battery? H'm! This fellow might be in's time a great buyer
of land, with his statutes, his recognizances, his fines, his double
vouchers, his recoveries. Is this the fine of his fines and the recovery
of his recoveries, to have his fine pate full of fine dirt? Will his
vouchers vouch him no more of his purchases, and double ones too,
than the length and breadth of a pair of indentures? The very
conveyances of his lands will scarcely lie in this box; and must th'
inheritor himself have no more, ha?

HORATIO
Not a jot more, my lord.

HAMLET
Is not parchment made of sheepskins?

HORATIO
Ay, my lord, and of calf-skins too.

HAMLET (remote)
*They are sheep and calves which seek out
assurance in that. I will speak to this fellow.*

They move off towards the GRAVEDIGGER. The GRAVEDIGGER
moves over to his skulls and starts to pack the bones into a bag as
HAMLET kneels down by the grave.

HAMLET
Whose grave's this, sirrah?

FIRST GRAVEDIGGER
Mine, sir.

(sings)
*O, a pit of clay for to be made
For such a guest is meet.*

A wry smile from HAMLET at that very, very funny remark.

HAMLET
I think it be thine indeed, for thou liest in't.

FIRST GRAVEDIGGER
*You lie out on't, sir, and therefore it is not yours. For
my part, I do not lie in't, and yet it is mine.*

All right, Mr Smarty, I can twist words with the best of them.

HAMLET
*Thou dost lie in't, to be in't and say 'tis thine. 'Tis
for the dead, not for the quick; therefore thou liest.*

FIRST GRAVEDIGGER
'Tis a quick lie, sir, 'twill away again from me to you.

FIRST GRAVEDIGGER, is enjoying this. He has found a much
better sparring partner than his usual stooge.

HAMLET
What man dost thou dig it for?

FIRST GRAVEDIGGER
For no man, sir.

HAMLET
What woman, then?

FIRST GRAVEDIGGER
For none, neither.

HAMLET
Who is to be buried in't?

FIRST GRAVEDIGGER
One that was a woman, sir; but, rest her soul, she's dead.

Christ, it's not possible to get a straight answer out of anyone in this country these days!

HAMLET
How absolute the knave is! We must speak by
the card, or equivocation will undo us. By the Lord, Horatio,
these three years I have taken note of it. The age is grown so
picked that the toe of the peasant comes so near the heel of the
courtier he galls his kibe.

HAMLET's very tone of voice, changes the mood. No larks for
a moment.

HAMLET (to First Gravedigger)
How long hast thou been a grave-maker?

FIRST GRAVEDIGGER
Of all the days i' th' year I came to't that day that our
last King, Hamlet, o'ercame Fortinbras.

HAMLET wants to be told. Reminded.

HAMLET
How long is that since?

FIRST GRAVEDIGGER
Cannot you tell that? Every fool can tell that. It was
the very day that young Hamlet was born — he that was
mad and sent into England.

A quick look to HORATIO. Has THE FIRST GRAVEDIGGER spotted
this new seafaring HAMLET?

HAMLET (cautious)
Ay, marry, why was he sent into England?

FIRST GRAVEDIGGER
Why, because he was mad. He shall recover his wits there;
or if he do not, 'tis no great matter there.

HAMLET
Why?

FIRST GRAVEDIGGER
'Twill not be seen in him there. There the men are as mad as he.

Actually, that's fair enough. HORATIO and HAMLET nod a smug
Danish agreement.

HAMLET
How came he mad?

Ooo. Into the very juicy gossip now. FIRST GRAVEDIGGER stops
what he's doing.

FIRST GRAVEDIGGER (quietly)
Very strangely, they say.

HAMLET joins him in this tone.

HAMLET
How strangely?

FIRST GRAVEDIGGER
Faith, e'en with losing his wits.

He should have seen that one coming. Still he'll press on.

> HAMLET
> *Upon what ground?*
> FIRST GRAVEDIGGER
> *Why, here in Denmark.*

A shared groan between them all. Still, quite jolly bantering fun, given that it's the middle of a cold wet night and the FIRST GRAVEDIGGER has every reason to be wary of two strangers interrupting his illicit work. But no, they like each other. After a beat,

> FIRST GRAVEDIGGER (continuing)
> *I have been sexton here, man and boy, thirty years.*

HAMLET, who has become more obsessed with the skulls now that he's closer, asks with keen interest.

> HAMLET
> *How long will a man lie i' th' earth ere he rot?*
> FIRST GRAVEDIGGER
> *I' faith, if he be not rotten before he die — as we have many pocky corpses nowadays, that will scarce hold the laying in — he will last you some eight year or nine year. A tanner will last you nine year.*

Seems weird.

> HAMLET
> *Why he more than another?*
> FIRST GRAVEDIGGER
> *Why, sir, his hide is so tanned with his trade that he will keep out water a great while, and your water is a sore decayer of your whoreson dead body.*

He fetches out yet another ex-person's head.

> FIRST GRAVEDIGGER (continuing)
> *Here's a skull, now. This skull has lain in the earth three-and-twenty years.*

HAMLET slightly dubious about how the FIRST GRAVEDIGGER recognizes someone in this condition, but intrigued just the same.

> HAMLET
> *Whose was it?*

FIRST GRAVEDIGGER is clearly amused by the remembrance of this one.

> FIRST GRAVEDIGGER
> *A whoreson mad fellow's it was. Whose do you think it was?*
> HAMLET
> *Nay, I know not.*
> FIRST GRAVEDIGGER
> *A pestilence on him for a mad rogue — he poured a flagon of Rhenish on my head once! This same skull, sir, was Yorick's skull, the King's jester.*

The name strikes HAMLET's ears like a blow.

HAMLET
This?

FIRST GRAVEDIGGER
E'en that.

HAMLET
Let me see.

He takes the skull and holds it very delicately, awe-struck. FIRST
GRAVEDIGGER is fascinated.

HAMLET (continuing)
*Alas, poor Yorick. I knew him, Horatio — a fellow of infinite
jest, of most excellent fancy. He hath borne me on his back a
thousand times; and now, how abhorred in my imagination it is!*

Cut to:

Interior / PALACE Day (Flashback)

We see the mobile face of this classic clown. The instant appeal of
a comic's vulnerability. YOUNG HAMLET appears behind YORICK
to grab him around the neck and YORICK pulls him onto his
knee, laughing.

HAMLET V/O (continuing)
*My gorge rises at it. Here hung those lips that I have kissed I
know not how oft.*

Cut to:

Exterior / GRAVEYARD Night

As before.

HAMLET
Where be your gibes now, your gambols,

Flashback again to see YORICK, in full swing, as OLD HAMLET,
GERTRUDE, CLAUDIUS and YOUNG HAMLET roar with laughter
at one of his jokes.

HAMLET (continuing)
*your songs, your flashes of merriment that were wont to set
the table on a roar? Not one now to mock your own grinning?
Quite chop-fallen? Now get you to my lady's chamber
tell her, let her paint an inch thick, to this favour she must come.
Make her laugh at that. Prithee, Horatio, tell me one thing.*

HORATIO
What's that, my lord?

HAMLET
Dost thou think Alexander looked o' this fashion i' th' earth?

HORATIO
E'en so.

HAMLET
And smelt so? Pah!

He throws the skull down and FIRST GRAVEDIGGER gets back on
with his work.

HORATIO
E'en so, my lord.

HAMLET
*To what base uses we may return, Horatio! Why may not
imagination trace the noble dust of Alexander till a find it stopping a
bung-hole?*

HORATIO
'Twere to consider too curiously to consider so.

HAMLET
*No, faith, not a jot; but to follow him thither with modesty
enough, and likelihood to lead it, as thus: Alexander died,
Alexander was buried. Alexander returneth into dust, the dust
is earth, of earth we make loam, and why of that loam whereto
he was converted, might they not stop a beer-barrel?*

He is now quietly taken by this idea of the cycle of greatness
and nothingness.

HAMLET (continuing)
*Imperious Caesar, dead and turned to clay,
Might stop a hole to keep the wind away.
O, that that earth which kept the world in awe
Should patch a wall t' expel the winter's flaw!
But soft,*

HAMLET throws the skull to the FIRST GRAVEDIGGER, then he
and HORATIO run off to hide behind a tree.

  SECOND GRAVEDIGGER rushes back to tell FIRST GRAVEDIGGER
to get a move on. They scurry out of the way, getting the grave ready
for the funeral.

HAMLET (continuing)
          *but soft, aside. Here comes the King,
The Queen, the Courtiers – who is that they follow,
And with such maimèd rites?*

LAERTES leads FOUR BEARERS who carry the coffin ahead of a
PRIEST, the KING and the QUEEN.

  HAMLET shocked at the hugger-mugger nature of this.

HAMLET (continuing)
                    *This doth betoken
The corpse they follow did with desp'rate hand
Fordo its own life. 'Twas of some estate.
Couch we awhile, and mark.*

The Coffin is laid on the planks and the PALLBEARERS move back.
CLAUDIUS takes off his hat, and LAERTES and the GRAVEDIGGERS
follow suit. The PRIEST closes his Bible. LAERTES snaps.

LAERTES
                    What ceremony else?

HAMLET (aside to Horatio)
That is Laertes, a very noble youth. Mark.

LAERTES
What ceremony else?

The PRIEST tries to make this conversation private and quick.

PRIEST
Her obsequies have been as far enlarged
As we have warrantise. Her death was doubtful,
And but that great command o'ersways the order
She should in ground unsanctified have lodged
Till the last trumpet. For charitable prayers,
Shards, flints, and pebbles should be thrown on her.
Yet here she is allowed her virgin rites,
Her maiden strewments, and the bringing home
Of bell and burial.

It still isn't good enough.

LAERTES
Must there no more be done?

PRIEST (harsh)
                              No more be done.
We should profane the service of the dead
To sing sage requiem and such rest to her
As to peace-parted souls.

LAERTES
                              Lay her i' th' earth,

The PALLBEARERS move in and lift the tapes. The GRAVEDIGGERS
move in and pull out the planks and the Coffin is lowered into
the ground.

LAERTES
And from her fair and unpolluted flesh
May violets spring.

LAERTES suddenly grabs the Bible from the PRIEST.

LAERTES
                              I tell thee, churlish priest,
A minist'ring angel shall my sister be
When thou liest howling.

HAMLET (aside)
                              What, the fair Ophelia!

The PRIEST moves off, passing CLAUDIUS and GERTRUDE and
leaving the graveyard. GERTRUDE steps forward.

GERTRUDE (scattering flowers)
Sweets to the sweet. Farewell.
I hoped thou shouldst have been my Hamlet's wife.
I thought thy bride-bed to have decked, sweet maid,
And not t'have strewed thy grave.

The GRAVEDIGGERS now start to shovel the earth into the hole.

LAERTES (uncontainable)
                              O, treble woe

Fall ten times treble on that cursèd head
Whose wicked deed thy most ingenious sense
Deprived thee of! – hold off the earth awhile,

He immediately jumps into the grave and throws open the lid of the
coffin to pull to his bosom the lifeless OPHELIA.

LAERTES (continuing)
Till I have caught her once more in mine arms.
Now pile your dust upon the quick and dead,
Till of this flat a mountain you have made
To o'ertop old Pelion, or the skyish head
Of blue Olympus.

HAMLET steps out, the group gasps.

HAMLET (coming forward)
                    What is he whose grief
Bears such an emphasis, whose phrase of sorrow
Conjures the wand'ring stars and makes them stand
Like wonder-wounded hearers? This is I,
Hamlet the Dane.

LAERTES
            The devil take thy soul.

He throws the Bible at HAMLET and then leaps out of the grave
attacks HAMLET, pushing him to the ground.

HAMLET
                              Thou pray'st not well.

I prithee take thy fingers from my throat,
For though I am not splenative and rash,
Yet have I something in me dangerous,
Which let thy wisdom fear. Hold off thy hand.

CLAUDIUS (to the Lords)
Pluck them asunder.

The PALLBEARERS weigh in.

GERTRUDE
            Hamlet, Hamlet!

ALL
Gentlemen!

The PALLBEARERS seize LAERTES. HORATIO and another
PALLBEARER lift the enraged HAMLET up onto his feet.

HORATIO
            Good my lord, be quiet.

HAMLET
Why, I will fight with him upon this theme
Until my eyelids will no longer wag.

GERTRUDE is a blur of emotions. Overjoyed to see her son again,
but terrified for him also.

GERTRUDE
O my son, what theme?

HAMLET (impassioned)
I loved Ophelia. Forty thousand brothers
Could not, with all their quantity of love,
Make up my sum. – What wilt thou do for her?
CLAUDIUS
O, he is mad, Laertes.
GERTRUDE
For love of God, forbear him.
HAMLET (to Laertes)
'Swounds, show me what thou'lt do.
Woo't weep, woo't fight, woo't fast, woo't tear thyself,
Woo't drink up eisel, eat a crocodile?
I'll do't. Dost thou come here to whine,
To outface me with leaping in her grave?
Be buried quick with her, and so will I.
And if thou prate of mountains, let them throw
Millions of acres on us, till our ground,
Singeing his pate against the burning zone,
Make Ossa like a wart. Nay, an thou'lt mouth,
I'll rant as well as thou.
GERTRUDE (to Laertes)
                    This is mere madness,
And thus awhile the fit will work on him.
Anon, as patient as the female dove
When that her golden couplets are disclosed,
His silence will sit drooping.

But now his puff has gone and only despair comes flooding in.

HAMLET (to Laertes)
                    Hear you, sir,
What is the reason that you use me thus?
I loved you ever. But it is no matter.
Let Hercules himself do what he may,
The cat will mew, and dog will have his day.

He goes.

CLAUDIUS
I pray you, good Horatio, wait upon him.

HORATIO follows his friend. GERTRUDE moves to watch them
leave. CLAUDIUS speaks to LAERTES.

CLAUDIUS
Strengthen your patience in our last night's speech.
We'll put the matter to the present push. –
Good Gertrude, set some watch over your son. –

GERTRUDE moves off to follow her son, the PALLBEARERS
escort her.

CLAUDIUS (continuing)
This grave shall have a living monument.

An hour of quiet shortly shall we see;
Till then, in patience our proceeding be.

CLAUDIUS moves away and LAERTES kneels down beside the grave
to pray. The GRAVEDIGGERS lower their heads in respect.

We dissolve to:

Exterior / ESTABLISHING-SHOT PALACE Day

A misty morning. We establish FRANCISCO back in place as formal
sentry by the gate. We note too that he is once again uneasy. He will
become for us, like the Gert Frobe character in *The Longest Day* – the
German soldier having his breakfast in the coastal bunker who then
sees the massive flotilla coming across the Channel at him.

We dissolve again:

Interior / STATE HALL BALCONY Day

HORATIO and HAMLET walk the balcony towards his apartments.

HAMLET
So much for this, sir. Now shall you see the other.
You do remember all the circumstance?

HORATIO
Remember it, my lord!

HAMLET
Sir, in my heart there was a kind of fighting
That would not let me sleep. Methought I lay
Worse than the mutines in the bilboes. Rashly –
And praised be rashness for it: let us know
Our indiscretion sometimes serves us well
When our deep plots do pall, and that should learn us
There's a divinity that shapes our ends,
Rough-hew them how we will –

HORATIO
That is most certain.

HAMLET
                    Up from my cabin,
My sea-gown scarfed about me in the dark,
Groped I to find out them, had my desire,
Fingered their packet, and in fine withdrew
To mine own room again, making so bold,
My fears forgetting manners, to unseal
Their grand commission; where I found, Horatio –
O royal knavery!

A grim look as we enter HAMLET's apartments. They walk along
the library gallery and down the steps into the apartment.

HAMLET (continuing)
                    – an exact command,
Larded with many several sorts of reasons
Importing Denmark's health, and England's, too,
With ho! Such bugs and goblins in my life,

That on the supervise, no leisure bated,
No, not to stay the grinding of the axe,
My head should be struck off.

This is genuinely shocking.

HORATIO

                           Is't possible?

HAMLET (giving it to him)
Here's the commission, read it at more leisure
But wilt thou hear me how I did proceed?

HORATIO
I beseech you.

HAMLET
Being thus benetted round with villainies –
Ere I could make a prologue to my brains,
They had begun the play – I sat me down,
Devised a new commission, wrote it fair.
I once did hold it, as our statists do,
A baseness to write fair, and laboured much
How to forget that learning; but, sir, now
It did me yeoman's service. Wilt thou know
Th' effect of what I wrote?

HORATIO

                         Ay, good my lord.

HAMLET
An earnest conjuration from the King,
As England was his faithful tributary,
As love between them like the palm might flourish,
As peace should still her wheaten garland wear
And stand a comma 'tween their amities,
And many such like as'es of great charge,

There is an awful glee in HAMLET's re-telling.

HAMLET (continuing)
That on the view and know of these contents,
Without debatement further more or less,
He should the bearers put to sudden death,
Not shriving-time allowed.

HORATIO

                         How was this sealed?

HAMLET
Why, even in that was heaven ordinant.
I had my father's signet in my purse,
Which was the model of that Danish seal;
Folded the writ up in the form of th' other,
Subscribed it, gave't th' impression, placed it safely,
The changeling never known. Now the next day
Was our sea-fight; and what to this was sequent

Thou know'st already.

HORATIO is still taking this information in.

HORATIO
So Guildenstern and Rosencrantz go to't.

A brief beat, before the new wiser, harder HAMLET speaks.

HAMLET
Why, man, they did make love to this employment.
They are not near my conscience. Their defeat
Doth by their own insinuation grow.
'Tis dangerous when the baser nature comes
Between the pass and fell incensèd points
Of mighty opposites.

HORATIO has little choice but to agree. Or change the subject.

HORATIO
                    Why, what a king is this!

HAMLET
Does it not, think'st thee, stand me now upon —
He that hath killed my king and whored my mother,
Popped in between th' election and my hopes,
Thrown out his angle for my proper life,
And with such coz'nage — is't not perfect conscience
To quit him with this arm? And is't not to be damned
To let this canker of our nature come
In further evil?

HORATIO will not give that final assurance to HAMLET, as after the play scene, that what he's doing could be right. He evades again.

HORATIO
It must be shortly known to him from England
What is the issue of the business there.

HAMLET recognizes the difference between them. It's OK. He knows he's on his own. And he knows now what that means. It's all right. He speaks to himself.

HAMLET
It will be short. The interim is mine,
And a man's life's no more than to say 'one'.
But I am very sorry, good Horatio,

And he truly is, however ironic it seems.

HAMLET (continuing)
That to Laertes I forgot myself;
For by the image of my cause I see
The portraiture of his.

You can say that again.

HAMLET (continuing)
                    I'll court his favours.
But sure, the bravery of his grief did put me
Into a tow'ring passion.

A knock at the door.

HORATIO

Peace, who comes here?

HORATIO stands and OSRIC enters and removes his hat.

OSRIC

Your lordship is right welcome back to Denmark.

HORATIO and HAMLET share a look, who on earth is this?

HAMLET

I humbly thank you, sir.

(to Horatio) *Dost know this water-fly?*

HORATIO

No, my good lord.

OSRIC remains in the doorway.

HAMLET

Thy state is the more gracious, for 'tis a vice to know him.
He hath much land, and fertile. Let a beast be lord of beasts,
and his crib shall stand at the King's mess. 'Tis a chuff, but,
as I say, spacious in the possession of dirt.

OSRIC throws him what he imagines to be a winning smile.

OSRIC

Sweet lord, if your friendship were at leisure I should impart a
thing to you from his majesty.

HAMLET

I will receive it, sir, with all diligence of spirit. Put your bonnet
to his right use; 'tis for the head.

OSRIC

I thank your lordship, 'tis very hot.

It's not of course, and anyway he's indoors.

HAMLET

No, believe me, 'tis very cold. The wind is northerly.

Tricky customers, these mad Princes. Humour them, I think.

OSRIC

It is indifferent cold, my lord, indeed.

He decides to humour HAMLET and puts his hat on.

HAMLET

Methinks it is very sultry and hot for my complexion.

OSRIC losing his way rapidly. And rather touchingly. He's not
so bad. A fashion victim with a talent for real estate.

OSRIC

Exceedingly, my lord. It is very sultry, as 'twere –

Taking his hat off again.

I cannot tell how.

Anyway, look, let me get on with this.

But, my lord, his majesty bade me signify to you that he has
laid a great wager on your head.

Which is rather exciting, isn't it?

Sir, this is the matter.

HAMLET

I beseech you, remember.

HAMLET points to the hat. OSRIC can't remember whether it's supposed to be cold or hot or what, but decides it'll be easier if he keeps the bloody thing off.

OSRIC

Nay, good my lord, for mine ease, in good faith.

Now please, let me get back to my speech.

OSRIC (continuing)

Sir, here is newly come to court Laertes. Believe me, an absolute gentleman, full of most excellent differences, of very soft society and great showing. Indeed, to speak feelingly of him, he is the card or calendar of gentry; for you shall find in him the continent of what part a gentleman would see.

Anything you can do ...

HAMLET

Sir, his definement suffers no perdition in you; though I know to divide him inventorially would dizzy th' arithmetic of memory, and yet but yaw neither, in respect of his quick sail. But, in the verity of extolment, I take him to be a soul of great article, and his infusion of such dearth and rareness as, to make true diction of him, his semblable is his mirror, and who else would trace him, his umbrage, nothing more.

Yes, all right I've got the point.

OSRIC

Your lordship speaks most infallibly of him.

HAMLET

The concernancy, sir? Why do we wrap the gentleman in our more rawer breath?

OSRIC

Sir?

HORATIO

Is't not possible to understand in another tongue?
You will to't sir, really.

HAMLET

What imports the nomination of this gentleman?

OSRIC

Of Laertes?

HORATIO

His purse is empty already. All's golden words are spent.

HAMLET

Of him, sir.

OSRIC

I know you are not ignorant —

HAMLET
I would you did, sir. Yet, in faith if you did, it would not much approve me. Well, sir?

OSRIC
You are not ignorant of what excellence Laertes is –

HAMLET
I dare not confess that, lest I should compare with him in excellence; but to know a man well were to know himself.

OSRIC
I mean, sir, for his weapon. But in the imputation laid on him, by them in his meed, he's unfellowed.

HAMLET
What's his weapon?

OSRIC
Rapier and dagger.

You see, didn't get me there, did you?

HAMLET
That's two of his weapons. But well.

Don't you just hate people like that? Never mind. I will go **on**.

OSRIC
The King, sir, hath wagered with him six Barbary horses, against the which he has 'imponed',

He **loves** saying this word. It's the kind of word that reveals his quite brilliant intelligence.

OSRIC (continuing)
                                        as I take it,
six French rapiers and poniards, with their assigns, as girdle, hanger, or so. Three of the carriages, in faith, are very dear to fancy, very responsive to the hilts, most delicate carriages, and of very liberal conceit.

HAMLET
What call you the carriages?

HORATIO
I knew you must be edified by the margin ere you had done.

Oh. Better make a stab at this.

OSRIC
The carriages, sir, are the hangers.

HAMLET
The phrase would be more germane to the matter if we could carry cannon by our sides. I would it might be hangers till then. But on: six Barbary horses against six French swords, their assigns, and three liberal-conceited carriages – that's the French bet against the Danish. Why is this 'imponed', as you call it?

OSRIC reckons he's got the measure of him now. Few sticky moments, but nothing he can't deal with.

OSRIC

The King, sir, hath laid, sir, that in a dozen passes between
you and him he shall not exceed you three hits.

He ends with a flourish.

OSRIC (continuing)

> *He hath laid on twelve for nine, and it would come to*
immediate trial if your lordship would vouchsafe the answer.

HAMLET (ominously)

How if I answer no?

Oh. That's thrown him. OSRIC-ian computer malfunction.
Wasn't he clear enough?

OSRIC

I mean, my lord, the opposition of your person in trial.

A beat. HAMLET knows what this is leading up to.

HAMLET

Sir, I will walk here in the hall. If it please his majesty,
'tis the breathing time of day with me. Let the foils be brought;
the gentleman willing, an' the King hold his purpose, I will win
for him if I can. If not, I'll gain nothing but my shame and the
odd hits.

Is that a 'yes' then?

OSRIC

Shall I re-deliver you e'en so?

HAMLET

To this effect, sir; after what flourish your nature will.

Thrilled to be getting away now.

OSRIC

I commend my duty to your lordship.

HAMLET

Yours, yours.

OSRIC bows, hitting the chair with his sword, and goes out.

HAMLET (continuing)

He does well to commend it himself, there are no tongues
else for's turn.

HORATIO

This lapwing runs away with the shell on his head.

HAMLET

He did comply with his dug before he sucked it. Thus has
he — and many more of the same bevy that I know the drossy
age dotes on — only got the tune of the time and outward habit of
encounter, a kind of yeasty collection which carries them through
and through the most fanned and winnowed opinions; and do
but blow them to their trials, the bubbles are out.

Cut to:

Exterior / PALACE Night

FRANCISCO, at the gates, still pacing. He stops and looks.

Movement in a bush? The sound of a horse? The flash of metal?
But there is nothing there.

Cut to:

Interior / HAMLET'S APARTMENTS Day

A YOUNG LORD steps in, unannounced. He gives off an atmosphere
that makes REYNALDO seem like Mother Theresa. He's here because
clearly no one trusts lovely OSRIC to get it right.

> LORD
> *My lord, his majesty commended him to you by young Osric,*
> *who brings back to him, that you attend him in the hall; he*
> *sends to know if your pleasure hold to play with Laertes, or*
> *that you will take longer time?*

The KING really is getting twitchy. The moment of truth is nigh.

> HAMLET
> *I am constant to my purposes; they follow the King's pleasure:*
> *if his fitness speaks, mine is ready; now or whensoever, provided*
> *I be so able as now.*

He still wants him to get a move on.

> LORD
> *The King and Queen and all are coming down.*

All right, I heard you the first time.

> HAMLET
> *In happy time.*

And on a more intimate note. Mum has a message.

> LORD
> *The Queen desires you to use some gentle entertainment to*
> *Laertes before you fall to play.*

> HAMLET
> *She well instructs me.*

The LORD goes, and a very anxious HORATIO turns to his friend.

> HORATIO
> *You will lose this wager, my lord.*

> HAMLET (distracted)
> *I do not think so. Since he went into France, I have been in*
> *continual practice. I shall win at the odds.*

He moves to the window.

> HAMLET (continuing)
>> *But thou wouldst not think how all here about*
> *my heart*

Snaps out of it a little.

> HAMLET (continuing)
>> *but it is no matter.*

> HORATIO (worried)
> *Nay, good my lord —*

> HAMLET (smiling)
> *It is but foolery, but it is such a kind of gain-giving as would perhaps*

161

trouble a woman.

HORATIO (very firm)
*If your mind dislike anything, obey it. I will forestall their repair
hither, and say you are not fit. But no. It's gone way beyond
that. This is a moment where his destiny will reveal itself.
Whatever, it will be the right moment.*

HAMLET
*Not a whit. We defy augury. There's a special providence in the
fall of a sparrow. If it be now, 'tis not to come. If it be not to come,
it will be now. If it be not now, yet it will come. The readiness
is all. Since no man knows aught of what he leaves, what is't to
leave betimes?*

He has spoken with the heart-rending simplicity of a man who
knows that he is going to die and probably very soon. He accepts
the inevitability of it. No more resistance, to people, to things,
to circumstance, to himself. No more suffering. Acceptance.
At last. Peace.

We cut to:

Interior / STATE HALL Day

Great shafts of light make the massive space look like a cathedral.
The Royal chairs have been placed in the middle of the hall, to one
side, placed to be right in the centre of the action. There is a sizable
CROWD of Courtiers. HAMLET and HORATIO stand at one end,
LAERTES and YOUNG LORD at the other. OSRIC will be judge.
The two opponents start to walk towards each other. It's a friendly
atmosphere with a little Dodgers stadium thrown in, in expectation of
the sport. Perhaps it is a chance at reconciliation. GERTRUDE waits
while the KING formally presents the men to each other.

CLAUDIUS
Come, Hamlet, come, and take this hand from me.

HAMLET (to Laertes)
*Give me your pardon, sir. I've done you wrong;
But pardon't as you are a gentleman.*

We cut to:

Exterior / PALACE Night

HAMLET V/O
*This presence knows,
And you must needs have heard, how I am punished
With a sore distraction. What I have done
That might your nature, honour, and exception
Roughly awake, I here proclaim was madness.*

This speech is intercut with images of the outside attack. Poor
FRANCISCO surprised from behind, just as we see FORTINBRAS's
Army crest the hill. Close on FORTINBRAS as he gives the order to
charge, ending on an epic view of the thousands of Norwegian troops
silently engulfing the palace.

HAMLET V/O (continuing)

Was't Hamlet wronged Laertes? Never Hamlet.
If Hamlet from himself be ta'en away,
And when he's not himself does wrong Laertes,
Then Hamlet does it not, Hamlet denies it.
Who does it then? His madness. If't be so,
Hamlet is of the faction that is wronged.
His madness is poor Hamlet's enemy.

Cut to:

Interior / STATE HALL Day

HAMLET

Sir, in this audience
Let my disclaiming from a purposed evil
Free me so far in your most generous thoughts
That I have shot mine arrow o'er the house
And hurt my brother.

LAERTES uncertain how to respond to what has been delivered
with great humility and heart.

LAERTES (slowly)

    I am satisfied in nature,
Whose motive in this case should stir me most
To my revenge. But in my terms of honour
I stand aloof, and will no reconcilement
Till by some elder masters of known honour
I have a voice and precedent of peace
To keep my name ungored; but till that time
I do receive your offered love like love,
And will not wrong it.

That is enough. How could he do other?

HAMLET

                I do embrace it freely
And will this brothers' wager frankly play.

CLAUDIUS leads the applause. GERTRUDE embraces both players.
She and CLAUDIUS return to their thrones.

HAMLET

Give us the foils. Come on.

They take off their gowns to reveal a sort of high-tech combination
of a modern fencing jacket with a Roman gladiator's breast plate
They could be two graduates of the Robocop academy.

LAERTES (to attendants)

Come, one for me.

HAMLET (jolly relaxed)

I'll be your foil, Laertes. In mine ignorance
Your skill shall, like a star i' th' darkest night,
Stick fiery off indeed.

LAERTES (jumpy)

                 You mock me, sir.

HAMLET (sincere)
No, by this hand.

CLAUDIUS
Give them the foils, young Osric.

OSRIC pushes his sword trolley towards the opponents.

CLAUDIUS

                 Cousin Hamlet,
You know the wager?

HAMLET (grinning)

               Very well, my lord.
Your grace hath laid the odds o'th' weaker side.

CLAUDIUS
I do not fear it; I have seen you both.
But since he is bettered, we have therefore odds.

LAERTES (taking a foil)
This is too heavy; let me see another.

We see LAERTES and HAMLET choose their weapons.

HAMLET (taking a foil)
This likes me well. These foils have all a length?

OSRIC
Ay, my good lord.

HAMLET and LAERTES move back to the mat and face each other.

CLAUDIUS (to attendants)
Set me the stoup of wine upon that table.
If Hamlet give the first or second hit,
Or quit in answer of the third exchange,
Let all the battlements their ordnance fire.
The King shall drink to Hamlet's better breath,
And in the cup an union shall he throw
Richer than that which four successive Kings
In Denmark's crown have worn.

He holds up the pearl which is to be the prize. The AUDIENCE
applauds.

CLAUDIUS

                 Give me the cup,
And let the kettle to the trumpet speak,
The trumpet to the cannoneer without,
The cannons to the heavens, the heaven to earth,
'Now the King drinks to Hamlet'.

More applause while he drinks.

CLAUDIUS (continuing)

                 Come, begin.
And you, the judges, bear a wary eye.

HORATIO and YOUNG LORD acknowledge CLAUDIUS. HAMLET

and HORATIO take their fencing masks and turn to face each other, the ritual almost complete.

HAMLET (to Laertes)
Come on, sir.

LAERTES
Come, my lord.

They cross their swords for the start of the First Bout.

OSRIC steps forward, glances at each of them, and splits the swords with his sword. Then, Boo!

HAMLET attacks with the speed of a greyhound, pushing and pushing LAERTES up the long mat. It's one long sustained aggressive surprise attack and it's successful. LAERTES falls on his back onto the mat and HAMLET touches LAERTES on the chest.

HAMLET
One.

LAERTES (standing up)
No.

HAMLET (to Osric)
Judgement.

OSRIC
A hit, a very palpable hit.

The Crowd erupts!

LAERTES looks to the KING. Things not going absolutely as to plan. He picks up his sword.

LAERTES (very eager)
Well, again.

No you don't. Let's do this properly. Let's poison him. **Now**.

CLAUDIUS
Stay. Give me drink. Hamlet, this pearl is thine.
Here's to thy health.

Drum and trumpets sound and shot goes off. The CROWD applaud. CLAUDIUS drops the pearl into the cup.

CLAUDIUS (continuing)
   Give him the cup.

A momentary pause. He suspects nothing of the poison, he just doesn't want anything from this man. LAERTES looks again at CLAUDIUS as do GERTRUDE and the CROWD. No problem.

HAMLET
I'll play this bout first. Set it by a while. –

They move back to the centre of the mat to begin the Second Bout.

HAMLET
Come.

                 Cut to:

Exterior / PALACE Morning

Quick Cuts of FORTINBRAS's Army taking complete control of the inner courtyard. Powerful, silent stealth.

Interior / STATE HALL Night

The Second Bout. Masks off. More cat and mouse this time. Lunges
and stretches and trips. The CROWD on the edge of their seats as the
pace builds. HAMLET falls! But yes, he's up again. LAERTES
increasingly aggressive, blades flashing at incredible speed. Finally,
LAERTES takes a great run at the Prince, who manages to swerve at
the last minute, LAERTES passes him and as he does so HAMLET
manages to make one last swipe at LAERTES's body.

> HAMLET
>> *Another hit. What say you?*

OSRIC throws himself down onto the floor to see and signals

> LAERTES
> *A touch, a touch, I do confess.*

The CROWD erupt. HORATIO moves over to HAMLET to help him
take off his jacket, and LAERTES goes over to CLAUDIUS.

> CLAUDIUS
> *Our son shall win.*

GERTRUDE grabs the goblet from CLAUDIUS before he has time to
stop her and makes her way over to HAMLET, and LAERTES moves to
the YOUNG LORD.

> GERTRUDE (smiling)
>> *He's fat and scant of breath. –*
> *Here, Hamlet, take my napkin. Rub thy brows.*
> *The Queen carouses to thy fortune, Hamlet.*

Whilst they do this to the delight of the CROWD, we see the
YOUNG LORD lift the tip of LAERTES's sword and wipe it
with poison.

> HAMLET
> *Good madam.*

She lifts the poisoned cup to her lips.

> CLAUDIUS (panicked)
>> *Gertrude, do not drink.*

This cuts across all the public chat. The CROWD listens.

  No. She is her own woman now. And for a moment, all too brief,
she and her son are happy.

> GERTRUDE
> *I will, my lord, I pray you pardon me.*

She drinks, then offers the cup to Hamlet.

> CLAUDIUS V/O
> *It is the poisoned cup; it is too late.*

HAMLET shakes his head.

> HAMLET
> *I dare not drink yet, madam; by and by.*
> GERTRUDE (to Hamlet)
> *Come, let me wipe thy face.*

LAERTES moves over to CLAUDIUS who is watching his wife
in horror.

LAERTES (aside to Claudius)
My lord, I'll hit him now.

CLAUDIUS (grim)
I do not think't.

We see the frightened face of a man who is not a natural murderer.

LAERTES
And yet 'tis almost 'gainst my conscience.

He moves back to the mat, the YOUNG LORD following and we see
GERTRUDE make her way back to CLAUDIUS, but suddenly she
begins to feel the effect of the poison, swoons slightly.

HAMLET and LAERTES are now jacketless and putting their gloves
back on.

HAMLET
Come for the third, Laertes, you but dally.
I pray you pass with your best violence.
I am afeard you make a wanton of me.

LAERTES (enraged)
Say you so? Come on.

LAERTES runs for HAMLET and as he passes him, he nicks HAMLET's
shoulder with the poisoned sword. He runs past and then stands to
face his opponent.

LAERTES (to Hamlet)
Have at you now!

For several seconds it's *High Noon* as they stand facing each other, the
MEN slowly moving in towards them, and then suddenly it's a free-
for-all, and now HAMLET chases LAERTES round the hall, in amongst
the CROWD. The MEN attempt to stop him and the WOMEN take
cover as they rush past them.

OSRIC takes cover against the wall.

HAMLET chases LAERTES over the throne dais, through hordes of
Courtiers. A great leap from HAMLET trips LAERTES up. His sword
skids away. HAMLET rushes for it. He looks at the tip – enraged. He
throws his own sword to LAERTES and retains the poisoned one.
This isn't over yet.

After a beat, they both make for the main stairs.

Meanwhile pandemonium has broken out in the hall, many of the
CROWD are escaping through the mirrored doors.

At the top of the stairs, the flight is messier. Kicks and lunges and
bites. HAMLET is thrown into a glass bookcase. Shards spray
everywhere.

OSRIC watches and shouts.

OSRIC
Nothing neither way.

CLAUDIUS (to Osric)
Part them, they are incensed.

HAMLET (possessed)
Nay, come again.

He races after LAERTES along the balcony, leaping over a torchère of candles LAERTES has pulled down.

  GERTRUDE tries to stand up but falls to the floor, among the running CROWD.

OSRIC
Look to the Queen there, ho!

Her ATTENDANTS rush to her as does CLAUDIUS.

  The fight continues along the balcony and onto the bridge. HAMLET kicks LAERTES in the stomach and as he doubles up, HAMLET manages to cut LAERTES on the shoulder with the poisoned sword. HORATIO sees this.

HORATIO
They bleed on both sides.

LAERTES stares at HAMLET in horror for a few moments and then races at HAMLET who steps out of the way and LAERTES, unable to stop, trips and falls over the balustrade and down onto the floor below. HAMLET stays aloft looking down at LAERTES. HORATIO calls up to him.

HORATIO (continuing)
                    How is't, my lord?

OSRIC rushes over to LAERTES, the YOUNG LORD joins them.

OSRIC
How is't, Laertes?

Close on him as he lies in his arms.

LAERTES
Why, as a woodcock to mine own springe, Osric.
I am justly killed with mine own treachery.

HAMLET moves across the balcony to check on his mother.

HAMLET
How does the Queen?

CLAUDIUS
                    She swoons to see them bleed.

She looks into the face of her husband.

GERTRUDE
No, no, the drink, the drink! O my dear Hamlet,
The drink, the drink — I am poisoned.

She dies.

HAMLET
O villainy! Ho! Let the door be locked!
Treachery, seek it out.

LAERTES pulls him up short.

LAERTES
It is here, Hamlet. Hamlet, thou art slain.
No med'cine in the world can do thee good.
In thee there is no half an hour of life.
The YOUNG LORD moves away.
LAERTES
The treacherous instrument is in thy hand,
Unbated and envenomed.
The few people who are left, stand round appalled.
LAERTES (continuing)
                    The foul practice
Hath turned itself on me. Lo, here I lie,
Never to rise again. Thy mother's poisoned.
OSRIC moves away from the dying man and runs for one of the
secret doors.
LAERTES (continuing)
I can no more. The King,
He rolls over to look at CLAUDIUS
LAERTES (continuing)
                    the King's to blame.
ATTENDANTS
Treason, treason!

                                                        Cut to:

Interior / ANTE-ROOM Day
OSRIC, still trying to escape, tries another secret door and closes it.
Safe! His eyes open wide and we gib down to see a knife embedded
in his abdomen.

                                                        Cut to:

Interior / STATE HALL Day
HAMLET stares at the rapier.
HAMLET
The point envenomed too? Then, venom,
All eyes go to CLAUDIUS. He starts to move slowly then runs towards
the throne dais. As he runs HAMLET moves across the balcony.
HAMLET (continuing)
                                    to thy work.
He throws the poisoned sword, javelin like, across the Hall.
WHOOSH! It goes through CLAUDIUS and pins him to the back of
the throne. He struggles to get away, trying to pull the sword out.
CLAUDIUS
O yet defend me, friends! I am but hurt.
And HAMLET picks up his fallen rapier, and severs a rope, which
sends the chandelier plummeting towards CLAUDIUS.
  CLAUDIUS manages to release himself from the sword and turns in
the chair to see the chandelier flying directly towards him. It hits him
with great force.

HAMLET swings down on the rope to the floor. He grabs the poisoned goblet, rushes to the helpless CLAUDIUS. He feeds the poison down his uncle's throat.

HAMLET

Here, thou incestuous, murd'rous, damnèd Dane,
Drink off this potion. Is thy union here?
Follow my mother.

LAERTES calls across the hall.

LAERTES

He is justly serv'd.
It is a poison tempered by himself.
Exchange forgiveness with me, noble Hamlet.
Mine and my father's death come not upon thee,
Nor thine on me.

HAMLET

Heaven make thee free of it! I follow thee.

LAERTES dies.

Cut to:

Exterior / PALACE COURTYARD Day

The Palace secured, we see the stately procession of FORTINBRAS through the courtyard, towards the massive front doors.

Cut to:

Interior / STATE HALL Day

HAMLET moves away from the dais, passing HORATIO and giving him the cup.

HAMLET

I am dead, Horatio. Wretched Queen, adieu!

He looks around the court.

HAMLET (continuing)

You that look pale and tremble at this chance,
That are but mutes or audience to this act,
Had I but time –

He has collapsed with pain.

HAMLET (continuing)

as this fell sergeant Death
Is strict in his arrest – O, I could tell you –
But let it be. Horatio, I am dead,
Thou liv'st. Report me and my cause aright
To the unsatisfied.

This is too much for his friend.

HORATIO

Never believe it.
I am more an antique Roman than a Dane.
Here's yet some liquor left.

HAMLET stops him with whatever power is left in his voice.

HAMLET
As thou'rt a man,

Give me the cup. Let go. By heaven, I'll ha't.

HORATIO throws it down. He continues quietly impassioned.

HAMLET (continuing)

O God, Horatio, what a wounded name,
Things standing thus unknown, shall live behind me!
If thou didst ever hold me in thy heart,
Absent thee from felicity a while,
And in this harsh world draw thy breath in pain
To tell my story.

Terrifying noises are heard outside the Hall.

HAMLET (continuing)

What warlike noise is this?

OSRIC emerges from one of the hidden doors. Dignity intact.

OSRIC

Young Fortinbras, with conquest come from Poland,
To th' ambassadors of England gives

OSRIC shows his bloodied hand.

OSRIC (continuing)

This warlike volley.

HAMLET (very quiet)

O, I die, Horatio!

The potent poison quite o'ercrows my spirit.
I cannot live to hear the news from England,
But I do prophesy th' election lights
On Fortinbras. He has my dying voice.
So tell him, with th' occurrents, more and less,
Which have solicited. The rest is silence.

And the Court is silent too.

HORATIO

Now cracks a noble heart. Good night, sweet prince,
And flights of angels sing thee to thy rest. −

A great drum beat.

HORATIO (continuing)

Why does the drum come hither?

Because it's to mark an attack. **Boom!** Through every door in the room, by force, emerges FORTINBRAS's Army in SAS style. The Soldiers from the top gallery break through the doors in a shower of glass, already on ropes with which they abseil down into the hall. Within seconds they are in control. Immediately we hear the sound of approaching footsteps.

They reveal FORTINBRAS marching towards us with military precision.

FORTINBRAS

Where is this sight?

HORATIO
What is it ye would see?
If aught of woe or wonder, cease your search.
The new ruler starts to take in the scene.

FORTINBRAS
This quarry cries on havoc. O proud death,
What feast is toward in thine eternal cell
That thou so many princes at a shot
So bloodily hast struck!

The ENGLISH AMBASSADOR enters through one of the mirrored doors. What he sees, shakes him to the core.

AMBASSADOR
The sight is dismal,
And our affairs from England come too late.
The ears are senseless that should give us hearing
To tell him his commandment is fulfilled,
That Rosencrantz and Guildenstern are dead.
Where should we have our thanks?

HORATIO
Not from his mouth,
Had it th' ability of life to thank you.
He never gave commandment for their death.
But since so jump upon this bloody question
You from the Polack wars, and you from England,
Are here arrived, give order that these bodies
High on a stage be placèd to the view;
And let me speak to th' yet unknowing world
How these things came about. So shall you hear
Of carnal, bloody, and unnatural acts,
Of accidental judgements, casual slaughters,
Of deaths put on by cunning and forced cause;
And, in this upshot, purposes mistook
Fall'n on th' inventors' heads. All this can I
Truly deliver.

FORTINBRAS
Let us haste to hear it
And call the noblest to the audience.
For me, with sorrow I embrace my fortune.

FORTINBRAS moves across the court to the throne, now vacated by CLAUDIUS. He sits in it, as if to the manner born.

FORTINBRAS (continuing)
I have some rights of memory in this Kingdom,
Which now to claim my vantage doth invite me.

A Crown is placed on FORTINBRAS's head,

HORATIO
Of that I shall have also cause to speak,

And from his mouth whose voice will draw on more.
But let this same be presently performed,
Even while men's minds are wild, lest more mischance
On plots and errors happen.

The ENGLISH AMBASSADOR slowly leaves.

FORTINBRAS

Let four Captains,
Bear Hamlet like a soldier to the stage,
For he was likely, had he been put on,
To have proved most royally; and for his passage,
The soldiers' music and the rites of war
Speak loudly for him.
Take up the body. Such a sight as this
Becomes the field, but here shows much amiss.
Go, bid the soldiers shoot.

We see the body lifted aloft. The CAPTAINS carry it away down
the hall. As they reach the end of the Hall we are high above
the body, held high in the crucifix position. As it disappears out
of the bottom of frame ...

Exterior / PALACE FRONT Day

Through the huge doors we Dissolve and see it again, but this time
fully dressed and in a coffin. As we pull back we see HAMLET lying
in state in front of the Great Palace. FORTINBRAS's Army pay their
respects. A line of Soldiers preparing to fire a volley above it.

We Dissolve to see a platoon of Soldiers, at a quick march away
from the palace towards the Monument. The Soldiers climb the statue
covering it in ropes. FORTINBRAS's men tear at the great statue,
hitting it continually with hammers, until with a mighty crash it falls.

Our final frame is the legend on the plinth, clear and strong for a
moment, before, in Slow Motion, the great broken pieces of stone
come falling into shot, the great head first, and gradually obliterate the
name HAMLET. For ever. As we ... fade to black.

THE CHOICE OF TEXT

The screenplay is based on the text of *Hamlet* as it appears in the First Folio - the edition of Shakespeare's plays collected by his theatrical associates Heminges and Condell and published in 1623 by a syndicate of booksellers. Nothing has been cut from this text, and some passages absent from it (including the soliloquy 'How all occasions do inform against me...') have been supplied from the Second Quarto (an edition of the play which exists in copies dated 1604 and 1605). We have also incorporated some readings of words and phrases from this source and from other early printed texts, and in a few cases emendations by modern editors of the play. Thus in I, 4, in the passage (from the Second Quarto) about the 'dram of eale', we use an emendation from the Oxford edition of the *Complete Works* (edited by Stanley Wells and Gary Taylor, 1988): 'doth all the noble substance *over-daub*' - rather than the original's 'of a doubt'.

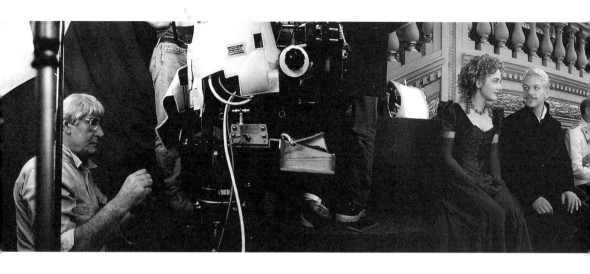

✠ THE FILM DIARY ✠

by Russell Jackson

What follows is taken from a diary of the rehearsals and shooting of *Hamlet*. In selecting from the three and a half months of work, I've tried to convey film-making's combination of the serious and the trivial, the glamorous and the mundane. I could have chronicled the picture's progress in terms of the catering (a film crew marches on its stomach, and we were well served by our caterers) but I will leave that to the reader's imagination. Because we had a 'running buffet' rather than fixed lunch breaks, a visitor to the set between twelve and three would have seen the Danish court in emotional crisis while most of the crew balanced bowls of salad or apple crumble in their laps. When the costumed actors have lunch, they are wrapped like deluxe skivvies in splendidly inelegant plastic aprons. I have also left out the truly dominant element of film-making, as vital an antidote to glamour as the ever-present styrofoam coffee cup: routine.

Every morning the crew assembles its trolley-loads of equipment, and the Director, the Director of Photography and their entourages arrange the set-ups for the first shots of the day. The actors rehearse the scene, and the stand-ins take their places so it can be lit. When each shot has been done, we move to another set-up. The actors either return to their dressing-rooms while this is being done, or stay on set to read, chat or do the crossword - though they need to keep their sense of the scene and the character, and may not want simply to pass the time of day. To make their job harder, scenes are often shot out of sequence. Sometimes even the shots that make up a scene are filmed out of order, and not always on consecutive days. At the end of every working day, when we hear the magic word 'wrap' and have tomorrow's call-sheet we can pack up and go home. (Though usually there are rushes to be viewed, and some people still have a lot of note-making and checking to do.)

I ought to explain briefly the function of a few members of the unit. The Script Supervisor keeps watch over dialogue or moves, logs photographic data for each take the director decides to have printed, maintains and is responsible (amongst other things) for the 'Bible' of the film, the marked continuity script. If we wanted to know what we were doing next (and in some cases what we had just done) Annie Wotton, our Script Supervisor, was the fount of all knowledge. The First Assistant Director (Simon Mosley) is responsible to the Director for the organisation of the set, and the Director of Photography (Alex Thomson) supervises the work of the camera team and the lighting. The props department has 'stand-bys' to place props on the set, go round with blowtorches lighting candles, and so forth. Costume and make-up have their own personnel on the set, so that the day's call-sheet might list half a dozen actors and still require catering for more than a hundred people. Two trolley-loads of electrical equipment are always in attendance, for sound and video, the latter providing video relay and a recording of each shot as the camera sees it.

So where do I fit into this labour-intensive artistic industry? Hugh Cruttwell and I have worked with Kenneth Branagh for some years on various projects, including his Shakespeare films. Hugh has a watching brief on Ken's own performance and is also part of the support system for the actors in general. I'm there to help with textual matters, which range from queries about specific words and lines to broader questions of interpretation affecting speeches or scenes. These can't (or shouldn't) be divorced from matters that are, strictly speaking, Hugh's department: we work together, as extra eyes and ears for the director. Most of the time during shooting, our place is by the video monitors, and what follows is largely *Hamlet* seen from that point of view - or, in the usual abbreviation, p.o.v.

Wednesday 3 January
REHEARSALS BEGIN

First morning in Shepperton. This may be one of the major British studios but it's not, on first sight, impressive. Located in a semi-suburban hinterland southwest of London, it seems at first like an industrial estate, a jumble of sheds, hangars, workshops, and what look like builders' yards, with a mansion trapped in the middle of it all like a genteel hostage from Edwardian England. Small electric trucks (some with '101 Dalmatians' blazoned on their cab) ferry lamps, equipment, food around between the offices, stages and workshops. The canine spectacular is well on in shooting: graceful white dogs with black spots are much in evidence.

One low white building, painted with Dalmatian-style spots, is the home of the puppies ('Caution - Puppies at play') and inmates in various sizes bounce or amble about in their runs. One is being trained to trot alongside a bicycle, another to follow a row of silver-paper covered boxes and then pounce on it at command.

We're in the elegant board-room of the old house, round a long green-baize covered table. First session is with Derek Jacobi (Claudius) and Julie Christie (Gertrude), plus Ken, Orlando Seale (his 'acting double') Annie Wotton (Script Supervisor), Simon Mosley (First A.D.), Hugh Cruttwell.

Ken distributes phials of a herbal 'Rescue Remedy' (only half a joke, admitting nervous apprehension). Everyone has read the screenplay, and the actors have already had some discussion of their roles with Ken, but these days of rehearsal before we begin shooting will give everyone time for reappraisal, adjustments and (most important) finding out how the story will be told by *this* company of actors, in *these* circumstances. We won't start with a read-through: better to edge towards the play. We discuss royal families (including the current one), privacy, politics, and draw towards a reading of the scenes when Claudius and Gertrude are together. There's talk about the issue of complicity between them (not at all, so far as murder is concerned) and the 'essential' Claudius, which she took (and part of him still takes) as loving, kind, a 'good' man. Derek goes along with this, though he and Hugh Cruttwell remind us of Hamlet's very different point of view. Gertrude and Claudius feel responsible for Hamlet but Claudius has another agenda she knows nothing about - concerning the potential threat posed by her son.

After lunch the Polonius family join us, with Horatio. By now we feel able to discuss frankly and simply (and off the record) our own experiences of family, bereavement, grief. (This is not just to canvass ideas about the emotions of the play to draw on them in performance: it also establishes common ground among us.) Then we try to imagine an 'ideal' family, successful and well-balanced according to current middle-class notions, professional but not competitive, materially well-off but not showy - which (we agree) turns out quite repulsive. Then on to the Polonius family.

Polonius (Richard Briers) was promoted by new king. Laertes (Michael Maloney) is in Paris getting the gentlemanly accomplishments (N.B. not at Wittenberg). Ophelia (Kate Winslett) and Hamlet have been having an affair (yes, they have been to bed together, because we want this relationship to be as serious as possible) since the death of Hamlet senior. (Effect of a surge of feeling in time of bereavement and crisis?) Then we visit the set, particularly the State Room, which fills the whole of Stage A. Actors seem to be getting the Elsinore air in their nostrils. Slowly, alone, Julie walks along one mirrored wall. Ken announces that in a fortnight's time he hopes to have a 'performance' of the whole play, if possible without scripts and certainly without set or costumes.

Thursday 4 January (morning)

Ken gives us all copies of a questionnaire, a magazine-style personality quiz ('Which of your characteristics do you most/least admire?', 'If you were to die and come back in another form, what would you like to be?' and so on). The actors fill this in as their characters, the rest of us as ourselves, and Tim Spall and Reece Dinsdale (Rosencrantz and Guildenstern) arrive half-way through as though coming late to a party – which may be exactly the position their characters are in when they get to Elsinore. Then we have to exchange the forms, and guess who wrote which. Some surprises among the 'characters' (Horatio wants to translate Virgil's *Aeneid* into Danish) but mainly a consolidation of the ideas we have been pushing round so far, a good way of taking stock of the court.

Later more on the Polonius family. Believable intensity in the Polonius/Ophelia talk about Hamlet: not simple oppression from him and rebellion from her, but she can't tell him what's been going on. After much talk, paraphrasing lines, trying moves, Ken runs the scene with them just sitting on chairs side by side: stronger, more frustrated, with a greater sense of her being cornered. Kate Winslett plays Ophelia as vulnerable but not cowed, Dickie Briers is getting more than anger in Polonius - some loving apprehension. We try having her present when Polonius tells the king and queen he has found the cause of Hamlet's madness, and to take this further by making her read out Hamlet's love-letter - usually read by Polonius. We decide this is (a) too cruel an ordeal for her to be put through by our Polonius (b) too extreme so early in the story - so we will split the difference and have her read some of it only.

Thursday 4 – Monday 8 January

We work through scenes, trying various approaches, finding snags, problems, opportunities. Ophelia's motivations in returning Hamlet's love-tokens are considered: she is going further than Polonius suggested in any instructions we have heard, and whatever her father and the king expect from this confrontation, she has her own agenda (perhaps to find out why Hamlet is behaving this way to her, to put him on the spot?). The kinder and more circumspect Polonius seems, the harder it will be for her to betray him - hence her lying to Hamlet ('Where's your father? - At home, my lord'). In 'To be or not to be' Ken wants to show Hamlet alone with his mirror image(s) in the vast space of the mirrored hall. He has to be careful not to give the soliloquy an energy or momentum that it does not need - those qualities are coming soon enough in what follows when he encounters Ophelia. Ken steers Derek towards seeming even more vulnerable as Claudius, 'quietly anxious' about Hamlet after 'nunnery' scene, rarely openly angry, even when Rosencrantz and Guildenstern have screwed up. So, when he does flare up, becomes desperate, it will be more shocking.

On 8 January we go over each actor's lists of their character's priorities. Claudius has specific aims: inspiring confidence and trust in himself; loving Gertrude; making Hamlet look indulgent and neurotic (and thus defusing him); creating a new, strong, triumphalist Denmark (a military regime). Gertrude's aims are more general: decorum, sense of behaving properly in public; *noblesse oblige*, etiquette; sense of culture, confidence; loving Hamlet. Old Hamlet (Brian Blessed) points out that when he was alive he never failed to let Claudius see how little he mattered - there has to be an underlying bitterness in what Claudius has done to get the crown, as well as intense love for Gertrude. We consider different ways of showing these relationships in a short flashback - perhaps Old Hamlet and his son playing chess, while Gertrude and Claudius watch, or some other activity (perhaps outdoors) that will focus their various feelings for each other.

As we go along we acquire actors, so that the 'family' grows daily. In the room next to the board-room we watch the actors murder in jest while the Dalmatians go through their innocent paces outside. The play scene is set up with chairs on tables, the doors to the board-room become the curtains in Gertrude's apartment. Actors pace the room imagining the long tracking shots. Even here we begin to sense the look and pace of the film. Julie remarks that after the play scene we see the characters 'moving from room to room so you get a feeling of the whole beehive tipped over'.

Wednesday 10 January
Rehearsal on set with Robin Williams (Osric), Nick Farrell (Horatio) and Ken, to set up Osric scene in Hamlet's study. This is our first exposure to a fully-dressed set, stuffed with the impedimenta of Hamlet's artistic and literary enthusiasms. For the first time there are discussions of camera set-ups, lighting, etc. Now we are no longer in the technical-free environment of the board-room. We discuss dividing up the scene, but agree that it needs to take place in this private room, except for the very opening (which we do on the hall balcony). Robin is inventive, full of comic 'turns' and voices but not aggressive or showy (at lunch he gives us, among other things, 'Gandhi, the musical'). He is careful to see Osric as a person - a landowning upstart, but with his own sense of place and purpose. Details: he looks round the room nervously (but only a brief glance) while waiting for Hamlet to answer him.

While we're rehearsing, a striking figure appears, ushered in by a bearded stranger: a woman in an extravagant art deco outfit, all angles and black-and-white lines from head to toe. At first I assume this is one of the ultimate fashion victims of the movie business on a day out - then realize it's Glenn Close in full fig as Cruella de Vil.

Thursday 11 January
Shoot the scene. Osric at first confident, not very flamboyant or

aggressive, but as the scene progresses he is less easily conciliatory with Hamlet, a bit surer of his own fashionable rightness, even when taunted about the fancy words he uses. (But it's still an ordeal: eyes show he's had enough, and he manages to collide with a chair when he bows.) Robin has found the physicality: the painfully restricting boots, tight new uniform, make him stiff and awkward, undermine the high status he has awarded himself. Proud at first of having been told to go to see Hamlet, by the end he is glad to get out. Lack of space in study means that we sit in our overcoats in the dimly-lit, cold State Hall, watching monitors, and thread our way through cables and lights to get into the set. Catering is in a tent against the outside of the stage, and feels like a garden-party gone wrong, with hot-air blowers fighting a rear-guard action against icy wind under canvas walls. Later (as a bonus and while we're in the study) we shoot Hamlet's scene with Horatio just before the fencing match - 'providence in the fall of a sparrow'. Somehow it doesn't work: Ken a bit too lyrical, not stern enough, too sorry for that sparrow? We'll come back to this in a couple of months' time, but it was worth having a go now.

Monday 15 - Wednesday 17 January

More rehearsal, some on the set. Among other things, a session with Derek and Julie and their attendants to get a sense of how this court works. Discretion, status, and the significance of living close to royals are discussed. We also work on Ophelia's 'mad' scenes. In the first she will be frightening, not all 'pretty', and almost beyond communication as Gertrude and Claudius try to get through to her. In the second (with Laertes) she is stiller, less confrontational. She is being treated with a mixture of shock treatment (using water) and fairly brutal confinement, partly in accordance with some nineteenth-century notions of how to deal with the insane, but also because she is a political threat that has to be contained.

Then, on Wednesday, the promised run-through takes place, with no costumes and a few props. A private 'studio' version. The acting area is a large square in the middle of the State Hall's tiled floor, marked off with candlesticks on stands, and the working lights are lowered so that we see it virtually by candlelight. The whole play is acted in sequence, with a five-minute break in the middle. Those not 'on' watch from the sides, along with heads of technical departments. When he's not on, Ken wanders round watching action from various angles - which somehow seems to embody both his two roles as actor and director, and Hamlet's own dual role as well (plotter/victim).

Some revelations: Claudius's 'goodness' is paying off, and the solution to the Hamlet problem seems to be displays of more love, apparently sincere and caring, until Hamlet has taken matters well beyond the bounds of acceptable (or excusable) behaviour by killing Polonius. Gertrude is well-defined, Horatio clear and passionate, Hamlet still a bit too sane in 'Fishmonger' scene with Polonius, the Ophelia/Laertes relationship not right (too playful?). This is an invaluable opportunity for us all to get a sense of the whole play, to see where there are strengths and weaknesses - and in a technology-free environment.

Tuesday 23 January
After four days off, back to rehearse the Players' scenes. Charlton Heston (Player King) is sitting at the end of the board-room, drinking coffee, when we arrive. He moves straight in on verbal queries about his speeches, which he has gone through with a fine-toothed comb. Ken and Rosemary Harris (Player Queen) arrive and we read through, then move into next room to get it on its feet. Heston becomes more relaxed, begins to see acting opportunities rather than possible problems. Quest for a quasi-Chekhovian feeling (intimacy, sadness) in the speeches between the 'play' king and queen, rather than starting out from a notion of their being in a quainter, more 'old-fashioned' style than the rest of Shakespeare's play (the verse will do that anyway). At lunch Heston and Harris are expansive, anecdotal, at home. Afterwards, on to the first meeting with the Players and the 'Pyrrhus' and 'Hecuba' speech. The size of the performance will come from Heston's natural command and physique: we work now on expressive detail. Players' background discussed: they used to run a theatre, but times are bad, and they have been forced to take to the road. Still an impressive bunch - though a command performance is just what they need right now. Actor-managerish names provided for them (Horatio and Ermingard Hamilton and two further generations of their family). We imagine that the actor who plays the poisoner fancies himself as an innovator and may have an eye on the Hamilton troupe for himself.

Wednesday 24 January
Last full day of rehearsals: work on the play scene and Hamlet's meeting with the Players, who begin to seem a sort of ideal, alternative family. (The only one we see that is not dysfunctional?) The dumb-show is choreographed, then run again and again to make it faster, snappier. The State Hall is now practically ready, and without realizing it we have slipped onto the 'real' set. At the end of the afternoon, everyone is called onto the State Hall set - all the crew, carpenters, painters, workshop staff, most of the principal actors, about two hundred of us. The play-scene bleachers are filled to overflowing. Ken makes a short speech. Some of us have worked with him since he started in the theatre, many (including several crew) have worked on his other films. This is the fulfilment of an ambition since 1972 when he was at school. We need to keep a high level of efficiency, attention, commitment. Then we have drinks, to 'wet the baby's head': tomorrow the long haul starts.

Thursday 25 January
FIRST DAY OF PRINCIPAL PHOTOGRAPHY
We start with the long tracking shot of Hamlet talking to the Players, 'Speak the speech, I pray you ...' with background activity (chandelier raised, attendants passing). A complex speech with a lot of detail in action around it. When Hamlet reaches group of Players in the corner, Heston remarks on the effect of his being with these people (warm colours in costume, family group), in contrast with starchy, well-drilled formality of our military court.

Friday 26 January
Snow outside, and icy wind. Inside the sound stage, flaring gas jets, high bleachers with ranks of courtiers in shades of red and gold. Bits of scene including dumb show. Shots from balcony down to stage. How we do this determines shots for succeeding days. Ken doesn't at first find the sense of 'antic' in his teasing Polonius before the play - it seems as though it's a sideshow they have both anticipated. Then it gets edgier, less amiable. Later Hamlet is angrier, cruder with Claudius, too. The Players now look picturesque and vaguely 'medieval' in costumes they must have carted lovingly across Europe.

Saturday 27 January
Back to the top of yesterday's scene, now with the arrival of the court. In one take the look in Gertrude's eyes suggests that she understands what Claudius is being accused of: which tells a different story (not ours) - with just one glance. Hamlet gets cruder with Ophelia ('country matters' etc.), and Kate registers the embarrassment and bewilderment that will carry her forward to madness. The last time she talked to him was the 'nunnery scene' (which we haven't shot yet, but which will have been a terrifying experience for Ophelia), so being singled out in this way is a dismaying trial for her.

Monday 29 January
More reactions of Claudius and Gertrude to the play. One close-up on Derek is a little *too* subtle, until fourth take, where we see a few moments of unsuppressed apprehension that will register with no one except the cinema audience and the concealed Horatio. Close-ups for Polonius (variations on surprise, sense of indignation at Hamlet's behaviour). In isolation these shots seem like comic 'takes'. Dickie's sense of the absurd gets the better of him and the rest of the crew: serious outbreak of 'corpsing' (involuntary laughter on set).

Later, royal party leaving the balcony, then Horatio's p.o.v. of various moments in the play scene. The monitors are down by the staircase behind the Players' stage - suddenly Gérard Depardieu materialises, quietly, behind us. Slighter and shorter than you'd expect. Cordial, direct. Likes resemblance between Ken and Derek, which he thinks striking, maybe a good plot point. We go to look at the royal apartments, and Polonius's room which is now dressed fully. Depardieu says he's impressed with the scale of the production - only the English studios can assemble in one place the resources for filming on this scale. How about his *Cyrano*? That was a while ago, and in any case most of it was filmed in Hungary. Depardieu looks around, gestures embracingly: 'This is the European cinema, here.'

After the dumb show is filmed, we go to B Stage to rehearse Depardieu's scene. While Dickie and Melanie Ramsey (as the prostitute) rehearse, Depardieu sits quietly watching. His lips move occasionally, he gestures as he follows action. Directing in his mind's eye? (No - this is him as Reynaldo, not D.) Moment of wonderful intensity when he grabs the prostitute, pushes her away. Actor's instinct: 'I grab her gently, but the violence is when I push her away.' After rehearsal: 'It's easy - well ...' (shrugs, raises hands) - meaning the outline is clear, we just have to shoot to find out more.

Tuesday 30 January

On B Stage all day for the scene itself, which ends with entrance of the distraught Ophelia. Set closed off with black drapes across the corridor. This is a hard scene for everyone: complex, oblique speeches by Polonius, and Depardieu's measured, murmured responses need to be fitted into rhythm. Cigars and drink mean that props stand-bys are constantly darting in to provide repeats for new takes.

At first, Polonius seems to be ordering Reynaldo around too firmly, and a less servant/master approach is suggested: more 'two men of the world'. Polonius's 'Fare you well' mustn't be too dismissive, and for a moment Dickie is saying 'Observe his inclination in yourself' as though he were warning Reynaldo (who in our version probably runs a chain of whorehouses) not to be naughty. Eventually the scene seems like part of (lost) Balzac novel. Depardieu is able to be evil, amusing, vulnerable all at once. He has Polonius's number, but also knows who is paying his fees.

Good work, but a bit tense. Ken (as make-up department makes the set wait a half-minute): 'Meanwhile, here on the set of Branagh's *Hamlet*, Hell freezes over'. Afterwards, a planning meeting for first big court scene, to be shot on Friday with scores of extras and confetti by the hundredweight.

Wednesday 31 January

Close-ups on play scene, then part of the aftermath of the play, on a single tracking shot, with Ken encouraged to be wilder and harder to Rosencrantz and Guildenstern (and they bite back - they are beginning to lose composure). These four minutes take an hour to set up and only 45 minutes to film, which is remarkably swift: Ken in good spirits, buoyant. Seems happy to be acting, able to release some energy.

First 'court' scene (2 February): in the State Hall. The Director and the Director of Photography (Alex Thomson) inspect the Guard of Honour with a viewfinder.

Thursday 1 February

Players greeted, in long travelling shot in our hall of mirrors, so that the few acting problems pale beside the logistical ones. Heston on epic form in 'Hecuba' speech, with a touch of Moses in a low angle shot where he is holding out his arms, but quiet - resonant, expressive voice and face made for the camera. (Like Depardieu, one of the great screen faces.) Chats about films and Shakespeare, including Olivier's abortive plans to do *Macbeth*, which he discussed with Heston several times.

(Question: how do you address a screen legend? Answer from camera crew, a mixture of deference and familiarity: 'A bit to the left please, Chuck, sir'.)

Friday 2 February

First big court scene. King and queen approach the dais down the corridor, then seen from corridor p.o.v., swishing towards thrones with their attendants, in eerie silence (music on sound track will make a great difference here). Later we turn round to film their departure, with multiple cameras and a snowstorm of confetti that we hope not to have to repeat.

This is a day dominated by logistics and problem of getting maximum effect from crowd. The sense of a public occasion with the extras in serried ranks produces different performances: Derek gives Claudius's speech with a brio (and he does the whole lot) that will be qualified in the close-ups. Finale is confetti snowstorm, with Hamlet alone on the dais, but the most striking sight of the day is after the lights have been switched off. Alone, holding a plastic bag with her belongings in

Claudius sends ambassadors to Norway. Kenneth Branagh and
Alex Thomson check the shot on the monitor (right).

one hand, and clutching her script and the train of her wedding dress
with the other, Julie stands pensively among heaps of confetti in the
dim and empty hall. (Unfortunately, no photographer is at hand.)

Saturday 3 February

Close-ups on Claudius, Gertrude and Hamlet, to be cut into yesterday's
grand gala event. Derek's first speech is now compassionate: 'Our cousin
Hamlet - and our son'. He caresses Hamlet with that momentary pause in
the middle of the line.

Claudius's later speech, 'Tis sweet and commendable...', has to be
feeling, but with undertow of pragmatism, thinking his way through the
particulars of the argument rather than reciting some commonplace. Ken
likes to sneak in an extra go at the end of a set-up, if there's enough film
in the camera. This is often a radically different version of what he's been
doing, sometimes with lucky effect. Here he gets the intensity of Hamlet's
responses to his mother and stepfather, feelings that start us off on the
film's journey. (An audience that doesn't know the story should want to
know *why* this man is behaving like this.) Hugh insists that Ken should
avoid conscious 'melancholy' in this scene.

Monday 5 February

Soliloquy, 'O that this too, too solid flesh ...', which must be welded to
the next beat of the action in a single shot, taking Hamlet the length of
the hall, then back again: three of the takes seem to hit the right notes of
savage anger, frustration, disgust, despair. Ken shoots a couple of close-
ups to cover the moment in the middle where he greets Horatio and the

others, in case the single shot doesn't work and we have to cut at that point. (Jack Lemmon passes through, ushered along mirror wall on his way to the make-up dept, then comes to sit in his chair to watch monitor: short, white-haired, compacter edition of younger self, with mobile, subtly expressive face.) In Hamlet's apartment: Hamlet learns details of the Ghost. The whole sequence is in three shots: they move across to the hidden door, then go through it, then we will follow Hamlet up staircase to upper level of shelves - but these will be done on three separate days.

Tuesday 6 February
Over to another, smaller sound stage for the first day in the woods. (Hamlet's first scene with the Ghost, and its aftermath.) Powdery snow outside (Dalmatians identifiable against it by their spots) and snowy powder (finely shredded paper) inside. At first it seems like Siberia, but with the doors closed and the lights it's soon like the Mediterranean, especially for actors in layers of heavy uniform. The woodland almost fills the stage, and is built over a cellar full of hydraulics. In the working lights it resembles a display in a garden centre, with trees and branches bedded in with loam and held up with wires and iron stakes. Smoke and the wonderful cold morning light arranged by Alex Thomson (Director of Photography) change it into a mysterious, haunted woodland. First contact with special effects: bursts of flame and shaking forest and floor. In the middle of all this, there's acting to be done. Hamlet has to seem in a state of high anticipation and apprehension. The mad or 'antic' behaviour has to come later when he warns that he may have to behave oddly, but now he mustn't seem too sober for a man fired by the need for revenge, awed by the Ghost's commands, horrified by the news of the murder. (Before each take, as the camera starts running, we hear Jack Lemmon murmur 'magic time' to himself.)

Wednesday 7 February
The Ghost (Brian Blessed) is a creature from one of Fuseli's weird paintings, with muscles moulded on the 'armour' (in fact constructed on a wet-suit). Brian is an expansive, larger-than-life personality out of costume, and his acting usually draws on this, but now Ken encourages him to go for a measured, whispered delivery. By seven o'clock Brian has spent hours propped against a tree in a neoprene suit, with blazing lamps trained on him, and a row of gas-jets providing a heat-haze, so we break for the day - but there's a sense of real achievement in him.

Outside, in the comparatively real world, the *Dalmatians'* facsimile of a London street is dressed and lit for filming, and a procession of 'extra' motors are driven on and off it. My grubby Nissan, parked nearby, gets a free car-wash in the overspill from their rain effect.

Thursday 8 February

Last night's scene is picked up and dispatched, with a refreshed actor and crew, then we film the components of the Ghost's departure and Hamlet's reactions. Shots of Hamlet running through the woods and Horatio and Marcellus (Jack Lemmon) finding him, which means moving everyone from the side of the stage and laying a track for most of its length. Day ends with birthday cake and champagne for Jack, who is seventy. It's a shame we can't be on the palace set for this.

Friday 9 February

Polonius's room: Ophelia reports on Hamlet's behaviour. A moment of quiet for Kate to collect herself - over the headphones we can hear Ophelia sobbing, then her distress propels her into the room. When Polonius asks if she had denied Hamlet access to her, she beats the door with her fists in frustration - that was exactly what her father *told* her to do. Kate in the rehearsal walk-through is matter-of-fact, joking with crew, then painfully distraught for the takes, then relaxes again. Ready to take risks in acting, admirably easy to work with.

Afterwards to Hamlet's apartments, for the exit of Barnardo (Ian McElhinney), Marcellus, Horatio. Part two of the single move that is being done over three days. As he ushers them through the door in the bookcase, Ken adds a moment's exchange of glances with Horatio, which helps to kick-start the rush into the soliloquy, with its excitement, anticipation, fear, confirmed suspicion.

Saturday 10 February

In Hamlet's room for 'O what a rogue and peasant slave am I'. After initial anger, release, self-abasement, he shifts ('About my brains...') to real plotting, with a manic edge, but not 'mad' or possessed. Argument gets clearer as passion subsides. Business with toy theatre, and Hamlet dropping figure through the trapdoor - which of course fails to function on first take, as any simple mechanical gizmo will at the end of a long single shot. Return to the hall for more from the end of the play scene, then back into study where the crew has set up crane shot to end the scene we left yesterday afternoon, on 'My father's spirit in arms'. So we have been backwards and forwards in the script twice in two days. Murphy's Law again: Ken, followed by camera on crane, rushes upstairs, along gallery, grasps book - and fails to find the right page.

Tuesday 13 February
BLENHEIM PALACE, FIRST DAY OF LOCATION SHOOTING

Cold wet morning in the grounds of Blenheim Palace. Our first set-up is outside the side gate of the extraordinary piece of English early eighteenth-century baroque that was the (enormously expensive) reward of a grateful nation for the military prowess of the first Duke of Marlborough. We will be spending a fortnight encamped in the grounds from early morning to late at night like a small army, with a base camp of trailers and tents and fleets of minibuses and off-road vehicles to ferry personnel and equipment about. Now a bitter wind cuts across the lake, blowing our snow around. This is mostly detergent foam sprayed by teams of men and women in oilskins who stand in rows supporting lengths of hose across their shoulders, linked to tanks and compressors on lorries: a cross between some arcane rural ritual and an airport firecrew.

The first shot has Rosencrantz and Guildenstern arriving by miniature train, which has been dressed up as a vintage steam locomotive. (Smoke charges like fireworks in chimney.) Polonius meets them first: 'You go to seek the lord Hamlet, there he is'. Radio microphone signal is faint. (Sound department, over headphones: 'Polonius isn't behaving very well. I'll probably have to change his aerial'.) Then Hamlet, doublet all unbrac'd, greets them. Chat turns serious when prisons are mentioned: smiles freeze in apprehension (as well as literally) and R. and G. are already out of their depth, their skin-deep jauntiness wearing thin. Ken needs to sustain Hamlet's mood from a scene we haven't shot yet ('Fishmonger') which precedes this immediately in the script. Hamlet is bitter, evasive, now backfooting them, now attacking, now genial - their job isn't going to be easy.

Set-up for these first lines of long conversation seems interminable, compounded by the need to get snow just right. The 'green-room', a mobile home parked nearby, is a refuge, but heated like a sauna, and every burst of shooting is heralded by an invasion from make-up and wardrobe, so that it soon becomes as crowded as the Marx Brothers' stateroom in *A Night at the Opera*. As everyone is wearing the most layers of clothing possible space gets even tighter. Catering now includes soup and bread at one o'clock, and evening hot snack: cold weather rations.

Blenheim in different lights: orangey glow to stone, responding to shifting sun, a formidable Winter Palace. Courtyard is covered in our snow, this time paper rather than foam. The great open space is bounded by the wings of the building, and guarded by a splendid wrought-iron gate to which our Art Department has added 'Danish' crests and flanking rows of 'iron' railings. There are also two very convincing sentry-boxes. (Blenheim, of course, was not built as a fortress, but we need to suggest that Claudius has taken some measures to defend his palace.) Rushes are shown in the Palace restaurant, and we sit snugly at tables watching the screen and eating lunch out of styrofoam trays. On the screen are events from another, warmer, indoor world. In the afternoon we set up for night's shooting at Palace gates, with sentry in snow. We finally reach the first line of the play. Snow on snow now, with close-up detail in salt and finely powdered paper which are dusted onto railings with a hand brush.

Wednesday 14 February
Into gateway for Hamlet confronting Rosencrantz and Guildenstern. Bright sunshine now, but problems with air traffic from nearby flying

In the snow at Blenheim: Hamlet gossips about the Danish theatre with Rosencrantz and Guildenstern. Annie Wotton, the Script Supervisor, follows the scene in the script, as grips propel the camera dolly along a track.

school. Reece Dinsdale (G.) more brazen, Tim Spall (R.) more sheepish in response to 'You were sent for' - distinction that will run through play. In the evening we get to Marcellus's arrival. On one take Jack Lemmon, bundled into a greatcoat, and burdened with a long and awkward pike, suddenly slides down the bank out of sight. Moment of alarm (have we slain a comic genius?) then voice from below: 'Marcellus is here on his ass'. Jack dusted off, gets back to greeting sentries.

Thursday 15 February
In colonnade looking over main courtyard for 'What a piece of work is man', which needs a lot of takes, including one spoiled by a mobile phone going off. Sentries changing guard in background rehearsed carefully, and seem right as bringing life to Palace, but may distract. Eventually 'elbowed' (important and frequently used expression on set, often replaced by simple mime of elbowing something out of the way). Mood good before we do this scene (banter in bus) but silent, preoccupied afterwards. In the evening, down at gate again for sentries and Horatio running away from Ghost, with crane and tracking shots. As they scamper backwards across the yard one voice says 'My money's on Horatio'. Another voice: 'Are there hurdles?'

Kate, who has been nominated for an Oscar for her performance in *Sense and Sensibility*, appears in the evening in the hotel bar in finely unglamorous array: hair in pins and curlers, tee-shirt, leggings, bottle of mineral water. There is a vague sense (in the evening at least) of being 'on holiday'. At Shepperton we all just finished work and went home: on location at Blenheim the feeling is more like a theatre company on tour with a hotel bar to call its home. Days are more gruelling than in the studio, but evenings in the welcoming warmth of the Feathers Hotel do something to make up for it.

Friday 16 February
The water-garden and the path from the portico: bright sunshine, some shelter from sharp wind. Chairs along garden exposed, but we pull them over to the shelter of the house. After we've settled in, a change of plan. An immense tract of fake snow is spread on the lawn, and a camera track has been laid to shoot towards it following Laertes and Ophelia as they walk. This looks fine but the wind gets up and blows away great sheets and flecks of foam, so we have to reverse the angle and shoot with building in background.

Kate and Michael are a playful brother and sister pair (but not skittish, as they had been in rehearsal). He is more anxious than hectoring, she has that secret about her relationship with Hamlet.

Night shooting. Jack Lemmon (Marcellus), Ian McElhinney (Barnardo) and Nick Farrell (Horatio) will run behind an urn on the terrace, then challenge the Ghost. After first section, they dodge round behind the urn for the passage that includes one of the play's 'ghost' characters, Marshall Stork ('Thus twice before, and jump at this dead hour/ With martial stalk hath he gone by our watch ...'). Inevitably this goes wrong, and at one point everyone gets hysterical as a new figure, Marshall Strange, intrudes. (Jack: 'Get me two fresh actors'.) Progress slower than hoped for. Ken a bit fed up, but philosophical. Not sure he got what he wanted out of 'What a piece of work is man' and considering a reshoot if we get time. (In the end it seemed O.K. in the rushes).

Monday 19 February
Filming in the colonnade in an icy wind: Horatio gets Hamlet's letter from sailors. Problems with sun, wind (which blows about a lot of the 'snow' in the courtyard) then real snow arrives. It sweeps in off the lake, blanking out visibility in a blizzard that covers us all. Nick acquires more and more clothes as the weather deteriorates, and can hardly read the letter for droplets that make the ink run. Respite in afternoon, then in the evening just as we have at last finished Horatio's long speech in the first scene – more snow with wind, and by the last shot of the Ghost's p.o.v. of 'stay, illusion', a blizzard whirls round the camera crane. With the lights behind it, and viewed from the shelter of the doorway where the monitor lurks, this looks doubly spectacular. Ken on Horatio's intellectualism: 'Jonathan Miller comes to Elsinore'. Fervour, curiosity, guts turning over, fascination with what has previously been theory and hearsay. 'Intellectual curiosity giving clarity to consonants'. Green-room trailer now seems like the hut in Chaplin's *Gold Rush*, especially when the door blows open. Rufus Sewell (Fortinbras) arrives, looking as farouche in his day clothes as he does at the head of the army. Production office

has issued him with an i.d. label (number 007) that reads 'Famous Film Star'. With Spall and Dinsdale ('the terrible twosome') he establishes a record for staying up late after shooting - it's getting even more like a theatre company on tour.

Tuesday 20 February

Dry, bitter wind. Frozen snow now like brittle wedding-cake icing, and mixed with our own foam, paper and salt. First unit begins with Francisco (Ray Fearon) down by gate – in various states of apprehension – then having his neck wrenched from behind by a Fortinbras soldier. (Fortinbras's soldiers are in grey blanket-like material, unshaven, guerrilla-like, while the Elsinore guard are spit-and-polish toy soldiers.) Eventually, and thankfully, unit moves into a corridor off the courtyard, for part of the dialogue before Hamlet's first encounter with the Ghost ('the air bites shrewdly'). At first this begins with a flurry of snow as the door opens: but it looks like what it really is, a handful of paper confetti blown with a hair dryer. (Elbowed.) Hamlet at first doesn't seem full enough of sense of what he might expect from the Ghost, his feelings about Claudius's behaviour etc. This improves as timing and moves become clearer. (Trailer heating fails: even more like *The Gold Rush*. 'Why wasn't it Hamlet, Prince of Tuscany?'). Night shooting begins with the conclusion of the play's first scene, 'It faded on the crowing of the cock'. Jack against a gate, with Barnardo and Horatio. Ken sits behind the sentry box with monitor, hunched against cold in a bright red padded anorak, relaxed, resigned - as camera quite literally freezes. We wait half an hour as lights are shone on it to thaw it out and a circuit board is replaced. Ken can see the film better now we've done some of the locations, feels he has a better idea of its *scale*. It seems more solid, and the sense of place from Blenheim helps.

When we start again, Jack gives fine reading of the 'Some say that ever 'gainst that season comes' speech. ('Magic time'.) Dawn on coat of arms is done by Alex Thomson moving two lamps by hand. Final shot of the evening is spear-throwing ('Jack Lemmon IS Tessa Sanderson in HAMLET...'.) Rubber-tipped spears are dispatched over crew's heads towards position of Ghost. (Jack, as he lunges forward: 'Take that'.)

Wednesday 21 February

Dusk: down to the gates again for Hamlet to meet the Ghost. The scene is simply staged, with Hamlet and the others first behind the gates, then coming through. Camera on crane (Ghost's eye view) yaws and dips alarmingly but smoothly. In the trailer during set-up for crane shot, Jack tells stories about his early career: being sacked by Bert Lahr from a comedy, *Burlesque*, because he could only play the piano by ear, and Lahr, with perverse perfectionism, demanded an actor who could sight-read; also his dealings with the President of Harvard, who each semester told Jack he would make nothing of himself, then, when Jack (already

Lying in state (23 February). The camera, remote-controlled, is mounted on the 'Adder' crane.

successful) came to Boston in a play that flopped, met him outside theatre and said, 'I told you so' - then took him to dinner. Evening ends with with Jack's farewell ovation from the unit.

Thursday 22 February

The Norwegians invade. (Call-sheet includes 'His Grace the Duke of Marlborough' as an officer.) The army charges across courtyard with fixed bayonets - only some of them rubber, and not the ones in front. We stand our ground in the portico, with Duchess of M. and her dog on the steps to repulse the invasion. Will the dog go for them? (No, it obviously thinks the whole business is further proof of human folly.) Then the cavalry make a statelier progress. Troops line up for tracking shots and close-up on Rufus (Fortinbras) and his Captain (Jeffrey Kissoon) and officers (including Duke of M.), as they ride up to take possession. Rufus looks as though he really wants it, but knows it's easily won. Intense eyes, darkly handsome, calmly self-assertive. (Ken: 'No glam spared on this film'.)

Friday 23 February

The morning starts with Hamlet lying in state. Billy Crystal (First Gravedigger) has arrived for make-up consultations, and comes on set while Ken is in the coffin: Billy gets up the stepladder beside catafalque and the corpse sits up to chat. Special motorized crane for camera movement (slow track back and rise/tilt) takes a lot of setting up. Ken as deathly as can be - but every now and then he sits up to look at the hand-held monitor. In the evening Ken starts 'Angels and ministers' but stops after a few goes: come back to it later when there's more juice in the batteries. Quiet in bar, everyone tired. A few people in the unit (including me) have a flu-like bug that's going round ('The *Dalmatians* unit had it before Christmas').

Saturday 24 February

Last day at Blenheim. Out in the driving rain and down to the bridge over the lake, for Fortinbras' men to demolish statue, bits of which (in ready-broken version) lie in a corner like fragments of a giant chocolate Santa Claus. As weather worsens, and our *ersatz* snow is threatened, this gets more urgent. We get a take in before a furious downpour. Tourists with umbrellas appear by the gate, all decanted from one bus, and brave the drizzle to snapshoot each other by the sentry boxes (which we have added, along with the railings). Our people up there shoo them away. Grim entrenched atmosphere down by the statue, constant discussion of weather reports (which are phoned in from the Meteorological Office). Most of what can be done with dialogue on location has been achieved, but we need shots like this for sense of place and scale. I go back to our hotel in Woodstock for lunch. Meet Nick Farrell and we spend half an hour at an antiques fair in the town hall. Odd moment of remembering we're just camped out on the edge of a busy little town where normal Saturday afternoon life goes on.

'Angels and ministers' at sunset, dealt with quickly and efficiently. Then other angles and close-ups, and close in on Ken for 'By heaven I'll make a ghost of him that lets me'. Ken thinks of saying 'stops' for "lets", anxious not to be misunderstood at this moment. Worrying, because it's a famous line and it seems a shame to compromise like this. After he's watched first take on the monitor I hear myself almost yelling, 'No, 'lets' is fine - it'll be clear enough what you mean!' Then odd silence and general laughter. 'Well, I think I know what you feel about that one'. (We go for 'lets'.) Wrap at about nine, back to hotel. Ken awards himself steak and chips with ketchup, breaking strict training regime, to celebrate end of location shoot.

Monday 26 February
RETURN TO STUDIOS

Rehearse gravediggers' scene and funeral of Ophelia. Straight onto the set (formerly woodland, now cemetery), with Ken, Billy Crystal and Simon Russell Beale (Second Gravedigger), and into the grave itself. Billy already on top of the text: first bit plays quietly, with Second Gravedigger anxious to get a move on, First more relaxed. We discuss how he should use the Latin legal phrase '*se offendendo*' Ken suggests analogy with the O. J. Simpson trial: everyone has an opinion, and has suddenly acquired the legal vocabulary. After lunch we go over the funeral details, logistics of getting coffin into grave, placing priest, fight. What to do with Laertes and Claudius at end: how conspiratorial are they? Derek suggests he should go off, leaving Laertes alone by the grave, keeping emphasis on grief, not plotting.

Tuesday 27 February

First section of graveyard scene. Snow, light through trees, crosses, broken fence. Billy fluent, in command of lines, inventive. Reasons for the Gravediggers' conversation: fascination with doings of 'great ones', but also element of contest between two men. Scene more 'magical' with lights in and around grave, seen through mist. Cardboard box of skulls in corner on props table, and bones set out alongside 'repeats' of Simon's sandwich (which he has to munch at between bouts of digging). Billy works on the song, then does a 'wild track' (sound only, for sake of cover) which becomes an improvised bit of cod *bel canto*. Lunch with Billy and Simon in the sunshine outside by the huts. Could pass for modern workmen, not overly Victorian in detail of costume. Simon a crossword wizard (though not as impressive as Derek). Billy quiet, thoughtful, quick-witted but not as much of a compulsive improv. artist as Robin Williams.

Wednesday 28 February

Hamlet now with gravedigger. Tone differs from gravedigger's chat with junior colleague. Now he's met his match, but is still able to talk about things he knows and prince doesn't. Placing this in context of Hamlet's mood (at first detached, then curious, then moved and intrigued). Ken encourages Billy to be simple then invites him to do a take 'for himself'. This one is more kindly, less cool and confrontational with Hamlet. Good variety to choose from. At lunch Billy talks about family's background in Yiddish theatre: but none since his grandparents, and no Shakespeare. Need to get through inhibitions about the language. He's giving us a real person, not a caricature, but comedy is a tricky, insecure business. Simon is currently in Stoppard's *Rosencrantz and Guildenstern* at the Royal National Theatre, and Billy has also been in the play. Simon suggests that during the funeral he and Billy will start tossing a coin in the background, and begin Stoppard's play. Various other background tributes to their previous performances are considered but not executed. After lunch, back to grave. Last hour takes us to Yorick: the close and medium shots on Hamlet have him encounter the first emotional shock of the scene – and more are on their way. Why does Hamlet ask how long a corpse will lie in the ground before it rots? Does he think about the death of his father, whom Gravedigger has just referred to? Hugh: 'There's an odd element of social satire, that has to be relished, despite circumstances. It seems to mark a change in Hamlet's state of mind.'

Affairs of state: Claudius and Gertrude hear the ambassadors' report. 'Checks' have been called for on make-up and costume in the moments before a take.

Thursday 29 February

Close-up, then in even closer for Hamlet's 'Yorick' speech. Hugh encourages Ken to be harsher, not at all pathetic about Alexander: unlike Yorick, Alexander is not part of his own experience. Billy and Simon do the Horatio/Hamlet p.o.v. shots, which look like a fine romantic painting with figures in foreground, trees, mist and crosses. Perhaps a Caspar David Friedrich? – but with man smoking and reading paper to spoil it.

Friday 1 March

More graveyard. Important to remember in the middle of all this where we have got to emotionally. So, when Hamlet says 'This is Laertes, a very noble youth' he isn't telling Horatio something he may not know: Hamlet thinks aloud, begins to take in the situation – and has deduced who is in the coffin. (Which raises question as to why Horatio didn't tell him before now that Ophelia was dead – to which there is no good answer). Julie's Gertrude is tragically adrift in her grief, which makes it doubly odd immediately before the takes, when the First Assistant calls for 'Checks, please' and make-up, hair, costume and props departments gather round her and adjust tiny details of her appearance (such as flicking the feather on her hat). Kate arrives in late afternoon, made up and costumed for coffin, but with her own big black boots on. Gets in so we can check lights. (Ken: 'The boots will be on either side of your head, Kate'). A runner from the production office comes with a telephone message from L.A. for Kate, but we don't know where she is, so messenger departs – then we remember she's in the grave.

'To be or not to be...' The camera operator (Martin Kenzie) lines up a shot against the mirror door, checking for reflections.

Saturday 2 March

Last day in the graveyard - general fatigue, because we've been in here too long. The funeral has become a series of bits and pieces, close-ups, different p.o.v.'s on and around Laertes who has to sustain and repeat the feelings again and again. The tension breaks when Horatio goes to separate Hamlet from his adversary: Laertes and the officers restraining him fall over in a heap, laughing, disappearing from view in the monitor. 'Get off Horatio, you great nancy'. Last shot: Claudius admonishes Gertrude, 'I pray you, Gertrude, set some watch upon your son'. On the second take, Derek narrows his eyes a little, and the moment is suddenly exciting and sinister: he recognizes his enemy and knows what has to be done. Gertrude's look back at him could kill.

Monday 4 March

Affairs of state once again, in the brighter, warmer world of the Palace sets. A long single shot from arrival of Rosencrantz and Guildenstern in the royal apartments, follows the actors down the corridor and onto the A Stage set, and moves through hall to the moment when Claudius and Gertrude are on the dais and ready to hear the newly returned ambassadors. When the camera glides into the Hall and gets ahead of Claudius and Gertrude, we are back with mirror and shadow problems, with the camera crew in guards' jackets just in case an elbow or a back gets reflected. Fluffs and faults on a very long shot make for multiple takes (Claudius suavely and authoritatively puts his hand in the cup of coffee handed to him by an aide: a moment of *Naked Gun*), but this will cover three and a half pages of script - a good daily figure.

Tuesday 5 March

Polonius tells Claudius and Gertrude he has discovered the 'cause' of Hamlet's madness: love for Ophelia. His long speech is in three parts, done in the order 1, 3, 2, because the first two of these share the same set-up. Dickie is at first a bit too hard, not relishing his news: he lightens tone, then gets the whole of the first section in one proud, urgent and oddly compassionate flow. This tells a more interesting story about Polonius and Ophelia. (Query: what happened to the letter the Ambassador gave Claudius? Continuity-friendly answer: he put it in a pocket when we weren't looking.)

Wednesday 6 March

'Fishmonger' scene, with Hamlet teasing Polonius: potentially most difficult in play for Hamlet? Easy to be amusing, but Ken is urged by Hugh to go for the bitterness: convincing imitation of 'madness', thoughts of Ophelia ('Have you a daughter?'), lingering impression of encounter with Ghost. The last of these is harder to perceive directly. First shot in chapel gallery, with skull mask. Then two shots, one on either side of hall balcony. In the second, Ken plays 'madder', positively playful, vicious in listing details of old man's appearance.

Thursday 7 March

Edging towards 'To be…'. First a long, complex circling shot to take us from R. and G. being quizzed on their success in sounding out Hamlet ('And can you by no drift of conference…?') to Ophelia being placed with a prayer book for Hamlet to 'affront' her. Acting and text all fairly secure, but reflection-dodging taxes the concentration. This takes its toll on lines and moves. Ken sits at the monitor, hunched forward on his chair willing them on with impatient involuntary gestures, like a punter at a racecourse - helpless, unable to influence his horse. Two acceptable takes, one very good.

For a time it seems as though we will never reach 'the' soliloquy, then suddenly we set up for it, with track to accompany Hamlet to mirror: the isolation we discussed in rehearsals, and (so far as possible) the sense of an infinite regression of mirror reflections. The first take is simple, but not shaped by sense of argument. This should seem the 'Wittenberg' mode of his mind, intellectually trained, reflective. Later takes are clearer in argument, more specific and vivid in details of the 'whips and scorns' a man must endure, getting a sense of wonder in the thought of the 'undiscovered country' after death. We sit by monitor in one of the side 'rooms' behind the doors, oddly quiet between takes. The unit (professional, pragmatic, not consciously inclined to any sentimental 'reverence' for the work in hand) seems to be affected by the aura of this speech - or perhaps simply by its power? Covers, like large quilts, are piled on the camera to damp down the sound of its motor: operator and focus-puller huddle under them.

Friday 8 March

Ken and Kate come in early to rehearse 'nunnery' scene with Hugh, then the camera and lighting teams are shown it and the crew set-up for the first section, up to his realizing she has betrayed him. There's a momentary pause after 'Well, well, well', then they giggle together, then kiss, then she offers the 'remembrances' (love-letters) and he flares up. How does she get to that point? Why does she return them? In rehearsal we reminded ourselves that she's not been *told* to do this by her father, so 'which I have longed long to redeliver' is spoken from her heart - or at least is what she is trying to convince herself of. What she has wanted for a long time is an explanation. But for a moment we see what the reconstruction of their love could be like. Then it gets worse, she can't go back now, she falters when he asks 'Where's your father?' Kate is stronger, tougher on the successive takes, but this is the moment of no return. At the end of the scene, Hamlet flings her down in doorway. Kate, in heap against the door frame, speaks 'O what a noble mind is here o'erthrown' in one shot, as camera moves in on her. (Between takes she darts into the side-room of the hall where we lurk with the monitors: 'Chaps, did you see my eyes? Did I have them open against the door?' 'Should I take "O heavenly powers restore him" in to myself a bit?')

Saturday 9 March

The same, from the p.o.v. of the watchers. (The room set is swiftly dealt with to accommodate lights and camera as if in some rapid and drastic bout of home improvement: 'Lose that wall, George...That ceiling's going too'.) Ken stands alone in the hall to rehearse, the complete post-modern prince with a dagger in one hand and the tiny remote monitor to watch himself with in the other. ('I could be watching the football now'.)

Monday 11 March

Into the chapel, and back some way in the script, for Polonius's advice to Laertes. ('Neither a borrower nor a lender be'). When Laertes leaves, father and sister watch him fondly, but the gates closing across them seem to mark a transition. Shades of the prison-house? If there is symbolism, it isn't intentional at this stage. Martin (Camera Operator) thought it would look good, and it's a legacy of an earlier plan to locate the scene behind closed doors in a boathouse by the lake at Blenheim.

Kate in the confessional. At first too 'modern', in being dismissive of her father at the end ('I will obey, my lord' too petulant), but she has after all just had to tell a lie again - since in our version she has slept with Hamlet, and hasn't given up the truth to her father. So the scene becomes more fraught, until Kate plays her with the first signs of the stress and strain that will eventually lead to madness. Sobbing, almost speechless (but - 'There's a tear here, is that O.K.?') Dickie getting a firm, angry manner: it's his prohibition to her and its consequences that affect her.

Tuesday 12 March

In the morning Cliff Richard visits set, suddenly appearing from one of the mirror doors. Slighter, taller than one imagined: intrigued, unpretentious manner. Crew behaves with studied professional nonchalance in the presence of a major British pop legend.

In the chapel again: Claudius tries to pray. Derek has to find the emotional argument: a man trying to come to terms with his guilt and his God. First take seems too meditative, but from then on he is the 'limed soul that struggles to be free.' Round on Hamlet's p.o.v.: in original draft of Ken's script the king would have been confessing and Hamlet would have impersonated a priest, but the implications of this seemed too complex. Instead Hamlet has happened across an opportunity to discharge his duty, and it is clear that Claudius came to the confessional simply to be alone. Claudius kneels, 'Bend stubborn knees...' ('Can you see my knees?' 'No, are they stubborn?')

As he leaves the set, Derek drops the centre of one of Claudius's cufflinks: suddenly the unit is walking round slowly with their eyes cast down, like so many melancholy Danes. Outside there is something of spring in the air. In the car-park a man in a baseball cap carries a birdcage in one hand and a startlingly convincing fibre-glass replica of a Dalmatian under the other arm.

Wednesday 13 March

Rehearsal at 10.00 for first sections of scene between Gertrude and Hamlet and the death of Polonius. Blood is a practical problem once he has been stabbed: we mustn't get any on the bedspread or her dress (no repeats available). At first Dickie is a little too brusque with queen - he marches in, tells her very sharply what to do. A brief bow is then added as he opens the doors, but Ken wants to keep it brisk, with sense that everything is falling apart, less time for politeness. We end the day with Hamlet heaving Gertrude onto the bed ('leave wringing of your hands'), which Julie does with a precisely placed flying lunge. ('Where do you want me?')

Friday 15 March

Gertrude and Hamlet sit together on sofa. A few minor adjustments, but plays well from first take. Tenderer now than in rehearsal, and in fact the only time when mother and son are seen together like this. Lull in the storm - then they look across to where Polonius lies in a pool of blood. The main acting decision is how to treat the section near the end, beginning at 'Not this by no means...', where Hamlet is sarcastically describing what he doesn't want her to do. In rehearsal we considered the possibility of this being despair and contempt, with Hamlet unable to trust her ('Oh, I know you'll give in and tell him') but we didn't follow that line, and now as we work on the scene it is clear that version couldn't be motivated by the way Julie asks 'What shall I do?', and that

Hamlet is in fact getting carried away with disgust for Claudius ('the bloat king') as he imagines what would happen if she gave his game away. As so often, Hamlet seems to relish in vivid detail any picture he conjures up for himself.

The final shots are of Polonius's body, looking towards the forlorn pair on the sofa, pool of blood in foreground. Job demarcation: blood on floor is props department, blood on clothes is costumes, blood on Dickie is make-up. Rules relaxed to let make-up pour the blood on costume and face. We soon get through all the 'blood donor' jokes.

This is the last of the series of 'big' emotional scenes between Hamlet and Gertrude or Ophelia. When we wrap, Ken is relieved, but will only allow himself big sigh of relief when rushes are O.K. (In the end they weren't - some shots had to be redone because of a processing fault).

Saturday 16 March

Long single shot to go down corridor as Claudius dashes to find out what is happening, then into his room with Gertrude, out into corridor again, into bedroom, back out to send off Rosencrantz and Guildenstern and then embracing Gertrude tightly as camera tracks back leaving them lonely and fearful. Decision that Claudius will be impatient with her for a moment as she tries to excuse Hamlet, then more comforting and finally himself insecure. When he goes into her room, should Claudius kneel by pool of blood? Doesn't it take a beat too long? Derek: 'No, I can do it all, kneel, look at pictures, move - just watch me!' While we rehearse shot in king's apartment, Tim and Reece do a soft-shoe shuffle routine in the doorway behind Derek's back. Julie, puzzled, asks Ken 'Will you be in this scene?' - 'No, I'll be over there' (behind camera) - 'Oh, I'd forgotten, you're the director too.'

All this takes three hours to light, but single shot here repays time in number of pages covered and impetus it gives to action. Court in crisis, and R. and G. have become even more haplessly embroiled: sent off to find a royal psychopath at large and armed. Another shot takes an hour to set up, but covers a long sequence from Claudius bursting into room ('It likes us not...') and sending R. and G. off to England with Hamlet, then the soliloquy that makes clear to the audience his anxiety to kill his nephew. R. and G. propitiate him. Tim is anxious about his elaborate speech ('massy wheel' etc) - but his anxiety feeds that of the character, wonderful moment of comedy as R. digs himself further into the mire and G. watches coolly. Relaxed atmosphere by end of day: a big sequence dealt with.

Monday 18 March

Two major shots, taking us from Hamlet hiding Polonius's body ('Safely stowed') to being apprehended – the second is a swift dash through a series of rooms, pushing extras and stunt artists out of his way, jumping over tables, surprising lovers, until he reaches his study, then (cut) he is inside and a rifle is lowered against his head. From our side of the tracks (literally) the set looks like rooms in a doll's house, with rails alongside for camera. Stunt arranger runs through first, then Ken does it for the takes - back panting to the monitor: 'It's like a testosterone farm out there'. Message from the stunt artists: would Ken mind pushing them harder? - then it's easier to fall well. As he reaches the last room before his study, some extra guards linger half-heartedly by the door ('Perhaps we should give them something to do, a cup of coffee and some sandwiches'). In first shot, Hamlet enjoys himself - the game is up, but he'll have a bit of fun with these people. Clowning in last lines, contempt for Claudius. Bloodhounds on set: gentle, friendly dogs, taking a lively interest - more curiosity than rabid pursuit of a victim.

Tuesday 19 March
Ken Dodd as Yorick, in flashback. One of the great British stand-up comedians, he is now resplendent in a costume that is a cross between a classic nineteenth-century clown (Joey Grimaldi) and the Mad Hatter. Royal family (plus child Hamlet) is looking years younger, with Brian Blessed in particular the picture of rude health after his ghostly pallor. Doddy entertains family at table in king's apartment set while camera semi-circles round. He does routines from his act including a joke about cat food that has the royals falling out of their chairs. A half-dozen of us have headphones, but most of the crew, standing in the corridor, can only hear the laughter. A close-up of Doddy with teeth displayed to match our shots of skull. In break he talks about variety comics he admires, particularly those who seemed like beings from another planet (Tommy Cooper, Frankie Howerd). Seen close-to in this make-up, his features seem strangely delicate. Talks about his stage performance as Malvolio in *Twelfth Night* - some people expected he would do his own act at the expense of the part, but he ad-libbed only once, one night when a prop necklace fell apart. Has photos taken of his name on a chair-back (which tickles him pink) and Yorick skull - which he is given as a memento.

Wednesday 20 March
Ophelia's first mad scene, shot on two cameras, one wide, one medium. At first little sign of the Ophelia we used to know, then, as she begins to recall Polonius, it changes, and the fullest effect is there in later shots, close-ups, with the hyperventilating, sobbing mania - she dips down below the camera's frame as though going *down* for air ('O.K. I'll go again' a few deep breaths, then up into view and sobbing). In the middle of all this Kate can change a word or a line-reading. (Ken: 'It's almost unbelievably painful. Once more with a higher eye-line').

Most important change is in her first entrance, which now begins as a run at full tilt into the hall, then is slowed down, and as a consequence twice as affecting - she seems to be looking for someone when she asks 'Where is the beauteous majesty of Denmark?' (Julie's hair and the high-ruffed collar on her dress make her look like Sarah Bernhardt: Derek points out that he has to make do with one haircut and three uniforms while she gets a different outfit in every scene.)

Kate, in her 'madhouse' combination of straitjacket and shift, jokes about having found her outfit for the Oscar ceremony (Vivienne Westwood?). Sitting on floor, during a respite, she waves, does 'potty' acting (lolling head, hands waving): thumbs-up cheerfully exchanged. Not a chatting day, though – everyone reading between shots, like a library or a doctor's waiting room.

Thursday 21 March
Laertes (Michael Maloney) comes back to Elsinore. Laertes' supporters seem too tidy and prompt in leaving when asked to: needs rethinking. Julie: 'They don't seem very threatening' (later re-shot). When they break for lunch, the rebellious mob line up in good order (like immigrants at Ellis Island) at props tables to hand in their cudgels and have names taken.

Ophelia is hosed down. Kate cowers in a corner of the sordid-looking tiled cell in a shift, with water played on her, then in close-up, we see her taking a key from mouth. Swathed in towels between takes.

Friday 22 March
Ophelia mad again. Ken wants this simpler, less extreme – instead of straitjacket she is in her nightdress, pursued down 'corridor' of rooms by Horatio and Nurse, crosses to Laertes and others, goes and sits by mirror. No distribution of 'real' flowers (though this was rehearsed). Instead she seems to have imaginary herbs and flowers in a bunch in her hand and all but two are offered to Laertes. After first take of 'flower' section (on floor, by mirror) which is fine but in the expected pathetic mode, Ken asks her to laugh through the whole thing – which she does, gently and not hysterically. So now the second 'mad' scene is radically unlike the first. In the song, she sits perfectly still and the camera slowly tracks in. Day's final shot, now through keyhole, of Kate being doused: then she is sent off to the Oscar ceremony!

In the morning Julie asks about poisons, so I phone the pharmacology department at Birmingham University, who are a bit bemused. Is this a practical joke? Decide on cyanide, which fits circumstances: physical symptoms discussed – sweating, unfocused eyes, loss of balance, stomach pains. Timing can be adjusted. This is the Agatha Christie side of *Hamlet*.

Saturday 23 March
Day of flashbacks and reactions. The most elaborate are to show relationships of Gertrude, Claudius, two Hamlets, Polonius before the murder. After much discussion of various ideas (including chess-game, archery) this has now become a compact indoor scene, in which the royals are enjoying a curling match on the marble floor. This includes opportunity for Hamlet father and son to wander off while Claudius is

solicitous in helping Gertrude throw a stone and Polonius exchanges an understanding look with him - and we cut to young Hamlet noticing something. Apart from a direct hit with a curling stone on the floor-level camera, no technical hazards. At end of day, we do reactions of Polonius, R. and G. and Hamlet to the 'Hecuba' speech (postponed from a month ago). End-of-week hysteria sets in: Ken cracks up every time he looks at Dickie, so we take five minutes for calming down. Player King's speeches 'off' are going a bit slow. ('Come on, we want to release before Christmas.')

Monday 25 March

King's speech, 'I have sent to seek him and to find the body', which we have made a soliloquy, with Derek alone at desk. Camera approaches round corner - and on one take, in unwitting homage to Mel Brooks, bumps into door like the camera hitting the window in *High Anxiety*. Important to get ruminative quality, progress towards this decision and action. (We agreed in rehearsal that Claudius doesn't decide to have Hamlet killed until this late stage, when Polonius has been murdered and the danger to his own life is too extreme to ignore. But this speech doesn't voice his intention: we have to wait until the end of the sequence when Hamlet has been sent on his way.) The next section, Claudius confronting and dispatching Hamlet, with the camera moving round the room, requires an hour to set up and ten takes to do, mainly for focus, but also to get the temper of the scene right, placing the slap, marking Hamlet's attitude to king. Earlier in the day we did Hamlet's scene with Horatio after his return from England, which informs the moment we've inserted in this scene where he asks his friend to stay behind in Denmark.

Tuesday 26 March

The call-sheet simply states 'The Fight Takes Place.' In fact this is a major operation, with a massive influx of extras, and attendant dressers, make-up, etc. Also a positive jamboree of mirror problems. The preliminaries of the fight are done. It's important for Laertes to seem a bit stiff - after all he's going to murder someone - but there's also a degree of sincerity, and at the same time we wonder (without coming up with an answer) how Hamlet can think he can excuse what he has done to the Polonius family. Props and art departments fuss round like houseproud caretakers, as the grand red carpet is constantly hoovered, cleaned, kept fresh and protected between shots with cotton cloths.

Wednesday 27 March

Fencing continues all day, with swordmaster's and stunt arranger's constant attention to detail - does it look as though the fencers really are trying to hit each other? On film (more than on stage) it has to convince from a series of angles, so needs adjusting from shot to shot. As fight goes on, moves get more complex, like three-dimensional chess:

a continuity nightmare. Fast camera (in case we want slow-motion) and two others for fight to give maximum choices in editing, so most of the time we hear whirring of fast camera reels, and clacking of swords, grunting and panting.

Thursday 28 March

Even more fight. Up and down carpet, with frequent false starts, so that overall shape is hard to remember. By 6.30 Ken and Michael Maloney have been fighting on and off since 8.30 a.m. (including their regular morning practice) - and tiredness shows, so we wrap. Between takes courtiers (up since early hours) slump against walls and snooze. Corridors outside set are full of ball-gowned ladies in cardigans over décolletages - knitting, reading, chatting, dozing.

Friday 29 March

Claudius and Gertrude react to it all: she drinks, Laertes gets the poisoned sword. Sudden rush of incident, plot and motive questions. Why doesn't he do more to stop her drinking? (Answer: moment of paralysis, instinctive self-preservation fights with loss of all he loves.) Should Derek say 'It is the poisoned cup, it is too late' out loud, or do a voice-over? (Answer: shoot both ways for choice when editing.) Queen sits down, queasy - we do various degrees of this malaise, and of attendants' reactions. Julie does fine puzzled, unfocused look. Next bout set up.

Final shot of the day is Ken lying on floor after a 'hit' - with camera at eye level. I find myself crawling in to advise him on an emphasis as he lies full length under a light and a reflector, while Tina (make-up) dabs at his face, Danny (dresser) rubs make-up off his costume, and Chynah (focus-puller) holds her tape-measure to his nose. Dignity of the Director? (And definition of my job on set: 'standby text'.)

Saturday 30 March

Yet more fight. At one point Hamlet and Laertes approach one another solemnly, like prize-fighters, down the long red carpet in front of the entire court, reach the middle - and crack up laughing. So 130 people 'corpse', all at once.

Desperate hacking and slashing upstairs. We never see the totality that will be there when the bits are joined together - indeed, there was never a 'complete' sword fight, but we now have enough components to show it twice over.

Julie's death - trying out each movement, turn of head at end, smile. Derek, reacting to fight, must remember to notice queen crumpling. Weary extras round staircase, more like a Victorian painting than ever - except for one lady prostrate at back with her legs only in view, which makes it more like the aftermath of an orgy. Another has taken her shoes off and used her fan to cool her feet. Rather than be slaughtered *en masse*, our Danish aristocrats flee - which shows how rotten the state is and also saves massively on stage-management and cleaning bills. Only a loyal band remains – determined by who can work on Monday. For one long shot we do the departure of the rest, which Simon orchestrates from the balcony with his loud-hailer: 'Pandemonium!!!' (lasts 30 seconds, then) 'Shut the doors as you go!' (for continuity).

Monday 1 April

A strangely desultory day, with Ken a bit withdrawn, anxious to get this done. Death of queen in detail, reactions – Derek has to get fear, desperation in 'she swoons to see them bleed' and also (tellingly) the fact that this is his last attempt to lie. Then we start on his death (which will involve several shots of varying degrees of complexity for swinging chandelier, sword flying at him, etc.).

Tuesday 2 April

Fortinbras' army arrives in the hall. Scaffolding towers and crash mats behind the set walls (for stunt men to swing through windows). Practice for troops crossing, closing doors, pointing guns downstairs, while the stuntmen will hurtle in above. Cameras shooting from several angles. Then Fortinbras stalks down the corridor. We probably have two goes at the invasion. Conferences with various departments: stunts, art dept, camera, effects. Decision needed on how many repeats of the 'sugar' glass window-panes we have. The stuff crumbles to powder underfoot, makes splinters that look nasty, litters floors on upper level, and the windows take a while to set back. Starting with a big shot helps the day. Ken: 'I'm making six films at once. This is *Diehard*.' Later shoot chandelier pinning Derek down in the throne: in fact it really does so, not stopping as soon as expected, giving a better shot than we could have asked for – luckily without really damaging Derek.

Wednesday 3 April

Derek's last day: Claudius plotting with Laertes. When we set up for Gertrude's entrance (with news of Ophelia's suicide) the positions of the table and sofa are 'cheated' to accommodate camera angles. Michael now sits on a box at the table, like a small boy allowed to sit with the grown-ups: Ken asks if camera crew would like to cheat anything else. 'We could put Julie on castors'. Meanwhile on the headphones we can hear her behind the door getting ready, summoning up distress.

The speech to be as little of an elocution piece as possible – numbed, shocked detachment, as camera moves in on her relentlessly. Then close-ups on Claudius. Laertes, grief-stricken, leaves quietly, not in a rush. Claudius is concerned merely to get him back on course for the sake of his plot – which Gertrude of course does not know about. He seems to blame her for upsetting Laertes. ('How much I had to do to calm his rage...') When Claudius leaves, she does not follow. She shows no sign of affection for him from now on.

A drama and a ceremony today. The first is a fire on set. As first scene is being set up, we hear shouts of 'fire', and see smoke and a red glow above ceiling of corridor. A drape has blown against one of the lamps and in these dry, dusty conditions, has taken fire. Stage cleared, blaze contained and doused by studio fire crew, then Surrey brigade arrive and Tim Harvey (Production Designer) persuades them not to hose down the whole set. Disaster has been averted, little time lost.

The ceremony: Derek completes his work on the film and there's the usual applause, especially strong in his case. Then he springs a surprise. He holds up a small red-bound copy of the play, that successive actors have passed on to each other with the condition that the recipient should give it in turn to the finest Hamlet of the next generation. It has come from Forbes Robertson, a great Hamlet at the turn of the century, to Derek, via Henry Ainley, Michael Redgrave, Peter O'Toole and others – now he gives it to Ken.

Thursday 4 April
Last day before the Easter holiday, includes Hamlet's brief dialogue with Fortinbras's Captain (on horseback). The beautiful, finely tuned and trained horse defecates on arrival, then urinates copiously during second take just before Ken says 'I thank you, sir'.

Tuesday 9 April
Several new haircuts after the Easter break. We've four more days 'over' to shoot, beyond original schedule, so a few changes in crew – and a new caterer as our regular firm has gone to Russia for another film. This causes some disorientation: everything is in a different place in the catering tent. ('Are we still doing the same picture?')

Back to the State Hall. Fight continues: up onto the balcony for the most desperate stuff, with breaking bookcase glass. Then reshoot arrival of Laertes and his mob. These now look more like revolutionaries and less like Central Casting peasants. Timing and speed of exit are paramount. Later crew members impersonate them for a reverse angle of Laertes, king and queen reacting. We rush in waving scripts and fists: only one take, which is a pity because we're beginning to enjoy it.

Wednesday 10 April
Laertes dies, followed by Hamlet. Hamlet's emotions? They include urgent need for Horatio to tell the story. Physical details a problem: Ken anxious to avoid being cradled by Horatio as in a *pietà*, or spending a lot of time on the floor. Problems carrying him out: getting the bearers to walk in step and not sway too much. (Unfortunately Fortinbras specifies *four* captains as bearers so we can't sneak in a couple more.) Should doors be shut, or Hamlet carried to end of corridor in shot? (Both tried.) Here for a session of publicity photos, Kate passes through from time to time

in a bewildering selection of Ophelia's costumes, like a rapid re-run of the play.

Thursday 11 April

First shot is Ophelia seeing Polonius dead. Kate is manhandled downstairs, and as body passes, she breaks away, grasps railings, screams, is dragged off. Three takes, with bloodcurdling screams on cue and jokes in between (aided and abetted by Pat Doyle, acclaimed film music composer and notable laugher).

Set-up for ambassador (Lord Attenborough). When he arrives, he greets and is greeted by various crew members (riggers, grips) who know him from other pictures. Genial but not effusive, businesslike. Nick then does Horatio's final speech in close-up and medium: one rehearsal, one take for each. ('Aha! One-take Farrell.') Simple, emotionally precise, unsentimental.

Meanwhile on another sound-stage, Kate is being drowned in a blue paddling pool, with various helpers in the water with her: a cross between a baptism and bath time (though not so pleasant for her). Large crew, much hilarity, tea tables, Elizabeth (hair and wigs) in the pool with Kate fanning out her hair in the water. Kate is later brought over, still dripping, to the State Hall set for the ritual of applause at end of her work on the film.

Friday 12 April

Hamlet and Horatio in the study (reshoot, as we anticipated way back in January). Ken now makes 'providence in the fall of a sparrow' simpler, with sense of resignation but not doom. (There was too much movement in earlier version: and Ken felt it needed more space between him and Horatio. Also, he wanted to come back to it with the experience of the play behind him.) Turn round on shots of Nick's reactions, then we say goodbye to him, and wrap. Slight sense of anticlimax - and postponed wrap party - because possible lens problems may mean that some shots in the hall and with Claudius and Laertes need reshooting. (Michael unavailable on some dates, Derek has shaved his beard off, and is already at Chichester Festival Theatre, where he is artistic director and is due to appear in an opening production).

Saturday 13 April

Final day. The news on the lens problems is better, and we won't need to save the State Hall set or even perhaps do any reshooting with Derek and Michael. (In the end, none was needed.) So this really is the final day of the complete unit.

Reshooting Hamlet and Gertrude on the couch. Her reactions made more specific by Julie. Dickie Briers in and bloodied for the last time. Gore spread again by the gallon, perhaps a bit thicker than last time, and Alfie (props) on his knees with a paintbrush, as Ken and Julie chat on a sofa in the background - so on the video monitor this looks even more like a do-it-yourself programme ('Be sure to use firm, even brushstrokes...').

Final shots of the film are in State Hall. First a 'cover' for Hamlet's turn to see Ophelia after 'To be or not to be...' During line-up for this an A.D. has been lashed to a post with a fireman's hat on his head and a banana in his flies - which is revealed to Ken in the rehearsal as he turns to where Kate should be. ('But soft you now - the fair Ophelia??') Then the last shot of all: he comes down the rope and grabs the poisoned drink from table. Ken is left dangling for a few seconds, then 'action' - he lands, gets the goblet, runs off out of shot - a couple of takes and suddenly that's it. 'Check that please'. 'Gate good'. Final wrap of film. Last farewell applause of the film. Short speech by First Assistant, then everyone is invited to a drink in Ken's dressing-room. Hamlet, coming off set: 'Well, we have a go, don't we?'

BARNARDO
Looks it not like the King? Mark it, Horatio.

HORATIO
Most like. It harrows me with fear and wonder.

HORATIO · MARCELLUS · BARNARDO

POLONIUS
This above all – to thine own self be true,
And it must follow, as the night the day,
Thou canst not then be false to any man.
Farewell – my blessing season this in thee.
LAERTES
Most humbly do I take my leave, my lord.
POLONIUS
The time invites you. Go; your servants tend.
LAERTES
Farewell, Ophelia, and remember well
What I have said to you.
OPHELIA
                'Tis in my memory locked,
And you yourself shall keep the key of it.

Previous page: The Wedding

Previous page inset: CLAUDIUS • HAMLET • GERTRUDE

LAERTES • OPHELIA • POLONIUS

GHOST

GHOST
     I am thy father's spirit,
Doomed for a certain term to walk the night,
And for the day confined to fast in fires,
Till the foul crimes done in my days of nature
Are burnt and purged away. But that I am forbid
To tell the secrets of my prison-house,
I could a tale unfold whose lightest word
Would harrow up thy soul.

POLONIUS • PROSTITUTE

REYNALDO

OPHELIA • POLONIUS

OPHELIA
My lord, as I was sewing in my chamber,
Lord Hamlet, with his doublet all unbraced,
No hat upon his head, his stockings fouled,
Ungartered, and down-gyvèd to his ankle,
Pale as his shirt, his knees knocking each other,
And with a look so piteous in purport
As if he had been loosèd out of hell
To speak of horrors, he comes before me.
POLONIUS
Mad for thy love?
OPHELIA
                    My lord, I do not know.
But truly I do fear it.

POLONIUS
I hold my duty as I hold my soul,
Both to my God and to my gracious King.
And I do think — or else this brain of mine
Hunts not the trail of policy so sure
As it hath used to do — that I have found
The very cause of Hamlet's lunacy.
CLAUDIUS
O speak of that, that I do long to hear!

Above POLONIUS • CLAUDIUS
Below OPHELIA • POLONIUS

POLONIUS
Th' ambassadors from Norway, my good lord,
Are joyfully return'd.

Above CORNELIUS • VALTEMAND
Centre OLD NORWAY
Below CLAUDIUS • GERTRUDE

GUILDENSTERN · HAMLET · ROSENCRANTZ

HAMLET • THE PLAYERS

HAMLET • LUCIANUS

PLAYER KING

FIRST PLAYER
'But if the gods themselves did see her then,
When she saw Pyrrhus make malicious sport
In mincing with his sword her husband's limbs,
The instant burst of clamour that she made,
Unless things mortal move them not at all,
Would have made milch the burning eyes of heaven
And passion in the gods.'

HECUBA

POLONIUS
Look whe'er he has not turned his colour, and
has tears in 's eyes. Prithee, no more.

HAMLET
'Tis well. I'll have thee speak out the rest soon.

PRIAM

POLONIUS • CLAUDIUS

HAMLET • OPHELIA

CLAUDIUS • GERTRUDE

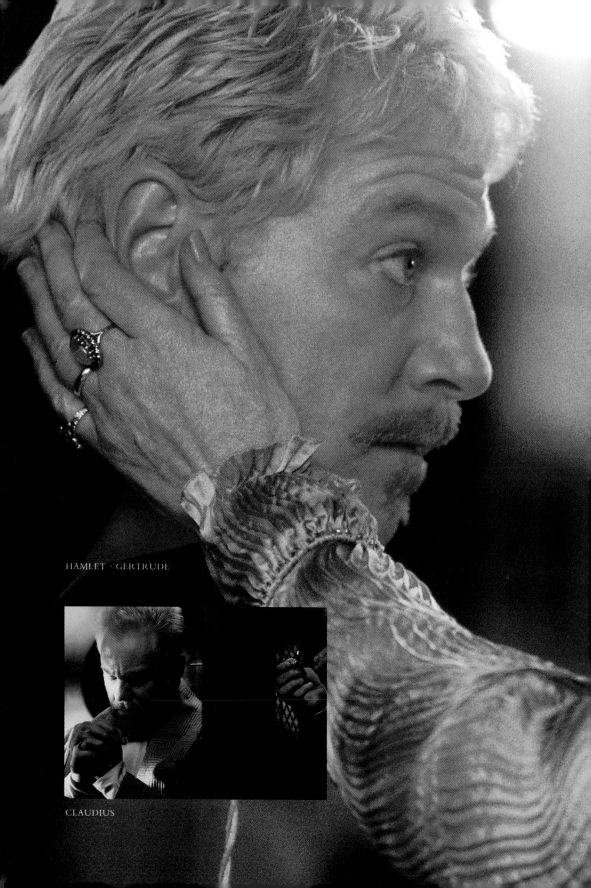

HAMLET · GERTRUDE

CLAUDIUS

GHOST

POLONIUS   OPHELIA · LAERTES

LAERTES
By heaven, thy madness shall be paid with weight
Till our scale turns the beam. O rose of May,
Dear maid, kind sister, sweet Ophelia!

LAERTES · CLAUDIUS

CLAUDIUS
Laertes, was your father dear to you?
Or are you like the painting of a sorrow,
A face without a heart?
LAERTES
                 Why ask you this?

OPHELIA

SECOND GRAVEDIGGER • FIRST GRAVEDIGGER

FIRST GRAVEDIGGER
Is she to be buried in Christian burial,
that wilfully seeks her own salvation?

SECOND GRAVEDIGGER
I tell thee she is, therefore make her grave straight. The
coroner hath sat on her, and finds it Christian burial.

FIRST GRAVEDIGGER
How can that be unless she drowned herself in her own defence?

YORICK

LAERTES · GERTRUDE · CLAUDIUS   HORATIO · HAMLET

HAMLET
There's a special providence in the fall of a sparrow.
If it be now, 'tis not to come. If it be not to come, it will be
now. If it be not now, yet it will come. The readiness is all.
Since no man knows aught of what he leaves, what is't to leave
betimes?

FORTINBRAS'S ARMY

ATTENDANTS TO GERTRUDE · GERTRUDE

LAERTES

HAMLET · CLAUDIUS

HAMLET

HAMLET
                    O, I die, Horatio!
The potent poison quite o'ercrows my spirit.
I cannot live to hear the news from England,
But I do prophesy th' election lights
On Fortinbras. He has my dying voice.
So tell him, with th' occurrents, more and less,
Which have solicited. The rest is silence.
HORATIO
Now cracks a noble heart. Good night, sweet Prince,
And flights of angels sing thee to thy rest.

The coup

ENGLISH AMBASSADOR

FORTINBRAS

FORTINBRAS
    Let four Captains
Bear Hamlet like a soldier to the stage,
For he was likely, had he been put on,
To have proved most royal; and for his passage,
The soldiers' music and the rites of war
Speak loudly for him.
Take up the body. Such a sight as this
Becomes the field, but here shows much amiss.
Go, bid the soldiers shoot.